A HISTORY OF
BOLSHEVISM

A HISTORY OF
BOLSHEVISM

FROM MARX
TO THE
FIRST FIVE YEARS' PLAN

By

ARTHUR ROSENBERG

Translated from the German by
IAN F. D. MORROW

New York
RUSSELL & RUSSELL
1965

FIRST PUBLISHED IN 1934
REISSUED, 1965, BY RUSSELL & RUSSELL, INC.
L.C. CATALOG CARD NO: 65-17919
PRINTED IN THE UNITED STATES OF AMERICA

PREFACE TO THE
ENGLISH TRANSLATION

THIS translation of the original German edition of my *Geschichte des Bolschevismus* (published in 1932) is an exact rendering and does not contain any alteration of any kind whatsoever. Events that have occurred since the appearance of the German edition fully confirm the views expressed in these pages. The collapse of the KPD without any show of resistance proved that the Communism of the Third International could no longer be looked upon as a living revolutionary force. The ruin of the KPD sealed the fate of the Third International, which has ceased, together with its affiliations in Czechoslovakia, France, &c., to be a factor in international politics. Moreover, the attitude displayed by the Soviet Government towards Hitlerite Germany shows that Stalin is no longer interested in the so-called world revolution. The Soviet Government did not in its negotiations with Nazi Germany allow itself to be actuated by any other consideration than that of self-interest, and displayed no regard whatever for the German Communists or the Communist International. Stalin thus indirectly proclaimed the dissolution of the Third International as an independent and active Labour movement. In Soviet Russia the course followed by events has been that indicated in the original German edition. At the same time the Soviet Government has revealed itself powerless to resolve the glaring contradictions in its governmental system

ARTHUR ROSENBERG.

ZÜRICH,
August, 1933

PREFACE

An immense literature exists on the subject of Soviet Russia and the Russian Revolution—documented and journalistic, scientific and sentimental, condemnatory and adulatory. This book does not attempt to compete with what has already been written and instead seeks to fill a definite gap. Up to the present there has not been available any history of the evolution of Bolshevism from its roots in Karl Marx through the individual stages traversed by Lenin, down to the theories and tactics of Stalin in 1932. It has thus come about that false notions are common in the widest circles on the subject of Bolshevism. It is either under-estimated or over-estimated and never appreciated for what it really is.

Ideas are the products of actual conditions and not of a vacuum. It is therefore necessary here to take note of the factors in the development both of Russia and the world in so far as they are essential for a proper understanding of Bolshevism. It would have been beyond the scope of this book to have attempted to describe fully any one event in the Russian Revolution or—for example—to analyse the Five-Year Plan in detail.

The problem which I have attempted to solve in this book is scientific and not a problem of Party politics. At the time of the split in the Independent Social Democrat Party in Germany in 1920 I joined the Communist Party in common with the majority of the USPD. I was for years a member of the Berlin Committee, the Central Committee of the KPD, and the Executive of the Third International. I was forced to resign from the Communist International in 1927, as so many Communists of all countries have been forced to do before and since. Since then I have not belonged to any political Party nor to any of the small groups comprising the Communist Opposition. I have not written this book to please any Party or group, and I am not conscious of any desire to make 'revelations' or to 'settle accounts'. Those who hope to find in this book anecdotes about Stalin and the 'torture chambers' of the GPU will be bitterly disappointed.

It is obviously necessary for scientific and political reasons to remove the problem of Bolshevik Russia from the atmosphere of petty strife and political debate. It will be shown that important issues depend upon our judgement of Bolshevik Russia, such as German-Russian relations, proletarian unity, and the relations between Russia and the international proletariat. It must be clearly understood that despite everything that has happened Soviet Russia is progressing and the Third International is irretrievably heading towards destruction. This book seeks to explain how this unique twofold situation has arisen.

As far as possible I have used Bolshevik sources. At the same time I have not hesitated to state my own opinions. I have throughout avoided giving this book an autobiographical character which would have been unsuitable for the task I had in view. Among German literature on Bolshevism I am specially indebted to the works of Karl Korsch

ARTHUR ROSENBERG

BERLIN-ZEHLENDORF,

June, 1932.

CONTENTS

I

MARX TO LENIN, 1843–1893

WHILE on a journey in Holland in March, 1843, the twenty-five-year-old Dr. Karl Marx wrote to his friend Rugge a letter in which he described the follies of Frederick William IV of Prussia. He added: 'The State is too serious a concern to be turned into a harlequinade. It is possible that a ship manned by idiots might run before the storm for a time. Its fate would nevertheless overtake it if for no other reason than that the idiots would not realize it. In our case this doom is the Revolution that is at our doors.'

This trumpet-blast was answered by Rugge in a mood of deep pessimism.

'Although it is a hard saying,' he wrote, 'I must write it because it is the truth. I cannot imagine any nation that is so disunited as the German nation. You see workmen—and not men; thinkers —and not men; masters and servants, young people and those who are already settled in life, but not men. Is that not a battle-field where arms and legs and mutilated bodies lie heaped on one another while the life-blood runs out upon the ground? Hölderlin in Hyperion. That describes my mood; and unfortunately it is not a new one. The same cleavage works at different ages in the same manner in all humanity. Your letter is filled with illusory ideas. Your courage only serves to intensify my lack of spirit. You say that we—the contemporaries of these Germans—are going to experience a political revolution? Your wish is father to your thought, my friend. Oh, I have lived through it all! Hope is sweet and disappointment bitter, very bitter. It takes more courage to despair than to hope. Nevertheless, it is the courage of commonsense, and we have reached the point at which we dare not let ourselves be disappointed any longer.'

Rugge went on to add: 'In so far as one can speak of a German spirit, it is contemptible, and it gives me no qualms of conscience to declare that it is owing to its contemptible nature that it appears as it does.' He concluded his letter with the words, 'Our nation has no future. What does our reputation matter?'

Marx refused to be discouraged. He agreed indeed with Rugge that a Germany of shopkeepers and fools could not be the scene of a revolution like the French or English revolutions. But in the eyes of Marx that only meant that a revolution in Germany must take on a special character; it must be no revolution of half-measures but must revolutionize the entire structure of society in a single effort. And Marx formulated his theory as to the nature of the coming revolution in Germany in his celebrated 'Criticism of Hegel's Philosophy of Law' which appeared in 1844 in the *Deutsch-französische Jahrbücher*. This review bore on its title-page the names of its two editors—Arnold Rugge and Karl Marx. Hence Marx's article was also a tirade against the pessimism of his co-editor.

In this article Marx asked the question, 'Can Germany accomplish a revolution that will not only raise it to the level of a modern nation but also to the pinnacle that will be attained in the immediate future by the other nations?' Marx went on to declare that the German middle class would certainly never be capable of carrying out this revolution, since it was nothing more than the type of the commonplace mediocrity that characterized all the other classes in the old Germany. But a new class was coming into existence in Germany which was no longer a part of the middle-class order of society, which was completely outside society, and which could only achieve its own freedom by overthrowing the entire existing world-order. This class was the industrial proletariat. In the course of its struggle the proletariat would attract to itself all the poor classes in society, in the country as well as in the towns, and by so doing would accomplish the truly great revolution—the German Revolution.

'The emancipation of Germany from medievalism', wrote Marx, 'is only possible in the form of a simultaneous emancipation from the effects of an incomplete liberation from medievalism. It is impossible to destroy any form of slavery in Germany without destroying all forms of slavery. Germany is too thorough-going to be able to revolutionize in any other way than from the very foundation of society. The emancipation of Germany means the emancipation of mankind. Philosophy is the directive impulse of this emancipation; its life-blood is the proletariat.'

The *Deutsch-französische Jahrbücher* reveal with an unmistakable clarity the psychological path trodden by the youthful Marx. It was not an overwhelming consciousness of the necessity for freeing the proletariat from its hunger and misery that caused Marx to regard revolution as the sole means to achieve that aim. He did not proceed from the proletariat to revolution. Indeed he chose a path proceeding in a directly contrary direction. His path had its beginning in his own intellectual and spiritual qualities, and his choice was influenced by the ideals that Hölderlin had implanted in the young German intellectuals of the *Vormärz*. He sought to free himself from the pressure exercised upon him and his intellectual equals by the mediocre German Police-State. And the way to such a liberation lay only through a German Revolution.

Marx was not actuated in these ideas by egotistic motives. It was not that he desired special privileges for himself and his friends. His aim was to raise the Germans from serfdom to freedom so as to make them men. It was in his search for a means by which to achieve this revolution that Marx discovered the proletariat.

A hasty consideration of these facts might lead one to think that the youthful Marx was a crafty or a would-be crafty Liberal. At first sight he seems to be a typical middle-class Liberal who recognized that his own class did not possess sufficient strength of itself to attain its ends and therefore looked around for allies. The feudal 'police and bondman' State was the enemy. The educated and propertied middle class was not powerful enough to overthrow this enemy by its own force. Other forces—the peasant and the industrial workman—must be called upon to help. It was thus that France in 1789 had stormed the Bastille with the aid of the poor. It was thus that the French *bourgeoisie* had hunted Charles X from his throne in July, 1830, with the help of the proletarian fighters on the Paris barricades. In the same way many Russian liberals sympathized in 1900 with the workmen's movement and accorded it an important share in the common task of overthrowing Tsarism.

It was Marx's lack of interest in the prosperity of the propertied middle class that distinguished him from this type of French and Russian Liberal. His aim was to raise humanity to philosophic heights and to make out of a bond-man a free and independent individual. This pinnacle of human development is as incompatible with the cash-books of a banker as with the castle of a feudal baron.

To this may be retorted: 'All these idealistic demands', 'philosophic heights', 'true humanity', &c., are only trappings to disguise a capitalistic striving after profits. The battle of Marxism against Capitalism is only a sham fight. Marxism and Liberalism are at bottom identical. They pursue a common aim: the destruction of a propertied, conservative order of society based upon family and tradition. That, however, is 'the fight against feudalism'. Are the reproaches justified which to-day are levelled against Marx and Marxism particularly in lower middle-class and anti-Semitic circles?

The social aspect of the middle-class revolution consists in the substitution of the rule of the propertied middle class and of the intellectuals who form a part of it for that of the feudal aristocracy with its following of officers, bureaucrats, priests, &c. The middle class, nevertheless, cannot simply denounce government by aristocrats and priests and praise that by manufacturers and lawyers, in order to achieve its aim. It is compelled to develop a radical criticism of the entire order of society that is bound up with aristocratic government. In other words, it must attack the existing order of society as a whole. The middle class cannot cry out against old fetters and then substitute new ones for them. It must demand the abolition of all fetters. Nor can the middle class substitute government by plutocrats for government by aristocrats. It must substitute the liberation of mankind.

It was ideas of this nature that inspired the middle-class revolutions of the seventeenth and eighteenth centuries. But the moment the middle-class revolution is victorious it must divorce itself from its own ideology. For in order to establish the power of money on the ruins of feudalism it is necessary to throw up fresh barriers against the unpropertied classes. The place of the old fetters must be taken by new fetters that are distinguishable from them only in shape. This transformation took almost grotesque forms in the policy pursued by the French Constituent Assembly from 1789 to 1791.

Nevertheless, there are always to be found in such a situation a number of radical minds who separate from their class and go ahead of it. These minds hold firmly to the theories which they propounded before the revolution took place. Their desire is to give the fullest possible practical expression to their theories of liberty and equality. Thus Robespierre still clung to his hope of realizing Rousseau's ideals after the fall of the Bastille and the collapse of absolutism. Such logical minds are forced to seek for new elements and classes in the population with whose aid they may complete the work abandoned by the middle class. Robespierre appealed to the poverty-stricken masses of the population; Marx to the proletariat.

In the eighteen-forties, when the German middle-class revolution was anticipated, Marx had before his eyes, in the examples of England and France, the attitude adopted after a successful revolution by the entire European middle class. Moreover, the theory and practice of contemporary German Liberalism showed only too clearly what would be the attitude of the German middle class after a successful revolution. He was not, therefore, labouring under any illusions.

A precisely similar example of the relationship between ideology and class-warfare is to be found in the Reformation in the sixteenth century. Princes, knights, and townspeople wanted to seize the revenues of the Church for themselves and to refuse to acknowledge priestly authority. In order to attain this aim they were forced, however, to call in question the entire social order that had been in existence in Europe for a thousand years. To papal dogmas they were compelled to oppose the principle of freedom and equality for every Christian. When, however, the new evangelical State Church rose from the ruins of the Roman Church, and the new faith came to take the place of the old, men like Thomas Münzer refused to be content with what had already been achieved. The task that had been abandoned by princes and merchants should be completed by the peasantry. It was for the peasants to throw off the shackles of serfdom and thus achieve the promised freedom. Robespierre and the youthful

Marx stood in the same relationship to middle-class Liberalism as Thomas Münzer stood to Luther—as fire to water.

Ever since the Revolution of 1688 the middle class had held the reins of government in England. In France it had finally grasped them in the July Revolution of 1830. But in central and eastern Europe monarchical feudalism reigned until 1848. It was the steady development of machinery and industry since the middle of the eighteenth century that conferred upon the middle-class movement its expansive force. At the same time the middle-class intellectuals sought to clarify and co-ordinate their ideas about their own class, aims, and duties. This tremendous intellectual task was attacked from two sides by the English political economists and the German philosophers.

The English political economists—especially Ricardo—discovered that the source of all values lies in the human capacity for work. Although they had also ascertained correctly the division of results as between employer and employed, i.e. that the former took the profits and the latter obtained a bare minimum on which to exist, they accepted this fact as a natural law which could not be broken or called in question. It was Hegel who discovered the schism in the middle-class society that sprang from the ruins of the old patriarchal order. He drew attention to the contrast between the small minority which grew ever richer and the great majority which steadily became more and more impoverished. This contrast seemed to him to proceed from an unalterable natural law. And in order to avoid a revolutionary solution of the problem Hegel proceeded to develop his conception of an omnipotent State founded upon Reason, in which the contrast between rich and poor afforded by the middle-class order of society would be overcome by a new and corporative order of society arranged according to professions. But Hegel's own teaching was contradictory of this artificial solution. He believed in an incessant spiritual progress that was always in opposition to itself. Each appearance of the world-spirit (*Weltgeist*) at a definite period in history of necessity gave rise to opposition. It was out of the conflict of power with power that a new and third force was born. This dialectic method when applied by Hegel to his own age clearly taught that the thesis (middle-class society) must be overcome by the antithesis (proletariat) in order to prepare the way for the new synthesis. In Hegel's eyes each period in history constituted a unity. The world-spirit displayed itself similarly in politics and philosophy, art and religion. If that be granted, then there is no longer any absolute historical value, since all the ideas of the philosophers, religious thinkers, &c., are the product of a definite historical period and must disappear with that period. Only the world-spirit itself is absolute in its eternal progression. In these ideas of Hegel are to be found the chief elements composing Marx's materialistic conception of history.

The critical minds among the middle-class *intelligentsia* in Germany as in England thus attained the uttermost limits of their self-analysis in the years preceding 1830. A single step farther must of necessity involve an upheaval of middle-class society.

In countries like France and England, in which the middle class had been politically victorious, it had drawn a sharp line of demarcation between itself and the poor and non-propertied masses. In England, as also in France under Louis Philippe, the suffrage was reserved for the proper-tied minority. The working classes, the peasantry, and the labourers, were the objects of law-making. The ruling middle class sought to conserve everything in the old feudal govern-mental system that could be of use in protecting the existing order against the masses. The English middle class retained the Monarchy, the House of Lords, and the antiquated feudal ceremonial. The French *bourgeoisie* also retained the Mon-archy in addition to the highly centralized administra-tive apparatus that had been set up under Louis XIV, destroyed during the Revolution, and resurrected in an even more centralized form under Napoleon I.

The disappointed masses did not wish to renounce the freedom and equality which had been promised by the prophets of the middle-class revolution. They wanted democracy; the self-government of the masses; and the abolition of all the privileges of the newly aggrandized middle class no less than of the old feudal nobles. Although demo-cratic ideas of republicanism and universal suffrage were at first purely political, it was not long before the conception of economic reform was added to them.

In the years preceding 1848 the rebellion of the workmen against their lot was obliged at first to take democratic form after the example of Robespierre and of 1793. Such of the young middle-class intellectuals as were radically inclined were also unable to reconcile themselves to the plutocracy which had come to occupy the throne formerly occupied by feudalism. These youthful Radicals set themselves at the head of the democratic movement. In England they formed the democratic working-class party known as the Chartists; while in France a number of opposition groups came into existence whose programmes embraced everything from purely political reform to its logical outcome, social revolution.

Feudalism still flourished in Germany. The Germany of 1847 stood politically where France had stood in 1788. The propertied middle class made ready to enter upon their inheritance. But behind the moderate Liberals rose the menacing figure of Demos intent upon substituting a complete revolution for the partial revolution which was expected to occur. The Radicals among the German intellectuals were the heirs of Hegel and developed his ideas to their logical conclusion. In the ranks of the young Hegelian revolutionaries stood Marx and Engels.

Karl Marx risked the final step and placed himself and his ideas outside the pale of middle-class society. He was now able to turn the economic notions of Ricardo to his own purposes. It was no longer a natural law that the factory worker should only receive a bare living-wage for his work; it was only the phenomenon characteristic of a particular historical period—the period of middle-class Capitalism. The capitalist law of wages would disappear with the downfall of Capitalism. Similarly the State is not the incorporation of eternal wisdom but only the political superstructure of a middle-class order of Society. The State falls with the destruction of that order of society.

The materialist interpretation of history consists in the application of dialectical criticism to all aspects of human life. The value of every activity and interest is carefully weighed in the balance and found wanting. Nevertheless, criticism alone did not suffice to bring about the disappearance of the middle-class State and the middle-class standard of wages. Philosophic criticism showed that no form of life was eternal. This did not indeed mean that the subjects of critical analysis were mere figments of the brain any more than air disappears because of the discovery by a scientist of the elements composing it. The police force maintained by the middle-class State and the cash-boxes of the capitalists are bitter truths which cannot be avoided by stripping them of their ideological coverings. The Revolution was the sole means of depriving the capitalists of power and of destroying them. And this last of all revolutions could only be carried out by the class which Fate had liberated from all the traditions, theories, and other restrictions imposed upon the feudal and middle-class societies—the proletariat.

The working class was thus in Marx's system confronted with a task that was as unique as it was vast—the consummation of a philosophy. It was to be their task to put the theories of the philosophers into practice. The middle-class intellectuals destroyed their own class in their final and most courageous conclusions by mobilizing a social underworld in order to prove the truth of their doctrines. Thus Marx saw an indissoluble association between theory and revolution. Theories are no more than intellectual toys without the revolution that gives them practical form. Marxism is a book of fundamental principles whose final chapter is revolution.

The working-classes in France and England, Belgium and Germany, were up to 1848 becoming daily more and more conscious of their peculiar situation. They sought in consequence to improve their miserable condition, and dreamed of a new and better order of society in which 'rich and poor' should no longer exist. Nevertheless, the European proletariat achieved little before 1848 in the way of independent thinking and organization. It contented itself with feeling its way slowly within the framework of the democratic movement. A few isolated and desperate outbreaks on the part of workmen did nothing to raise the working-class level.

Once Marx had made up his mind on the subject of his own system it became necessary for him to seek the support of the working class. Europe was faced with a democratic revolution. It was hoped that the proletariat would play the part in this revolution that Marx had assigned to it. Marx visited Brussels, Paris, and London, in company with his friend Engels, in order to establish contact with the various democratic and proletarian groups. He sought to bring home to the German workmen abroad the nature of the historic mission which they were called upon to fulfil, and he founded the Communist Party with a mere handful of supporters. On the eve of the Revolution of 1848 Marx published his Communist Manifesto, which contained the Party's programme.

In this Manifesto Marx drew a clear line of demarcation between the great task awaiting his Party in the future—the overthrow of capitalism—and its more immediate work of assisting in ensuring the success of the coming democratic revolution in Europe.

On the subject of Germany the Communist Manifesto runs:

'As soon as the *bourgeois* revolution begins in Germany, the Communist Party will make common cause with it against the absolutist monarchy, the feudal landed proprietors, and the lower middle class. At the same time the Party will lose no opportunity for making apparent to the working class the enmity that exists between middle class and proletariat. It will do this in order that the social and political conditions which must of necessity arise out of the rule of the middle class, may be used by the workers as so many weapons to be turned against that class so as to ensure that the moment the reactionary classes have been overthrown in Germany the battle against the middle class will begin. The eyes of Communists are turned towards Germany because it is there that the middle-class revolution is about to break forth which will be carried out with the help of a far more advanced proletariat and under the more progressive influence of present-day European civilization than were the revolutions in England and in France in the seventeenth and eighteenth centuries. For this reason the German middle-class revolution will only be the prelude to a proletarian revolution.'

The Communists in England were to support the Chartist Movement, in France the Social Democrat Party, and in Poland the nationalist revolutionaries who also desired an agrarian reform. In short, the Communists were to support all revolutionary movements that were directed against existing social and political conditions. Marx set before the Communists the duty of working everywhere for the unification of the democratic movements throughout the world. International co-operation among democrats in the Europe of 1848 was only natural in view of the fact that the feudal and monarchical governments had united themselves beneath the banner of the Holy Alliance. Nevertheless, Marx did not intend to supplant nationalism by internationalism.

In the Communist Manifesto is to be found a sentence that is frequently torn from its context: 'The working class knows no country.' The sentences that follow reveal what these words were intended to mean, namely, that the working class had no country simply because others were in possession of it—it was for the working class to conquer it for themselves. This does not mean that the conception of patriotism is senseless and something which ought to be combated. In the present political state of the world the idea of nationality exists and must be respected as a political reality. It cannot be destroyed merely by creating in the working class a feeling of belonging to no country in particular. Its disappearance will only come about through a social and economic development that will gradually unite the European States after a successful proletarian revolution.

The fall of the feudal Monarchy and the middle-class Liberals was to be followed by the rule of democracy—self-government by the proletariat. In Marx's view true democracy in a modern industrialized State can only mean the government of the proletariat in the sense that the working class assumes the leadership of the middle class and the peasantry. Through 'autocratic attacks upon the right of property' common ownership would gradually be established. Marx concluded by painting in glowing colours a picture of the disappearance of the State itself as the final step in this evolutionary process.

'When in the course of evolution class differences vanish and production is concentrated in the hands of the community, governmental authority will lose its political character. In its essence governmental authority is the utilization of the organized force of one class for the suppression of another. But when the proletariat of necessity forms itself into a class in its fight against

the middle class and through a revolution becomes the governing
class itself and then abolishes the old methods of production, it
abolishes with these old methods of production the fundamental
causes of class differences, class differences themselves, and therefore its own authority as a class. In place of the old middle-class
order of society with its class divisions and differences there comes
into being an association in which the free development of the
individual is the preliminary condition for the free development
of all.'

After the overthrow of the kings, nobles, and great
capitalists, a democratic government in the sense of 1793
would have to suppress counter-revolution with an iron hand
and carry out the abolition of ownership. Nevertheless, the
authoritarian State was not an end in itself. At the last the
State—that vehicle of middle-class and feudal government—
would dissolve itself and in its place would appear voluntary
association. Hence the 'ideal State' is not one of Marx's
ideals, since in his view there should no longer be any State in
the future, and its place should be taken by a voluntary
association of independent individuals. It was thus that he
hoped to realize the highest ambition of the eighteenth-
century revolutionaries—the perfect freedom and equality
of mankind.

The tasks actually facing Germany in 1848 were naturally
far less ambitious. The immediate problem was the destruction of princely and aristocratic power. Marx and Engels
actively participated in the Revolution, and in Cologne in
1848–9 they published the *Neue Rheinische Zeitung* as 'a
mouthpiece of democracy'. It proved to be the most daring
and most influential newspaper at the disposal of German
democracy. In its columns Marx and Engels preached a
revolutionary war on the part of the German nation against
Russia, as well as against Denmark and against the Austrian
Slavs, in the hope that in such a war a dictatorship similar
to that of 1793 would be established that would still farther
carry on the revolution. The *Neue Rheinische Zeitung* was
both nationalist and militarist in an actively democratic
sense. It was not a workman's paper in the customary meaning of the word. Indeed the various occupational and class
interests of the workers received scant attention in its pages.

This was left to Stephan Born, who in 1848-9 in Berlin and Leipzig sought to pursue a truly working-class policy—a policy founded upon conditions of work, wages, and hours of work that defined the position of the working class within democracy in general and more especially within the middle-class order of society. Although he was a member of the Communist Party, Born worked independently of Marx and Engels, and his great services were ignored by Marx despite the fact that they were conducted along strictly revolutionary lines. For Marx as a practical German politician only the coming democratic revolution was then of importance. This revolution could only succeed through a merciless criticism and showing-up of the middle class. This criticism, however, must concentrate for the present upon the great political problems and not upon proletarian problems of wages, hours of labour, &c. At this stage in the revolution it was necessary to reveal the 'treachery' of the middle class in the Danish, Polish, agrarian, and constitutional questions rather than in the wages issue.

In sentences in the Communist Manifesto that have become famous Marx defined the relations between the Communists and the working class.

'The Communists are not a special Party as compared with the other Labour Parties. They have no interests that are not those of the entire proletariat. . . . The Communists are therefore the most determined and propulsive element in the Labour Parties in all countries. They simply possess a clearer insight into the conditions, course, and results of the proletarian revolution than the majority of the proletariat.'

Who were in fact the Communists of 1848? The choice of the title is to be explained as follows: In those days the term Socialist merely denoted in general any one who was interested in questions of property-ownership and in criticism of the existing order of society. A Communist was a more revolutionary type of workman who was engaged in fighting Capitalism. The only organized Communists were the members of the Communist Party. Nevertheless, the policy of the Party was not determined by the wishes of its members.

The only true Communism was the teachings and opinions of Marx himself. The only equal whom Marx then and subsequently recognized was Friedrich Engels, whose views he listened to. All the others who worked with Marx and Engels in promoting the movement were treated by them with contempt. In proof of this it is only necessary to recall the expressions used by Marx and Engels in their letters to one another in speaking of Lassalle and Wilhelm Liebknecht. The Party organization was looked upon by Marx and Engels simply as a medium through which they could better influence the working class as a whole. And never once in any serious issue did they ask what were the wishes of 'the rebels'. If the Party were to make difficulties, or to fail to perform its functions, Marx and Engels believed it would be better either to abandon it or to dissolve it, and to confront the masses alone without the restrictions imposed by co-operation with a petty-minded deliberative body. On February 13, 1851, Engels gave open expression to these views in a letter to Marx. He wrote:

'At long last and for the first time for years past we have an opportunity for showing that we do not need either the support or the applause of any Party in any land and that we are wholly independent of such foolishness. From this moment onwards we are answerable for ourselves alone. When the time comes in which they have need of us, then we shall be in a position to dictate our own terms. Until then at least we have peace. . . . Moreover, we have no need to lament because the *petits grands hommes* avoid us. Have we not pretended for many years that Krethi Plethi was our Party, although we had no Party there, and those whom we at least officially recognized as members of our Party . . . did not comprehend the very ABC of our movement? How can men like ourselves, who avoid official positions like the plague, belong to a Party? What would become of us scorners of popularity if we began to be popular? What have we to do with a Party that is nothing more than a herd of asses, and that swears by us because its members look upon us as their equals?'

This letter was written by Engels in the bitterness of exile, and after the failure of the Revolution, at a time when Marx and Engels were ostracized by the other refugees. Although this fact explains the presence of many forcible expressions in the letter, the general tone is a faithful echo of their views. The two men invariably remained loyal to this principle and never bowed before the authority of their 'Party' in any weighty question. The 'Communists' of the 'Manifesto' were in truth only Marx and Engels themselves.

It may be discerned clearly from this how in those days Marxism was introduced into the working classes as something extraneous to them. Out of the working class itself sprang with elemental force only criticism of existing conditions, especially of their own living conditions, as well as a naïve Utopian belief in a better future and in the great uprising of the peoples which was to effect the overthrow of all proud and oppressive rulers. The working man himself did not realize, before his eyes had been opened for him by non-working-class counsellors, that he was himself to take over the leadership of this revolution and to advance by definite stages towards the realization of the communal order of society. The working class was indeed prepared to play its part in a national revolution at the side and under the leadership of the radical middle class. Hence the bitter disappointment aroused in the German working class in particular by the 'betrayal' of the common cause by the middle classes in 1848-9.

The naïve and inexperienced working class was thus in accord with Marx and Engels in its belief that the first necessity was the middle-class—the national—revolution. Although the working class was prepared to participate in this revolution loyally and obediently at the side of the middle class, Marx and Engels informed it that the middle class would prove itself incapable of bringing even its *own* revolution to a successful conclusion, and that therefore the national revolution must be conducted in a way in which the *Neue Rheinische Zeitung* had sought to secure the intellectual leadership of the Revolution of 1848-9. The theory of the political mission of the working class was thus inoculated into that class by the two most radical minds among the middle-class intellectuals—Marx and Engels. Since, however, the working masses were unaccustomed to such a task, it was obvious that it could not be achieved by the workers alone and unaided; and that it was only to be brought to a successful conclusion by means of a strongly disciplined organization that blindly followed the orders of its intellectual leaders. If the organization should prove itself unwilling to submit to so stern a discipline, then it must be destroyed and a new organization built up in its stead. It was out of this unique and variable relationship between the radical intellectual leaders and the proletarian masses that there emerged the dictatorship of the leaders over the proletariat. The purpose of the Communist teaching was that the workers should gradually come to recognize their historic mission in the doctrines of Marx and that they should themselves achieve their own liberation. Meanwhile they were very far from such knowledge, and until they had attained to it Marx and Engels were compelled to lead autocratically the infantile working-class movement.

After the collapse of the Revolution of 1848-9 Marx and Engels went to England. The Communist Party broke up in consequence of the failure. Marx saw no possibility for decades to come of putting his theories into practice. The life had gone out of Marxism and the loss was not compensated by Marx's theoretical work on 'Capitalism'. The First International, which was founded by Marx in 1864, was not a revolutionary Party in the Marxian sense. It was not even a united political Party. It was no more than a loose international union of working men's organizations of all kinds. Its membership included the Liberal and middle-class English Trade Unions and Latin anarchists. Two small Labour Parties founded by Lassalle and Wilhelm Liebknecht in Germany in the 'sixties were among the closest supporters of Marx within the International—a fact that did not prevent Marx and Lassalle from criticizing their leaders in a forcible and unjust manner.

Throughout the constitutional struggles in Prussia from 1862 to 1866, when Bismarck was making war upon the Liberal Majority in the Prussian Diet and ruling unconstitutionally as a dictator, Marx indulged once more in hopes of a middle-class revolution in Prussia and Germany, and he looked upon Lassalle's refusal to share this hope as little short of treachery. But Lassalle no longer believed in the German middle class as a means to revolution, and his object in a non-revolutionary period was to organize an independent class-conscious Proletarian Party that should be clearly distinguished from the Liberals. Nor was Lassalle's conscience in the least disturbed by the fact that in pursuit of his great aim he was temporarily brought into tactical association with Bismarck. Marx demanded from the Prussian working class that it should fight against the Hohenzollerns and the Junkers in the sense laid down by the *Neue Rheinische Zeitung*; and once again he reminded it that the democratic middle-class revolution was its first objective. All subsequent criticism by Marx and Engels of the Social Democrats in Germany, up to Engel's criticism of the Erfurt Programme of 1891, is based upon a single reproach—the reproach of insufficient preparation for the middle-class revolution, of suppressing the republican principle, of an indefinite attitude towards 'the State', &c.

The year 1871 saw the great workmen's uprising known as the Paris Commune. Marx had no part in preparing this rising and its leaders were not Communists. The fact that among these leaders were to be found members of the International does nothing to prove the contrary; for the loose and varied nature of the International has already been explained above. The Commune proclaimed the substitution of self-government and free association for the centralized authoritarian State. The masses were to be represented in the municipal and provincial administrations by representatives who were not to receive more than a workman's wage. These representatives were to incorporate the deliberative, law-giving, and executive powers. Modest 'communal' officials were to replace the parliament and bureaucracy of the ancient feudal and middle-class State. An armed nation was to act as its own army and police.

The Paris Commune took a course that was very different from that visualized by Marx. Marx had postulated a centralized and ruthless revolutionary Government, inspired by the mentality of 1793, which should beat down all enemies of the people by means of a concentration of all revolutionary forces. To proclaim a federalist and communal organization of society in the middle of a civil war seemed to Marx sentimental folly. The Commune started to realize its plans at the very point where Marx made his revolution end—with the destruction of the State and the establishment of the rule of liberty. This served at least to bring the ideals of the Commune into some sort of connexion with those of Marx.

After the defeat of the Commune Marx induced the Committee of the International to place itself unreservedly on the side of the Paris workmen. In his famous pamphlet, published in 1871, Marx proclaimed that the cause of the Commune was his own cause. All differences in theory and practice were ignored and only praise accorded to the revolutionary achievement of the Paris workmen and the destruction of the State. Marx had adopted the Commune of 1871 for his own purposes, an action unique in history in that the Commune was neither politically nor theoretically the work of Marx.

Marx thus took a fateful step. It was thus—and thus only —that he acquired for Communism a real revolutionary tradition. It was then that Communism became for the first time the creed of all revolutionary workers throughout the world. This great success was bought at a price: the immediate dissolution of the centralized State authority became the classical model for a working-class revolution.

The First International broke up in the 'seventies in consequence of its own internal dissensions and Marx's autocratic methods. All prospects of revolution had vanished not only in central and western Europe but also in America. Governmental authority had become so firmly established in Germany and France, Austria-Hungary and Italy, England and the United States of America, that armed revolt seemed to have no chance of success. Capitalism became more and more powerful everywhere. At the same time the numbers and importance of the industrial proletariat experienced a concomitant increase. The political working-class movement again became daily more evident; and especially in Germany, where in 1890 the laws against the Socialists had undergone modification. Nevertheless, the European proletariat in the heyday of the Second International after 1889 no longer had the democratic revolution as their political objective as had their forebears of 1848. Instead, their energies were devoted to improving their social and economic condition within the capitalist State. It is true that the Second International adopted Marx's theories.

These, however, were forced to undergo a singular change to make them adaptable to a non-revolutionary age. Communism now served, above all else, to enable the proletariat to differentiate itself ideologically from the middle class. In other words—to secure for itself an independent class existence within capitalist society. The Socialist working class—the Marxist Parties now adopted the designations 'Socialist' or 'Social Democrat'—no longer permitted itself to be dictated to by individual intellectuals in its Party organizations and trade unions. The organized workman now claimed for himself the right of self-determination within his organization.

Thus Communism changed from a revolutionary doctrine used by the extreme Radicals among the middle-class intellectuals to drive the working masses onwards, to a professional ideology with whose help the class-conscious workman defended and improved his position within the middle-class order of society. Although this change in Communism between 1848 and the Second International indicated a great development in the personal activity and the self-confidence of the working class, it was at the same time a definite step backwards on the revolutionary path. There was, nevertheless, still a great country in the Europe of the 'nineties where Communism could regain its position of 1848, and where it was not obliged to evolve any farther in a western European form. This country was Russia. There the middle-class revolution was imminent and the finest brains among the intellectuals desired to perfect the revolution in a Marxist sense with the help of the working class. Revolutionary Communism of 1848 thus found the path to further development open to it in Tsarist Russia.

The young revolutionary Lenin arrived in St. Petersburg from the Volga in 1893 to put the theories of Marx into practice.

II
REVOLUTION IN RUSSIA, 1893–1914

A CRUDE modernity characterized Tsarist Russia in the eighteenth century. At a time when almost the entire European continent bore the stamp of Absolutism Peter the Great and Catherine II were progressive rulers. And in days that saw the Congress of Vienna, Alexander I could afford to be more liberal in European politics than either Metternich or the King of Prussia.

The scene underwent a change during the reign of his successor, Nicholas I. The ideals of the French Revolution began more and more to penetrate Russia, where they were enthusiastically welcomed by the *intelligentsia*, which from this time onward walked step by step with the radical theorists of western Europe. Moreover, the criticism of existing conditions on the part of the *intelligentsia* found its justification in the misery of the vast Russian peasantry, which was still cumbered with the chains of serfdom.

Russia in the nineteenth century was still a feudal State. On the one side were the Tsar, the aristocratic landowners, the Church, Army, Police, and bureaucracy; on the other were the serfs. Between these two opposing forces stood a numerically small commercial and industrial middle class and a proletariat that was slowly coming into existence. The *intelligentsia* in Russia played a very important role in hastening the development of events. For the most part the educated and independent Radicals were aristocrats by birth. A father would sit in his office as Chief of Police or Governor while his daughter stood at a street corner throwing bombs. The social and intellectual history of the Russian Revolution reveals the very strong suicidal tendency at work in the Russian nobility as a class. Young students of noble birth themselves destroyed all that their fathers had constructed and venerated. The French aristocracy destroyed itself in a similar fashion in the eighteenth century before the outbreak of the French Revolution. As soon as the feudal organization of the State was felt to be intolerable by the masses, and once the historical development of the *ancien régime* had publicly revealed itself as outworn, its leaders faded away and opened the doors to revolution.

Tsar Alexander II sought to stem the tide by the so-called liberation of the serfs in the 'sixties. The peasants thus acquired legal freedom. Nevertheless, the land itself remained for the most part in the hands of the landowners and the village police were as powerful and brutal after the 'liberation' as before. The liberation of the serfs only testified to the strength of the revolutionary movement without solving a single one of the problems confronting Russia. The bomb that blew Alexander II to pieces in 1881 was the revolutionaries' reply to the comedy of the liberation of the serfs.

Who were the men and women who assassinated the Tsar? They were conspirators belonging to the great and many-sided movement that for close on fifty years, from about 1870 to 1917, constituted the driving force of the Russian Revolution, and manifested itself under every kind of title and organization. This movement as a whole can best be described as the 'popular' or 'national' movement. The characteristic common to all *Naródniki* ('democrats') was a frenzied hatred of the Tsar and his Government and a firm belief in Russia and especially the Russian peasant. Their aim was to overthrow the brutal governmental bureaucracy and replace it by a popular government in which the chief power should rest in the hands of the peasantry, as forming the great majority of the nation and embodying its special characteristics. The last vestiges of communal ownership among the peasantry that had survived the Tsardom and serfdom should perhaps be used to form the foundation of a Russian agrarian Socialism. Russia should learn from western Europe without necessarily adopting its theories in their entirety.

It was clear that the stupid and uneducated Russian peasant could not attain to this knowledge by himself. For this purpose he needed the assistance of the *intelligentsia*. Hence the self-sacrificing young aristocrats and intellectuals went 'among the people' and into the villages in order to indoctrinate the peasantry and prepare the revolution. There thus came into existence the type of educated Russian revolutionary who fought with all the means at his disposal, who did not hesitate to use terrorist methods against the hated representatives of the Government, who pursued the same ends in Switzerland and Siberia that he had followed in St. Petersburg and Moscow, and who served the cause of the Russian people in prison and on the gallows as well as in the editorial office of a prohibited newspaper and in the deliberations of his Party. The 'popular' movement created the professional Russian revolutionary who knew no other end in life except revolution, and who was ready to sacrifice his life in the popular cause. This type, however, was very far removed from the peasant. The finest characteristic of the 'democrats', who subsequently became generally known as 'Social Revolutionaries', and other groups allied with them, was their revolutionary heroism. Their weakness lay in their confused ideology. They refused obstinately to recognize that Russia could not remain for ever an agrarian paradise in the midst of a modern capitalistic world. And they could return no answer to the question as to what change would be wrought in Russia by modern industrialism.

The romanticist policy of the Social Revolutionaries was blind to facts and sought either to ignore Capitalism in Russia, or to exclude it. In the 'eighties and 'nineties of the nineteenth century, however, industries rapidly arose on a large scale that were called into being by the military requirements of the Tsarist Government and under the stimulation of foreign capitalists. The modern employer appeared at the side of the old half-Asiatic type of Russian merchant. Out of the villages came an industrial working class that at first maintained a bare existence under miserable conditions and then began to fight against their exploiters.

The greater the importance for Russia of the industrial and proletarian problem the greater was the interest displayed by a part of the Russian *intelligentsia* in Socialism and Marxism. Since public and legal activity on the part of Russian Socialists in associations or trade unions was forbidden by the Tsarist police, an illicit Social Democrat Party came into existence.

There is a surprising resemblance between Russia in 1895 and Germany in 1845. In both countries a middle-class revolution was imminent; the majority of the population was engaged in agrarian pursuits, although industry was increasing; the governmental system was the object of intense hatred on the part of all courageous and independent thinkers; and in both countries the majority of the nation was filled with an overwhelming desire for liberty. In Germany the youthful disciples of Hegel appealed to the nation to aid them in realizing their philosophical ideals in the same way that in Russia the *intelligentsia* turned to the masses in the hope of stirring them into rebellion against the Tsar. Finally, the mass of the population in both countries, and especially the working class, was politically ignorant and incapable of acting independently without receiving guidance from another source.

For this reason all the conditions preceding the revolutionary Marxism of 1848 made their appearance again in the Russia of 1895. The inculcation into Russia of Marxism in its original form nevertheless presented grave difficulties. For Russia in the 'nineties did not make acquaintance with Marxism in the form of the 'Union of Communists' but in the great Labour Parties—especially the German Social Democrat Party—of the Second International. A twofold development of Russian Socialism thus became possible: either through alliance with contemporary central and western European Labour movements or in a revival of the original Marxism of 1848. In choosing the latter path Lenin created the Bolshevism that stands in sharp contrast to western European Social Democracy and that claims with some justification to have resurrected the old revolutionary Marxism.

Lenin was descended from an ennobled family of Russian State officials. His brother took part in a conspiracy against the life of the Tsar and was executed. Lenin himself was filled with the same fiery hatred of Tsarism. Although he admired the heroism of the *Naródniki*, Lenin could not join the Social Revolutionary movement since his logical mind and scientific education prevented his sympathizing with the vague and sentimental ideals of the 'democrats'. He recognized that Russia could not escape industrialization and that Marxism as a scientific system towered above the fantastic notions of the *Naródniki*. He saw his mission as the task of allying a number of clear-thinking, realist, and determined revolutionaries with the industrial proletariat. It was only in this way that Tsarism could be defeated. Lenin thus took over from the *Naródniki* the organization of revolutionary 'cells' which live among the masses and are entrusted with the task of influencing and directing them. To await a spontaneous uprising of the masses would mean that revolution would be postponed for ever.

The development of Russian Social Democracy took the same course that had been followed by the Social Revolutionary Parties. Enthusiastic young revolutionaries in the 'eighties and 'nineties went among the industrial workers instead of the peasants. Armed with the writings of Marx and Engels, they abandoned their luxurious homes in the fashionable districts of St. Petersburg and Moscow and went to live in the slums of the working-class districts where they 'discovered' the proletariat. At first they contented themselves with winning the confidence of the working class by means of night-schools and free instruction, before attempting to inculcate them with Socialism.

What a different picture from that presented at the same time by the Socialist Labour Parties in western Europe! It was, nevertheless, the same method that had been followed half a century before by Marx and Engels in order to win over the German manual workers in Paris and Brussels to the revolution.

The further development of the infant Social Democrat Party in Russia depended now upon what they decided on as their principal aim. Two courses were open to them: to lay the greatest emphasis in their work either upon the special class interests of the workers—the social and political questions of wages, hours of work, conditions of work, housing, &c. —or upon the political struggle against the Tsarist Government. If they chose the former course, then the industrial workman became the decisive factor in the movement. The right of each individual member of the organization to vote would be preserved and the revolutionary impetus would be weakened. If, however, they adopted the second course, the professional revolutionaries would have control of the movement and the ordinary workman would have to obey them.

Under the first of these two alternatives it might indeed have been possible to achieve a partial legal existence for Socialism even under the Tsarist régime. The second alternative meant a life and death struggle with the Tsarist Government after the fashion of the struggle waged by the *Naródniki* Terrorists.

Lenin unhesitatingly decided upon the second course. In 1902 he wrote:

'We often say that the workman does not possess an inherent socialist democratic feeling and that this must be inculcated in him from without. Yet the history of every country shows that the working class is capable by itself of attaining Trade-Union consciousness, that is to say, of attaining to the conviction of the necessity to unite in Trade Unions, to fight against employers, to demand the passing of this or that law by the Government in the interests of the working class, &c. The theories of Socialism have developed from the philosophical, historical, and economic theories that have been the offspring of the brains of the educated elements in the propertied classes—the *intelligentsia*. Even the founders of modern scientific socialism—Marx and Engels—belonged socially to the middle-class *intelligentsia*. The theory of Social Democracy in Russia arose in a similar manner and wholly independent of the tremendous growth of the Labour movement. It came into being as the natural and inevitable consequence of the intellectual development of the revolutionary socialist mind.'

Lenin continued:

'The workman can only grow class-conscious outside the influence of the economic struggle and of his relations with his employer. The only sphere in which this knowledge can be gained is that of the relations between all classes in the State and the Government —the sphere of the interplay of relationships between all classes. It is for this reason that the question "What is to be done to make the workman politically intelligent?" cannot always be answered with the simple reply that satisfies many practical minds: "Associate with and teach the workmen." In order to make the working class politically intelligent Social Democrats must go into all classes of the community and must send out divisions of their army in all directions.'

Lenin firmly rejected the type of Labour movement which he called Trade Unionism after the English Trade Unions that were then specially typical of this movement. It was not enough that the proletariat should fight for their own class interests. The Russian Social Democrats must introduce their propaganda and carry on their agitation in all classes of the community and especially among the peasantry. The daily discontent of the workman with factory conditions, &c., must be developed into a general dissatisfaction with Tsarism as the source of all evils.

Again Lenin wrote:

'We possess neither a Parliament nor freedom of assembly. Nevertheless we are able to hold meetings of workmen who wish to listen to a Social Democrat. We must, however, manage to hold meetings for all classes desirous of hearing what a Democrat has to say. For he who forgets that "Communists support every revolutionary movement", and that we are therefore bound to make clear to the people the common task of democracy without for a moment concealing our Socialist convictions, is no true Social Democrat. Nor is he a Social Democrat who forgets his duty to go a step ahead of all others in the formulation, provocation, and solution of every general democratic problem.'

Lenin regarded Social Democracy as the great leader of the Russian nation in its struggle for freedom. If, however, that was to be its task, then it could only adopt one form of organization—the close, strongly disciplined Party of professional revolutionaries. The great mass of the working class should be influenced by the Party without being members of it. In Lenin's eyes a Labour Party in the western European sense of the term was impossible in Russia for the simple reason that the police forbade it. The real reason was of another and deeper nature: such a Party would not be able to carry out its revolutionary task. Russian Social Democracy must not be inspired by the ideas of a Trade Union secretary but by those of a tribune of the people. Let us listen once again to the voice of Lenin speaking in 1902:

'Our principal failure in the matter of organization has been that through our dilettantism we have lowered the prestige of the Revolution in Russia. Weak and undecided in questions of principle, possessed of a narrow mental outlook, excusing his own dilatoriness by the unruliness of the masses, incapable of drawing-up broad and daring plans, inexperienced and clumsy in the pursuit of his profession, i.e. the fight with the political police, a man who can respect his opponents and who reminds one of a Trade Union official rather than a tribune of the people—such a man, I tell you, is no revolutionary but only a contemptible amateur. No professional revolutionary need feel himself insulted by these bitter words; they apply to myself above all others in so far as inadequate organization is in question. I was an active member of an organization that was busied with far-reaching plans and every individual member of that organization suffered heavily from the consciousness that we were only amateurs, at a time when it is possible to say in a variation of the well-known phrase: "Give us organized revolutionaries and we will liberate Russia!"'

Marx would have been in complete agreement with these sentiments of the youthful Lenin, which were, nevertheless, rejected by a large number of the Russian Socialists. Out of their refusal to follow Lenin arose two opposing parties within the framework of Russian Socialism in general. The first believed that the Russian Social Democrat Party should be a Labour Party whose object was the improvement of the social condition of the proletariat. This did not mean that they were not to participate in the political struggle with Tsarism. Since, however, the approaching Russian Revolution could only be a middle-class revolution, the rate of its progression must be determined by the middle class itself. The second and opposing party believed that the Social Democrats should become a secret society of professional revolutionaries whose task it would be to persuade the proletariat to seize control of the middle-class revolution.

These two tendencies in Russian Social Democracy first became evident at the Congress of the Party which was held in London in 1903. In those days Russian Socialists could only carry on their deliberations undisturbed in foreign countries. The split came over the wording of Paragraph 1 of the Party Rules. Lenin proposed that this should read: 'Any one is a member of the Party who participates in the organization of the Party.' Martov introduced a counter-proposal which ran: 'Any one working under the supervision of the Party is a member of the Party.' Russian Social Democracy split into two groups over this to all intents and purposes not very important difference of opinion. In the voting that followed, Lenin's proposal received a couple more votes than that of Martov out of a total of some three dozen voters.

From that day onwards his supporters called themselves the Majoritarians (Bolsheviks), while those of Martov styled themselves Minoritarians (Mensheviks). A small handful of Russian refugees in London thus made world-history by their hairsplittings; for that day was the birthday of Bolshevism.

What was the actual difference between the proposal of Lenin and that of Martov? Socialists and their sympathizers in the Russia of those days were divided almost of necessity into two groups: the active Party workers who prosecuted the political work of the Party in secret; and the far greater number of those who sympathized with them and supported them as far as lay in their power without giving up their own private activities. If Martov's proposal had been adopted, this vast body of sympathizers would have automatically become members of the Party in so far as they—students or workmen—worked regularly for the Party and under its supervision. As members of the Party these would have the right to determine the policy of the Party and the appointment of its executive officers. Lenin's proposal was of quite a different nature. He deprived this large body of sympathizers of all influence over the fortunes of the Party. In Lenin's eyes the Party meant the small circle of active conspirators—and nobody else. Even in the then unfavourable conditions obtaining in Russia Martov wanted to uphold the principle of the right of self-determination for the masses. Lenin was of a directly contrary opinion. Martov was anxious to give to Russian Social Democracy the character of a western European Labour movement. Lenin utterly repudiated any such proposal. Certain sentences out of one of Lenin's speeches to the Congress serve to reveal clearly his attitude at this time. His words were directed against Trotsky, who had taken the part of the Mensheviks in the discussion over the wording of Paragraph 1.

'Comrade Trotsky', said Lenin, 'shows that he has completely misunderstood the basic idea of my pamphlet, "What shall be done?" by saying that the Party has no conspiratorial organization. Others have also reproached me similarly. . . . He has forgotten that the Party is only an advance post and the leader of the great mass of the working class which in its entirety, or virtually in its entirety, works under the supervision and direction of the Party organization without, however, belonging or being able in its entirety to belong to the Party. Let us consider the conclusions arrived at by Comrade Trotsky in consequence of his fundamental misunderstanding. He said that if after numbers of workmen had been arrested all were to declare that they were not members of the Party our Party would be shown up in a singular light. Is it not in fact the exact contrary? Do not the arguments of Comrade Trotsky show up in a singular light? He deplores what every more or less experienced revolutionary should applaud. If hundreds and thousands of workmen who had been arrested in the course of strikes and demonstrations were to prove that they were not members of Party organizations, this would only demonstrate the efficiency of our organization and that we have properly understood our task of forming a more or less small circle of conspiratorial leaders and of indoctrinating as many of the proletariat as possible with the ideals of the movement.'

Here were two wholly opposed worlds. In the eyes of Trotsky and Martov the politically active workmen and the Party are identical. Lenin looked upon the Party as a secret and directive power that stood behind and above the workers. In the course of the debate Lenin said less about the fact that his proposal would mean the exclusion of the proletariat from the Party itself than that he refused to accord the honour of membership of the Party to weak-kneed intellectuals who refused to take any risks. This, however, does not in any way alter the nature of Lenin's fundamental reason for opposing Trotsky and Martov.

Lenin did not look upon workpeople as being of little account. He was firmly convinced that the future belonged to the proletariat and he welcomed former factory-hands among the ranks of the professional revolutionaries. In his eyes, however, the immediate task of the Russian proletariat was to assist in achieving a middle-class revolution. Everything else was secondary to this political aim.

Notwithstanding many attempts to restore the unity of the Russian Socialist Party the breach between the Bolsheviks and the Mensheviks remained until 1917 and continues to the present day. It is true that the simple Socialist workman in Russia only thought of himself as a Social Democrat until 1917 and did not attach much importance to the differences of opinion between the various groups within the Socialist Party. The leaders of the movement both at home and abroad nevertheless remained opposed to each other despite a few temporary resolves to re-unite. For his own part Lenin devoted himself from 1903 onwards to organizing a revolutionary Party in accordance with his own ideas. In 1905 Bolshevism received its baptism of fire.

The Russian Revolution in 1905 did not begin as the result of an order on the part of a Party executive. It began in a sense directly contrary to Lenin's wishes with a spontaneous upheaval of the masses. The nation revolted after the defeat of Russia in the Russo-Japanese War had undermined the authority of the Tsarist Government. Lenin himself was under no illusion as to the real character of the uprising. His widow tells in her *Memories of Lenin* how Lenin said in October, 1905: 'I would postpone the revolution until the Spring. But we shall not be asked.' The Revolution began with the 'Bloody Sunday' on which the St. Petersburg workmen under the leadership of the priest Gapon demonstrated before the Tsar's palace. The troops fired upon the demonstrators. A thousand dead bodies covered the square. All Russia rose in fury. Every month of that year until December was filled with strikes and demonstrations on the part of workmen and civil servants, with peasant revolts and with mutinies in the Army and Navy. The Tsar was forced to concede Russia a parliament—the Duma. The zenith of the Revolution was reached in the great strike in December of the Moscow workmen; this was broken by the Government. From that moment the Revolution was a failure. The bravery of the revolutionary workpeople was not of itself sufficient to achieve the downfall of the Tsar. Peasant revolts and the mutinies in the Army and Navy were too sporadic and too lacking in cohesion to prove successful. The Government was able to restore discipline in the armed forces and to suppress the peasantry. The efforts of the workmen were thereby deprived of all prospect of success.

Lenin recognized clearly the true character of the Revolution in 1905.

'The peculiarity', he wrote, 'of the Russian Revolution consisted in the fact that while from a social standpoint it was middle class and democratic, it was proletarian in its choice of weapons. It was middle class and democratic because the democratic Republic was its immediate aim, which it sought to achieve with its own strength. It sought to achieve the eight-hour day, the confiscation of the vast estates of the nobility—in a word, all that the middle-class Revolution in France in 1792–3 had in great part accomplished. At the same time the Russian Revolution was proletarian not only in the sense that the proletariat formed the advance-guard of the Revolution and gave it its leaders, but also because that specially proletarian weapon—the strike—was the chief means used to stir up the masses and was the outstanding characteristic of the wave-like progression of the decisive events.'

Of the last months of the Revolution Lenin wrote: 'The proletariat formed the head of the movement. It had taken upon itself the task of achieving an eight-hour day by revolutionary means. The battle-cry of the St. Petersburg proletariat was "Eight-hour day and arms!" The steadily increasing number of workmen realized that the fate of the revolution could and would be decided only by force of arms.' In those days the workmen of St. Petersburg were the most intelligent and most revolutionary element in the Russian nation. If their object were the eight-hour day, it served to show that they were prepared to accept the continued existence of their employers after a successful revolution and that they looked upon the revolution as a middle-class revolution
The two Social Democrat groups (Bolsheviks and Mensheviks) took part in the Revolution beside the Social Revolutionaries (*Naródniki*) without paying any regard to the differences of opinion between their leaders. It cannot be shown that the Bolsheviks in 1905 worked harder and exercised a greater influence over the masses than did the other Socialist and revolutionary groups. It was, indeed, the Mensheviks who took the initiative that led to the establishment of the famous Workmen's Council in St. Petersburg in October 1905. In truth there was in those days no special group of revolutionaries who could lay claim to a monopoly of political wisdom. The working class was for the most part revolutionary in a general sense and not inclined to divide itself into groups. And this was still more true of the peasantry, soldiers, civil servants, and students.

On the subject of the creation of the Workmen's Council in St. Petersburg Trotsky writes:

'Although the Social Democrat organization only held together a few hundred workmen in secret and only exercised any considerable political influence over a few thousand workmen in St. Petersburg, it nevertheless contrived to set an aim before the masses by illuminating their primitive experience with the searchlight of political thought. Their strength was not, however, sufficient to enable them to unite hundreds of thousands of men and women through a living bond with their organization because the greater part of their work was accomplished in conspiratorial "cells" that were concealed from the eyes of the masses. The organization of the Social Revolutionaries was paralysed in a similar manner and was rendered still more impotent through infirmity and want of resolution. The establishment of a non-Party organization was rendered indispensable by the rivalry between the two Social Democrat groups as well as by the conflict between these two groups and the Social Revolutionaries.'

The Council of Workers' Delegates in St. Petersburg was so constituted that every five hundred workers were represented by a delegate. The great industries elected their delegates according to this principle, whilst the lesser industries were combined for the purposes of an election. The Trade Unions were also represented in the Council, which was a revolutionary fighting organization for the purpose of accomplishing the downfall of Tsarism. At that time nobody thought that a system of Workers' Councils would come to take the place of the Russian Parliament. All Russian revolutionaries, including the Bolsheviks, were unanimous in 1905 in thinking that after a successful revolution an all-Russian Constituent National Assembly elected on the widest possible suffrage would be called upon to determine the destinies of the nation. The Workers' Council was only intended as a means towards the realization of the National Assembly and not as a substitute for it.

In an article dated November 25, 1905, Lenin set forth his views on the system of Workers' Councils. His views at that time were wholly different from those he subsequently entertained in 1917. The Committee of the Workers' Council in St. Petersburg had just refused a request from the Anarchists to be represented on the Council—a refusal which Lenin upheld for the following important reason.

'There can be no question'—Lenin wrote—'that if one desired the Soviet of Workers' Delegates to be a Workers' Parliament or the Executive of a self-governing proletariat, the refusal to admit the Anarchists was wrong. Although the influence of the Anarchists over our working classes is fortunately slight, there can be no doubt that they can reckon a certain number of workmen among their supporters. . . . The fact that the Anarchists, who repudiate political warfare, themselves wish to enter an institution devoted to conducting such a warfare only serves to illustrate once more the tactics and unstable attitude to life of the Anarchists. Of course it is true that instability is no ground for exclusion from a parliament or the executive of a self-governing organization.'

Lenin looked upon the Workers' Council 'neither as a Workers' Parliament nor the organ of a proletarian system of self-government—indeed in no sense an organ of self-government—but as a fighting organization for the attainment of a definite aim'. In consequence of a temporary agreement this militant organization was the common property of the Russian Social Democrats, the Social Revolutionaries, and the non-Party revolutionary working men. The Russian Revolution was carrying on its fight 'for urgent democratic demands recognized and approved by the overwhelming majority of the nation'. Since the Anarchists disapprove of political reform, they have no place in the fighting union that 'carries out our democratic revolution'; and were they admitted to it they would only prove an obstacle and a disintegrating influence. It is clear that the basic principle of the Soviet—the right to self-determination of the proletariat, including the non-Party revolutionary working men—could easily be reconciled with Menshevism and scarcely reconciled at all with Bolshevism. Lenin refused absolutely to believe that spontaneous action on the part of the proletariat could lead to a real and lasting revolutionary victory. A Workers' Council constituted on this model must appear to him as a centre of disintegration. Although the state of affairs in 1905 compelled the Bolsheviks to accept the Workers' Council, they themselves would never have established such an organization.

In his extremely interesting speech in Zürich in January 1917, in commemoration of the twelfth anniversary of the Bloody Sunday in St. Petersburg, Lenin contented himself with a few casual words on the subject of the Workers' Councils. At the beginning of 1917 the Councils still played a secondary part in the revolution in Lenin's estimation, and it was the experience gained since February 1917 in the new Russian Revolution that caused Lenin radically to alter his view of them.

It is typical of the feeling prevalent in 1905 that the Workers' Council in St. Petersburg should have elected the young non-Party lawyer Nosar-Khrustalev to be its first chairman. Of this election Trotsky says:

'Very shrewd and alert in practical matters, clever and forcible as a chairman, a speaker of no special talent, but an impulsive temperament, a man without any political past, and without the bearing of a politician, Khrustalev revealed himself as born for the position to which he was elected at the close of 1905. Although the masses of the working class were revolutionary and possessed of a strong class feeling, they were in the majority not sympathizers with any particular Party. What has been said of the Council applies equally to Khrustalev: all Socialists with a political past were possessed of strong Party feelings and the candidature of a member of a definite Party would have given rise to dissensions at the establishment of the Council.'

Thus the St. Petersburg proletariat which had entrusted itself to the mysterious adventurer Gapon in January, now in October placed its confidence in the Radical Khrustalev who belonged to no Party. It is clear that it is impossible to speak of a Bolshevik leadership even among the most advanced Russian workmen at this time. After Khrustalev had been arrested in December his place as Chairman of the Council was taken by a Committee of Three of which Trotsky was politically the ablest. On the subject of his opinions on the Russian Revolution—opinions that differ absolutely from those of Lenin—more will be said presently.

As early as the spring of 1905 discussions took place among the leaders of Russian Social Democracy as to the character of the revolutionary Government that would be set up after the downfall of Nicholas II. Events belied these optimistic views. Nevertheless, the discussions are of extreme importance in that they show with great clearness the opinions then held by both Bolsheviks and Mensheviks.

The Mensheviks, whose principal spokesman was Martynov, thought as follows: The Russian Revolution is a middle-class revolution. On the overthrow of the Tsar the Constituent National Assembly will establish a middle-class republican government entrusted with the task of putting democratic reforms into operation. A Socialist Russia is for the time being impossible, owing to the small percentage of industrial workers in the Russian population and the backward economic state of agriculture. Nevertheless, suppose that a few Socialists are to be found in the new government—they will be in a position of great delicacy. If they content themselves with the measures of their middle-class colleagues, they will take upon themselves in the eyes of the working class a certain measure of responsibility for all the evil aspects of the capitalist system that will not only continue to exist but will for the first time manifest its full strength; and thus Social Democracy will be discredited in the opinion of the proletariat. If, however, they continue the Socialist battle within the Government by demanding strong measures against employers for the protection of the workers, then the Government will be forced along the path of Socialism against its own will; the middle class will come to fear Socialism; and it will be driven into the ranks of the reaction. The working class must of necessity be defeated in a forlorn fight for Socialism in a country that is not sufficiently developed for it. The consequence might even be a return to Absolutism, which would appear a lesser evil than Socialism in the eyes of the middle class. These two dangers could only be avoided by the Social Democrats through refusal to participate in a provisional revolutionary Government. Their task would be to further the Revolution by all the means in their power; to leave to the middle-class Parties the task of constructing a Government after the Tsar's downfall; and to oppose that Government in the capacity of a Labour Opposition entrusted with the defence of the special interests of the working class.

It is obvious from the foregoing that the Mensheviks were an extreme Labour Party in the western European meaning

of the term that repudiated any attempt to bridge the gulf
between proletariat and middle class and that designated the
entry of Social Democrats into a middle-class Government
as 'Jaurès-ism'. This expression 'Jaurès-ism' owed its origin
to the lively discussions then taking place in the International
over the thesis of the French Socialist, Jaurès, that the French
working class must be prepared to co-operate in a middle-
class republican Government for the defence of the Republic.
The intellectuals in the Second International were sharply
divided among themselves over this question. The Congress
of the Second International in Amsterdam rejected Jaurès's
tactics, and it was in the spirit of this decision that the
Mensheviks formulated their policy.

Lenin was sharply opposed to this Menshevik policy. His
standpoint was one that seemed that of the 'Right' in comparison to the 'Left' Wing Radicalism of the Mensheviks. In
reality his views only served to show that for him there
existed no differences of opinion within western European
Social Democracy. His dislike of all forms of non-Russian
Socialism in 1905 was so profound that confronted with it
all disputes over matters of policy between Radicals and
Revisionists disappeared. In 1905 Lenin championed a revolutionary and democratic dictatorship of the proletariat
and the peasantry. This was a genuine Marxian conception
which could not have been formulated by even the most
radical Social Democrat in the western Europe of those days.
Lenin wrote:

'Wherein lies the cause of the Martynov chaos? In mistaken
notions of the democratic and the Socialist revolution, in forget-
fulness of the part played by that section of the people standing
between the proletariat and the middle class—the partly lower
middle-class, partly working-class inhabitants of poor districts in
the towns and the country, in a misunderstanding of the true
meaning of our minimal programme. [This programme contained
the demands made by Socialism of the middle-class State.] . . . It
is only necessary to recollect the political and economic reforms
contained in their programme—demands for a republic, for the
right to carry arms, for the disestablishment of the Church, for
full democratic liberty, for radical economic reforms. Is it not
clear that the fulfilment of these demands is impossible in a middle-
class order of society without a revolutionary and democratic

dictatorship of the lower classes? Is it not clear that this is not a question of the difference between proletariat and middle class but of the entire lower class which gives the impulse to every democratic revolution? These lower classes are the proletariat with the addition of millions and millions of poor townspeople and villagers whose mode of life is just above that of the very lowest.'

The difference between Lenin and all other Social Democrats consists in his including in his plans, in addition to the proletariat and the middle class, the immensely powerful class lying between them. He believed that this intermediate class under the leadership of the proletariat could be won over to revolutionary democracy although not to Socialism. Lenin thus revealed his comprehension of the paradox of a middle-class revolution against the middle class which had been in 1848 the basic principle of Marx and Engels.

Sincere Socialists have always been agreed that a national revolution is only possible if supported by the majority of the nation. Among the Great Powers in 1905 it was only in England that the industrial workers formed the majority of the nation; they were a powerful minority in the United States and Germany; whilst in France, Italy, Russia, Austria-Hungary, and Japan they formed only a relatively small minority. Apart from England, where special conditions obtained, the working class could only attain to power by allying themselves to the other classes in the nation. Such an alliance existed, or at least seemed possible, in 1848, under the common banner of Democracy. The disappearance of revolution from the Continent about the year 1850 dissolved this alliance. The peasantry and the middle-class townsfolk joined with the middle-class parties or even with agrarian feudalism. It thus came about that extreme Socialists in western Europe saw the 'one reactionary body' in everything that was not Socialist and proletarian, and any pact concluded with any part of this composite body appeared in their eyes to be tantamount to desertion to the ranks of their class enemy, the middle class.

In contrast to this situation in the rest of Europe there still existed in 1905, in Russia, an enormous intermediate class capable of revolution. This was, above all, true of the millions of peasants. In so far as they were capable of political thought

these millions looked upon the *Naródniki*, Social Revolutionaries, &c., as their mouthpieces. Only if this army of
millions could be mobilized would the overthrow of Tsarism
be possible in Lenin's view, since the Army was for the most
part recruited from the peasantry—and unless it mutinied
no revolution could be successful. In company with such
allies private property could not indeed be abolished. But
the great landlords and the Church could be dispossessed of
their property, the old Tsarist authority destroyed, and the
Radical-Democratic Republic set up in its place. With such
an aim in sight, it was not possible to shrink from an alliance
with these democratic intermediate classes, even when men
like Gapon appeared as leaders of the 'popular' movement.
If this coalition were to prove victorious, Social Democracy
need have no anxiety in taking over the Government in
company with revolutionary Democracy. Nor need it become
fearful if the upper middle class returned to Tsarism and
feudalism in its terror of naked Democracy; for the working
class in alliance with the peasantry, manual workers, and
soldiers would be capable of destroying such an enemy. It is
true that this would not mean the introduction of Socialism
into Russia, and the country would still be living under
the economic laws arising out of the right to private ownership of property. Nevertheless, the establishment of pure
Democracy would in itself mean a great achievement on the
part of the working class and would provide the best foundation for future development along Socialist lines. There can
be little doubt that in those early days Lenin had already
formed in secret the belief that the well-disciplined and purposeful Bolsheviks would be able, within the limits of such a
coalition, to oust from power both the vague and romantic
Social Revolutionaries, and the weak and helpless Mensheviks.
The Bolsheviks would then become sole rulers of the democratic Republic.

It is clear that the difference between Bolshevism and
Menshevism is not to be defined by such phrases as 'right'
or 'left', 'radical' or 'moderate'. The Mensheviks in 1905
were modern and western European in their ideas. The
Bolsheviks were thinking in the terms of 1848. Only the
future could reveal which of the two was right. It alone could

show whether the lower middle classes in Russia were prepared to join in a democratic revolution against the middle
class as well as against the Tsar. Was not, perhaps, the
dictatorship of the working class and the peasantry a mere
figment of an overheated imagination? Would not the
peasantry repudiate their alliance with the proletariat the
moment that they became owners of their farms and therefore citizens? Would not the workman advance still farther
along the path that led to Socialism the moment he had the
reins of government in his hands? Was not Lenin's theory
of democratic stages between the various classes a dream
that could not be reconciled with the intensification of class
divisions everywhere? These questions could not be answered
in 1905.

With brilliant revolutionary eloquence Lenin defended his
theory against his Menshevik critics:

'Let us take another remark of *Iskra* [the newspaper of the
Mensheviks] on the subject of the war-cry "Long live the provisional revolutionary Government". *Iskra* says significantly:
"The combination of the words 'Long live' and 'Government' is
blasphemy." Is not that empty phraseology? They talk of overthrowing absolutism and at the same time are afraid to sully their
tongues with a salutation to the revolutionary Government. . . .
Just think of it! The revolt of the St. Petersburg workmen has
proved victorious. Absolutism has been overthrown. A provisional revolutionary Government has been proclaimed. The
workmen are joining in cries of "Long live the provisional revolutionary Government!" with their weapons still in their hands.
Among them stand the staff of the *Iskra*, turning their tearful
eyes up to Heaven, beating their breasts in self-righteousness and
crying aloud: "We thank Thee, O Lord God, that we are not as
these sinners and that we do not sully our lips with these words!"
It is a marvel that these people are not afraid to sully their
lips with cheers for the Republic. The Republic presupposes a
Government and—of this no Social Democrat has ever been for a
moment in doubt—a middle-class Government. What then is the
difference between cheering for the provisional revolutionary
Government and for the democratic Republic? No. A thousand
times No, Comrades! Do not be afraid of defaming yourselves
by supporting a republican revolution to the uttermost of your
power in common with revolutionary, middle-class democracy. . . .
If the Russian working class was able after January 9, under

conditions of political slavery, to mobilize more than a million of the proletariat for a resolute and deliberate collective action, we shall be able under a revolutionary-democratic dictatorship not only to mobilize millions and millions of the non-propertied classes in the towns and in the country but also to make the Russian political revolution the prelude to a European Socialist Revolution.'

For the present Lenin's hope that the victory of the democratic revolution in Russia would prove the prelude to that of Socialism throughout western Europe was compelled to await fulfilment in the future; for the defeat of the Russian Revolution in 1906–7 made an end to all these plans.

Lenin bore the defeat of his hopes with unshakable calm. Once more he was forced to continue his work beyond the Russian frontier. Throughout the years 1912–14 he directed the activities of his Party from his place of refuge in Galicia, close to the Russian frontier. He taught his supporters to fill in the days of the Counter-Revolution with such activities as were legally permissible. The Bolsheviks published daily newspapers that sought to evade the watchful censorship and they were represented in the Duma by half a dozen deputies. At the same time they organized illegal and subversive associations. They bided their time until the outbreak of the World War in 1914 once again resuscitated the possibility of a Russian Revolution.

III

THE WORLD WAR

August 1914 to February 1917

On the outbreak of the World War Lenin left Galicia and took up his residence in Zürich on the neutral soil of Switzerland. He was accompanied by his colleague, Zinoviev, a brilliant orator and writer, but not his equal in political ability. From November 1914 to the beginning of 1917 Lenin and Zinoviev collaborated in editing and publishing a Russian newspaper called *The Social Democrat*.

Lenin was convinced that Russia's participation in the War was only the prelude to the revolution in Russia itself. Since, however, the revolution would arise out of special conditions created by the War, it was necessary for him to study carefully the War and its effects upon society at large, and then to draw the necessary conclusions. Lenin was successful in bringing his study of the War to an end within a few months of its outbreak. The result of his meditations and studies was the brilliant essay that appeared in the spring of 1915 entitled 'Imperialism as the latest stage in Capitalism'. In order that this pamphlet might evade the Russian censorship Lenin expressed himself with great caution. The reader was left to glimpse its revolutionary purport between the lines. If read in conjunction with his other writings at this period, this essay on Imperialism affords a clear insight into Lenin's opinions.

Lenin distinguished between two stages in the development of Capitalism. Early Capitalism was based upon free competition. This was replaced in the later stages by trusts, cartels, and syndicates. The production of vital necessities for entire countries, and even for an entire hemisphere, was concentrated in a single organization. Free competition had been superseded by monopolies. In early Capitalism the industrialist had been the propulsive element; now he was replaced by the great banks and financial concerns. The industrial trusts allied themselves with the great banks.

Production became secondary to the financing of production. Thus the typical capitalist of the later stages in capitalist development was no longer the industrial pioneer but the wealthy speculator. Capitalism had brought into existence a parasitic class of *rentiers* living upon tribute exacted from humanity at large. The progressive element in Capitalism came to an end with the emergence of this parasitic monopolism. Capitalism no longer had any interest in increasing production and was content to assure itself of its profits by forcible methods. A modern Great Power is nothing but a collection of great financial institutions within national frontiers. Modern international politics are no more than the struggle between these centres of financial power for domination over all countries and all races.

The appearance of monopolistic Capitalism destroyed the liberal and tolerant character of the capitalistic middle class. Moreover, the State as an expression of monopolistic capitalism can only maintain itself internally and externally by an unscrupulous use of force. The newest form of Capitalism involved of necessity the maintenance of great armies and navies. It compromised with the monarchical system of government; it enlisted into its service the bureaucratic Civil Service; and it turned to its own account the last vestiges of feudalism.

Thus it came about that an agriculturally backward State like Tsarist Russia fitted in admirably with the modern imperialist system. For during the years 1906–14 that saw the counter-revolution in Russia industrial and financial Capitalism made mighty strides forward in that country and were helped in their advance not a little by the millions loaned by France to Russia. The corrupt and avaricious ruling class was now composed both of the old feudal elements and the new financiers and industrialists. The Duma was the scene of a compromise between these two forces. In Russian eyes the World War was a predatory expedition on the part of this imperialist ruling class from which the nobles hoped to gain new estates and the financiers still greater profits.

The outbreak of war seemed superficially to strengthen immeasurably the power of Capitalism. In Lenin's opinion, however, it also created entirely new possibilities for revolution.

At first the War united all forces in the nation in the hands of the ruling caste. War-time economics meant the triumph of the monopoly system. The entire economic life of the country was absorbed into one gigantic organization which controlled everything, according to definite regulations, from St. Petersburg down to the tiniest village. The State had become the finished and most complete expression of centralized authority and could not tolerate any form of 'freedom' within its boundaries.

In the Anglo-Saxon countries the middle-class order of society had up to this allowed the individual a certain liberty of movement and thought. The War made an end to this in England and later in the United States, both of which became centralized governmental machines under the political dictatorship of Capitalism and the all-powerful unitary system of war-time economy. The imperialist ring round the world had been completed and no longer showed a single gap. Each month of war, however, saw an intensification of the burden placed by monopolistic Capitalism upon the masses. In times of peace Capitalism had been able to distribute largesse to the populace from its ample profits. Indeed, in countries like England and Germany, the profits earned by the great capitalist organizations were so great that it was possible to admit the intellectual and official classes, the agriculturists, and even some of the industrial proletariat, to a share in them. This had the result, in Lenin's opinion, of raising the standard of living of these classes and of giving them an interest in the continuance and prosperity of Imperialism.

The War dissolved these illusions. The vast majority of the townsfolk and the peasantry were driven into the trenches and forced to sacrifice their lives on a scale unprecedented in history. At the same time food control and famine made their appearance among the civilian populations. The oppression of the masses on the part of Capitalism knew no limits and became unbearable. The only road to salvation left to the proletariat was revolution.

These theories on being applied to Russia strengthened Lenin in the beliefs he had entertained in 1905. The alliance between the working class and the lower middle class for the purpose of achieving a democratic revolution had become closer than ever before. The whole burden of the War was borne by the villages and the peasant-soldiery. If the revolutionary proletariat pointed the way to salvation, it would be followed by the entire nation. The gulf separating the workman at a machine and the workman behind a plough, the poverty-stricken man deprived of all means of production and the poverty-stricken man in possession of only the barest possible means of production—this gulf had been bridged by their common misery. And they possessed in common one single enemy—the Tsar and the imperialist ruling class.

The Russian Socialist Workers' Party could only lead a successful national revolution on condition that it did not allow itself to become enmeshed in the imperialist machinery of war. This machinery embraced the army, the administration, and the entire economic life of Russia; and it had its own peculiar ideology—that of the defence of the Fatherland and of a political truce between the parties. The ruling and imperialist class taught the masses of the people that they must obey and suffer for the sake of the Fatherland. If they were to refuse to obey, then the defence of the country would no longer be possible and the country itself would become a prey to the enemy. Every individual Russian would in that event find himself in such a condition of misery that it would make the sufferings of war appear as nothing by comparison.

Lenin combated this imperialist ideology with might and main. He staked his all upon the argument that in an imperialist war Social Democracy must overthrow the Government in every country and transform the war against the external foe into a war against the enemy within the gates. How is this extremist notion to be reconciled with the acceptance of nationalism by Marx in 1848—that Marx to whom Lenin looked as to his great exemplar? In 1848 Marx and Engels did not advocate the defeat of Germany; they demanded, on the contrary, the victory of Germany in a revolutionary war against Russia. What, then, was Lenin's attitude to the problem of nationality during the years 1914 to 1917? It is obvious that the greatest figure and leader of the Russian democratic revolution must accept the Russian nation. Here Lenin could not divest himself of the pure and original Marxist doctrine. On December 12, 1914, Lenin wrote a brilliant article on 'The National Pride of the Greater Russians', in which he said *inter alia*:

'Is the emotion of national pride foreign to the Greater Russian class-conscious proletariat? Certainly not. We love our language and our native land. It is we who strive most strenuously to uplift her [Greater Russia's] workers, i.e. nine-tenths of her population, to living the class-conscious existence of class-conscious Socialists. It is we who are most distressed by beholding our native country subjected to the violence and oppression of Tsarist hangmen, landowners, and capitalists. We are proud that this violation should have met with resistance in our midst, in the heart of Greater Russia . . . that the large Russian working class has organized a powerful revolutionary Party out of the masses, and that the peasant in Greater Russia has at the same time begun to become democratic and to free himself from the priests and the landowners.

'We are filled with national pride and it is for that reason especially that we regard with a peculiar hatred our past of serfdom . . . our present serfdom. . . . A nation cannot itself be free whilst it oppresses other peoples—such was the teaching of the great representatives of logical Democracy in the nineteenth century, Marx and Engels, who have become the teachers of the revolutionary proletariat. And we Greater Russian workmen, because we are filled with national pride, want to see a free and independent, a democratic and republican and proud Greater Russia whose relations with its neighbours shall be inspired by the humanitarian principle of equality and not by the servile principle of prior or exclusive rights degrading to every great nation.'

Here Lenin is speaking the language of national revolution, the language of the *Neue Rheinische Zeitung*, and that of the revolution of 1905. It is clear that the theories Lenin built up from his observation of the World War are not to be explained by his rejection of the principle of nationality any more than it is possible to give a moral content to Bolshevik war-time policy. It was not moral indignation with Imperialism and its allies that caused Lenin to demand the overthrow of his own Government. Lenin invariably regarded political problems from a realistic standpoint and in his eyes the end justified the means. He would have allied himself with the

Devil in order to serve the cause of the revolution. And it is nothing less than absurd to declare that Lenin advocated the dissolution of the International out of moral indignation with the patriotic Socialists. For the same reason Lenin steadily refused to be associated with so-called pacifism in so far as that implied the rejection of the use of force in disputes. Like Marx and Engels, Lenin was an advocate of the use of force and weapons to the end of his life. Hence it is impossible to explain Lenin's attitude during the World War on any other than the realist ground of the interests of revolution and more especially of the Russian Revolution. Lenin did not work for the downfall of his own Government—the Tsarist Government—because it was a bad Government or because the war it was waging was an indefensible war. He sought to effect its overthrow because without that there was no possibility of success for revolution.

A Party that adopts the motto 'Down with the Government' in a country that is waging war without at the same time possessing the means and the energy to accomplish a revolution is acting foolishly. It is merely helping the enemy to conquer its own country. If in a world war powerful political parties in every belligerent country were to proclaim the same end without seeking to promote a revolution their action would amount to criminal folly. If all States were to 'lose' in the war, what would be the ultimate outcome? Lenin's action would have been senseless if it had not been the first step to revolution. A Party cannot carry out a revolution in time of war without overthrowing its own Government and the administrative and military machine of that Government. To do that is tantamount to promoting the defeat of its own country, or at least its temporary defeat, by disorganization of the conduct of the war. Such a result is the inevitable consequence of such an action. At the time of the French Revolution the Mountain risked the defeat of France in overthrowing the Girondist Government. It was only thanks to the feeble resistance offered to the Mountain by the Girondins that the defence of the country did not collapse. If in 1848-9 the German Democrats had successfully carried out the revolution preached by Marx and

Engels the resultant problem would have been the same. The military and civil administration of Prussia and Austria would first have been destroyed. Since Prussia was then at war with Denmark and also engaged in putting down a Polish rebellion, and since Austria was fighting against Italy and Hungary, this would have involved the defeat of both those countries. After their seizure of power the revolutionaries cannot at first alter the situation.

Suppose that a revolutionary Party accuses the Government of conducting war badly and half-heartedly and declares that were it to come to power matters would take on a very different aspect. It is always possible for the Government to retort that the activities of the Party itself have paralysed the military conduct of the war, and that notwithstanding their loud protestations of patriotism, they themselves have been guilty of treason and of bringing the possibility of defeat upon their own country. Similar reproaches can be brought by a Government in time of war against such groups in the Opposition as criticize the actions of the Government and continue their political activity even without entertaining any revolutionary plans. These groups can be accused of disseminating mistrust, promoting civil dissension, and destroying the will of the people to prosecute the war. The whole object of a political truce in time of war is to heighten the national determination to pursue the struggle by artificially suppressing all political differences of opinion within the nation. Every opposition, or indeed revolutionary Party, in a belligerent State must be prepared to take upon itself the responsibility for a disturbance of the political truce that may result in paralysing the military conduct of the war and even lead to national defeat. Every determined oppositional group in a belligerent State acts at least temporarily as if no war were in progress. For the overthrow of the Government can only be effected by breaking the political truce and ignoring the patriotic obligations imposed upon all parties by the existence of a state of war. When Lenin as a Russian came forward in 1914 with his battle-cry 'Down with the Tsar', that did not mean that he desired the victory of William II in any form whatsoever. It did mean that in Lenin's opinion the real interests of the Russian nation demanded that the revolt against the Tsar should be carried on at this instant by every possible means.

If the defeat of the Russian armies should result from this revolutionary action, such a defeat must be regarded as the lesser of two evils; and in any case the victorious Russian Revolution would subsequently settle accounts with the German Emperor under very different circumstances.

There is indeed another way in which a revolutionary Party can seize the reins of government in time of war. It can support the conduct of the war and participate in it to such an extent that it eventually excludes all other elements in the nation from the control of the nation's destiny. This would seem to be the way in which Engels visualized the German Social Democrats seizing power in the course of a world war. Many Liberals and Democrats in Russia entertained similar notions long before the outbreak of the World War and therefore sought to incite the Tsarist Government to the pursuit of an aggressive foreign policy and even to war. In such an event they believed that the Tsar at any rate would be overthrown. If Russia were to suffer a defeat, the Government would collapse. It was only necessary to recall what had happened after the Russo-Japanese War. Even if the war were to end in a Russian victory, it would nevertheless involve the entire nation in such an expenditure of blood and energy, and impose such a strain upon all the national forces, that the Russian people would no longer tolerate the old type of Tsarist Government. The transformation of Russia into a middle-class and Liberal State would be the inevitable consequence of such a tremendous conflict. For this reason far-sighted Russian Conservatives invariably advocated a pacific policy in the interests of Tsarism and feudalism and declared that the Pan-Slav Movement was nothing else than a revolutionary movement in disguise. The fact that during the World War the entire Liberal middle class, virtually the whole of the completely democratic 'Popular' movement, and also some Social Democrats, ardently supported the prosecution of the war and the defence of the country did not mean that they did not believe that in any eventuality Tsarism was doomed. Nevertheless, Lenin resolutely refused in 1914 and the succeeding years to have anything to do with this plan of achieving a revolution by prosecuting the war to a successful end. According to Lenin it was imperative to distinguish sharply between Nationalism and Imperialism and between nationalist wars and imperialist wars.

It is clear that the Russian nation, the French nation, the British nation, &c., existed as such in 1914. Nevertheless, they were to some extent the prisoners of the imperialist system. The war which was conducted by the imperialist machine was not a war of nations; it was a war of conquest on the part of the ruling classes. Once more the phrase 'A workman has no country' acquired fresh meaning since the imperialists 'had' a country. A national war on the part of Germany or Russia would only be possible after the mass of the population had regained their country through revolution. Moreover, the imperialist war-machine could only be broken by those who refused to become involved in its cogs. Any one who allowed himself to be captivated by the imperialist ideology became the prisoner of the imperialist system. In Lenin's opinion it was impossible for a Labour leader to aid in defending his country in an imperialist war and at the same time organize a revolution. For with every revolutionary action he injured that effective defence of his country which he held to be of primary importance. Lenin indeed thought that the Russian proletariat should refuse its support to all who assisted in the defence of the country or the maintenance of the political truce throughout the World War. A supporter of the war was in Lenin's eyes identical with a counter-revolutionary. Hence he preached a ruthless crusade against the *Naródniki* and those Social Democrats who supported the political truce. Nor was he any less rigorously opposed to the Mensheviks and the group led by Trotsky, who refused to participate in a fight to the finish with the Democrats and the Socialist supporters of the political truce, although they themselves were opposed to this truce.

A new grouping of the Left Parties in Russia resulted from the outbreak of the World War. In 1905 the Mensheviks refused to participate in a democratic revolutionary government in contrast to the Bolsheviks who were prepared to co-operate. Now, in 1914–15, the position was reversed—the

Bolsheviks stood alone and the Mensheviks were prepared to co-operate with the Socialist supporters of the political truce, and, above all, with the Democrats. In 1905 Lenin's conception of the path to be followed by the revolution was wholly different from that which he entertained in 1914–16. In 1905 he believed that the overthrow of the Tsar could be effected by means of a great coalition of the democratic and *Naródniki* Parties. In the World War he believed that the supporters of the political truce had become prisoners of Imperialism and therefore were no longer capable of revolution. It remained for the Bolsheviks to set aside the democratic leaders and to obtain control over the masses themselves.

The Mensheviks indeed never assigned to themselves, either in 1905 or subsequently, the leadership of the Russian Revolution. In 1905 they were prepared to fight in the revolutionary ranks and to leave to the middle class the task of governing the middle class and democratic State that was to be established on the ruins of Tsarism. During the World War the old and recognized Menshevik leaders living in exile carried on their struggle against Tsarism. The Mensheviks who continued to work within Russia itself were divided in their opinions. Although the Menshevik leaders were determined to support with all their might any new revolution that might occur as a result of the War, they refused on account of the different opinions held as to the nature of the War itself to split the Russian working class into two inimical camps. Nor did the difference between the Mensheviks and the Bolsheviks undergo any real change; it merely took on new guises at different times for tactical reasons. The Mensheviks felt themselves to be representative of the Russian working class with their small range of influence in relation to the political life of the vast Tsarist Empire. The Bolsheviks felt themselves to be the leaders of a national Russian Revolution. When, in February 1917, the Revolution overthrew the Tsar, the great majority of the Russian nation, including the Russian working class, followed the lead of the Mensheviks and *Naródniki*; and despite the possibility that was now theirs of indulging freely in propaganda, the Bolsheviks remained in the minority. It was the fateful course

taken by events in 1917 that first placed Lenin at the head
of a majority of the Russian nation.

On October 11, 1915, Zinoviev published an important
article entitled 'The War and the Revolutionary Crisis in
Russia'. Throughout the entire period of their sojourn in
Switzerland from 1914 to 1917 Zinoviev was Lenin's mouthpiece and never once wrote anything that did not tally completely with Lenin's opinions. In this article Zinoviev drew
up a balance-sheet for the fifteen months of war. He began
by showing how the victory of Russian arms in Galicia in
1914 increased the authority of the Tsar and promoted the
idea of a political truce. In 1915 came a change. That year
saw an overwhelming defeat of the Russians by the German
armies, the loss of Galicia, and the conquest of Poland and
Vilna. The immediate result was an outbreak of violent
recriminations between the Russian Government and the
Liberals. Strikes took place and the peasantry rose in rebellion. Some democratic leaders like Kerensky and Plekhanov
raised the battle-cry 'Revolution for Victory'. In those days
Kerensky was the most respected and powerful man in the
Naródniki movement, and Plekhanov was a celebrated Social
Democrat, a founder of Russian Social Democracy, who before 1914 had on many occasions collaborated with Lenin.
On the outbreak of the War Plekhanov declared himself in
favour of defending his country from its enemies. Thence-
forward Lenin regarded him with irreconcilable enmity.
Kerensky and Plekhanov were of the opinion in 1915 that
Tsarism could be destroyed by being made to appear as the
chief obstacle to victory and that Russia could only be saved
from defeat by revolutionary Democracy. On the subject of
their views Zinoviev wrote: 'Kerensky and Plekhanov raise
the cry of "Revolt for Victory", clothe themselves in the toga
of revolutionary Jacobinism, and light-heartedly summon
from the shades the ghosts of the great leaders of the Wars
of Revolution. But in truth they are bondmen of the Tsar.'

Such tactics during an imperialistic war were in Lenin's
opinion sheer folly and those who pursued them became the
slaves of the imperialistic system. The Mensheviks had put
forward their plan of a Constituent National Assembly which
received Zinoviev's approval with the reservation that it did

not go far enough. Now was the time in which to set the goal of a republic and an expropriation of the great estates before the masses of the people. Zinoviev concluded his article by saying:

'To-day as yesterday revolutionary Socialist democracy continues the struggle for a democratic revolution in Russia. The imperialistic World War has indissolubly united the cause of revolution in Russia with that of the growing proletarian Socialist revolutionary movement in the West. . . . The interests of the millions of lower middle classes and semi-proletarian classes in Russia are irreconcilable with monarchy and with a landed aristocracy that is a relic of the age of serfdom. . . . It is not the task of the proletariat to neglect the democratic interests of the masses but to free the masses from the influence of the middle class and to confute former Liberal and present-day patriotic illusions by the teachings of experience. Long live the second democratic Revolution in Russia that opens the age of the proletarian World Revolution! Long live the victory over the Tsar that leads to the continuance of the proletarian and Socialist revolution in the West and not to victory over Germany! These are the mottoes inscribed on the banners of Russian Revolutionary Socialist Democracy.'

On October 13, 1915, Lenin took up his pen and beneath the modest title, 'Some Ideas', laid down eleven principles that should serve as guiding-lines in the work of Russian revolutionaries. This essay ranks among the greatest of Lenin's writings.

As his first principle he declared that a 'Constituent Assembly' alone did not suffice as a solution of the revolutionary problem. It depended upon who was to elect this Constituent Assembly. If, for example, the possibility was left open to the Tsar himself of calling a National Assembly into life, then that would place an obstacle in the path of the revolution. Instead of adopting a Constituent Assembly as the revolutionary motto Lenin advised the adoption of the three demands: a democratic Republic, confiscation of great estates, and an eight-hour working day.

His second principle was that the workers should not participate in the committees that had been set up with a view to speeding up production in munition factories and other industries supplying war materials.

In his third principle Lenin advocated the extension of Social Democrat propaganda to the agricultural proletariat, the poor peasantry, and the Army. Moreover, strikes must be encouraged and a demand made for the immediate conclusion of peace. Among other demands put forward by the proletariat must be one for the liberation of the Bolshevik members of the Duma whom the Government had banished to Siberia shortly after the outbreak of the War.

His fourth principle ran: 'Councils of Workers' Delegates and similar bodies must be looked upon as instruments of revolt and of revolutionary power. These bodies can only be of use in conjunction with a development of political strikes on a large scale and with revolts, and only in proportion to the preparation, development, and progress of each individual strike or revolt.' It is clear that Lenin did not at that time entertain any notions that the Councils would become the organic bodies in a future democratic or even Socialist State.

The fifth and sixth principles were concerned with the social character of the coming revolution. Lenin remained faithful to the convictions he had held in 1905, that the coming revolution in Russia must be of a middle-class character and not destructive of the right to private ownership.

In his seventh and eighth principles Lenin sought to make clear to his Party in Russia the reasons that had led him to alter his theory of a possible coalition that he had held in 1905:

'It is to be regarded as permissible for Social Democracy to enter a provisional revolutionary Government in company with the democratic lower middle classes; but not with the Chauvinists of the revolutionary movement. . . . Revolutionary Chauvinism is based upon the situation of the lower middle class as a class. This class always fluctuates between the middle class and the proletariat. At the present moment it is hesitating between Chauvinism and proletarian Internationalism—and it prevents the former from being truly revolutionary in the sense of a democratic Republic.'

Thus the Bolsheviks might enter into a coalition with the democratic Parties only upon the condition that these Parties were opposed to Chauvinism, i.e. the imperialist system. In the then circumstances this amounted to a refusal to join a coalition, since the *Naródniki*, as well as the Social Democrats under Plekhanov, favoured the prosecution of the war and the Mensheviks would not participate in any Government whose policy was directed against the other democratic Parties. By ignoring the actual facts Lenin thus daringly designated his own supporters as the only true proletarians in Russia and branded the Mensheviks, Plekhanov's Party, &c., as lower middle class. In reality, both then and until 1917, the majority of the Russian proletariat were members of the so-called lower middle-class Parties, while the intellectual strength of Bolshevism itself was not among the workmen but in a small circle of revolutionary intellectuals.

The events of 1917 lend a great importance to Lenin's ninth principle: 'If the revolutionary Chauvinists were to gain the upper hand in Russia, we should be opposed to a defence of their country in this war. Our battle-cry is "Down with the Chauvinists, even if they are also revolutionaries and republicans; and support for the union of the proletarians of the nations in the name of the Socialist Revolution!"' Lenin here takes into consideration the possibility that a revolution in Russia might not only destroy the Tsardom but also the Liberal middle class. The Government would then fall into the hands of the *Naródniki*, Kerensky's Party, the Social Revolutionaries, &c. In 1905, and indeed in any similar situation up to 1913, Lenin would have welcomed such a Government and have offered to co-operate with it. Now he was prepared to fight it as he fought the Tsarist Government. Before the War a coalition Government of *Naródniki* and Socialists would have been the expression of a true revolution and have signified the assumption of power by the broad masses of the people. A democratic Government, however, at the time of the World War, that simply continued to wage war, seemed in Lenin's eyes to be a pure farce.

For such a Government would be forced in the defence of the country to collaborate with the former Tsarist officers and the industrialists. It would be compelled to maintain law and order by means of the former Tsarist police force and it could not attempt to carry out any serious democratic reforms. For this reason Lenin saw in such a Government only a screen behind which the feudal and capitalistic imperialist system would continue to govern. Hence the necessity for combating it like every other imperialist Russian Government.

If the situation as between the various Parties in Russia were actually as depicted by Lenin, then the Bolsheviks would obviously have to reckon seriously with the possibility that they would have to effect a democratic revolution alone and in opposition to every other Party. Hence Lenin in his tenth principle says: 'To the question whether it is possible for the proletariat to play a leading part in a middle-class revolution in Russia the answer must be as follows: Yes, it is possible. But only if the lower middle class inclines towards the Left at the decisive moment.' As a political force the proletariat is here identified by Lenin with the Bolsheviks. A movement towards the Left on the part of the lower middle class would mean that the peasantry would abandon the *Naródniki* and join themselves to the Bolsheviks in some way or other.

The last and eleventh principle already contains the entire plan for a so-called World Revolution.

'To the question,' writes Lenin, 'what would be the attitude of the proletarian Party in the event of its attaining to power through a revolution during the present war, the answer must be: We would propose peace to all belligerents on condition that all colonies and all oppressed, enslaved, and dependent nations received their freedom. Under their present Governments neither Germany nor England nor France would accept this condition. As a consequence of their refusal we would be forced to prepare and wage a revolutionary war. In other words—we would not only carry out with the most ruthless methods the least part of our programme [the demands put forward by Russian Social Democracy for the creation of a democratic Republic], but we would stir up all the peoples oppressed by Greater Russia as well as all colonies and dependencies in Asia, India, China, Persia, &c., and, above all, incite the Socialist proletariat of Europe, in spite of the Chauvinists among it, to rebellion against its Governments.'

It is first of all necessary to explain here in what fashion the revolutionary war which Lenin proposed to wage as a consequence of the rejection of his peace proposal by Germany and the other Powers, differs from that which

Kerensky and Plekhanov were then engaged in preaching. For Lenin himself thought of Russia as a radical middle-class democratic State and not as a Socialist State. And in this he was in agreement with Kerensky and Plekhanov. The fact that events followed another course after the assumption of power by the Bolsheviks in 1918 is not of material importance here. Even Lenin in 1915 only contemplated achieving a middle-class revolution in Russia. The difference between Lenin's revolutionary war and that of Kerensky is to be explained as follows: On taking over the reins of Government Lenin proposed to destroy completely the whole imperial system of government with its officers, civil servants, police, and war organizations, even at the risk of temporarily para- lysing the further conduct of the war. On the other hand, Kerensky and Plekhanov wished to continue the fight with the old governmental machine in order to avoid any break- down in the military apparatus. It would in that event be impossible for them to revolutionize Russia. After their own victory Russian democracy would have to fight two imperial- istic groups of Powers—Germany and the Entente. In order to do this it would be necessary for them to secure the help of two allies—the oppressed nations of the East and the Socialist workmen of the West. Far from repudiating the idea of nationality Lenin desired to make of it the chief weapon in his warfare. And in this he reveals himself a true middle-class revolutionary of the 1848 type.

In the first place Lenin proposed to raise in rebellion the oppressed peoples of Tsarist Russia—Ukrainians, Poles, Finns, Caucasians, Turkistans—and to make of the middle classes in all these nations (peasants, manual labourers, intelligentsia, &c.) allies of the great Russian Democracy. A renunciation of the forcible methods of government employed by the Tsars would not injure Greater Russia in a national sense, since she would occupy a far more secure position than formerly at the head of a federation of liberated peoples. Revolutionary-democratic movements had followed in Asia upon the Russian Revolution of 1905 that had for their common characteristic a nationalist opposition to European rule. China became a republic. Parliaments were set up in Persia and Turkey. In India opposition to English rule

increased. After the fall of the Tsar, and in the crisis produced by the World War, these movements would be redupli-
cated. In all Asiatic lands, however, only nationalist and
democratic, and nowhere proletarian and Socialist, revolutions were possible. The revolt of the millions of Asia would,
nevertheless, strike at the heart of European Imperialism.
For such a revolt would mean the loss to the parasitic monopolistic capitalists, especially in England, of the tribute which
they had hitherto drawn from the East. Here Lenin's theory
of Imperialism as the latest manifestation of the capitalistic
age once more reveals itself. The tribute-paying slaves of
Imperialism are not only the European factory-hands but
90 per cent. of mankind. Hence Imperialism could only be
overthrown by a World Revolution that would only be
proletarian in a small degree.

According to Lenin it was the task of Russian democracy
to organize a world revolution against Imperialism. The
nationalist peasantry of Russia were to attract to their side
the Asiatic peoples, and the Russian proletariat was to make
allies of the western European working class. The idea of a
European revolution current in 1848 had developed by 1915
into that of a world revolution. The basic ideal remained
unchanged — the liberation of mankind. The proletarian
class interests of the western European working class were
satisfied with common action with the working class in Russia,
India, and China. It is indeed open to question whether the
European working class is called upon to sacrifice itself for
the establishment of middle-class nationalist States in Asia or
for the prosperity of the Russian peasantry. Such problems,
however, were in 1915 only matters of academic interest for
Lenin and the Bolsheviks. The immediate task was the overthrow of Tsarism—all else must be left to the future.
Throughout the years 1914–17, in which he was in Switzerland, Lenin was denied all opportunity for conducting a
propagandist campaign in Asia. But he was in the centre of
western Europe and therefore devoted his energies, in addition to planning the Russian Revolution, to indoctrinating
western European Socialism with his ideas. It will be necessary
in the next chapter to examine the extent of the success which
attended Lenin's endeavours in this sphere of action.

Although the Bolsheviks and the Mensheviks were strongly opposed to each other from 1903 to 1917, they shared the conviction that the coming revolution in Russia could only be a middle-class revolution; and this opinion was also held by the Russian Social Democrats who supported the prosecution of the war. There was, however, another and very remarkable Socialist theory as to the form to be assumed by the approaching revolution in Russia; its spokesman was Trotsky.

In the course of the nineteenth century Marxism had undergone two changes. The first was the organization of the workers for the purpose of completing the middle-class democratic revolution. At this stage in the development of Marxism the working class acted under the direction of a small group of professional revolutionaries sprung from the radical middle-class *intelligentsia*. This was the Marx-Engels and Bolshevik type of revolution. In the next stage the working class had so far developed as to have a voice in their own organizations and to seek to improve their condition as a class within the middle-class and capitalistic organization of society. The revolutionary ideal faded into the background and, in countries in which a middle-class revolution was imminent, the working class followed in the footsteps of the middle class. This type of revolutionary movement is represented by the western European groups in the Second International and by the Mensheviks in Russia. A logical forecast of the further development of the proletarian movement leads to a third stage in which the working class consciously determines its own fate. It is now no longer concerned with the improvement of its condition within middle-class society and seeks to attain to power through revolution. This revolution, however, is no longer the radical democratic revolution of the first stage; it is now a Socialist revolution with the object of substituting communal for private ownership of property. In such a revolution the workers would not merely execute the commands of their Party leaders but would act on their own independent initiative.

This third stage is the realization of the Marxist ideal. It is the fulfilment of Marx's dream of a society freed from class distinctions. In order to render the attainment of this third stage possible an immense development of Capitalism must first take place, and those classes that stand between the middle class and the proletariat must also be destroyed. The disappearance of these plebeian classes renders unnecessary the pursuit on the part of the proletariat of a policy of co-operation on a nationalist and democratic basis, and leaves the tiny minority of capitalist exploiters face to face with the overwhelming majority of the exploited. Moreover, the attainment of this third stage necessitates the development of a very highly-trained proletariat capable through intelligence and self-discipline of building up a new world for themselves.

The European working class at the time of the World War was not yet capable of achieving this third stage. For this reason the idealists and political leaders who were the embodiment of this third stage were only able to gather round them a very small band of supporters. These leaders and their groups were: in Russia, Trotsky; among the Polish and German Social Democrats, Rosa Luxemburg and her followers; and, finally, Gorter's band of Marxists in Holland. All the great working-class parties in central and western Europe were at this time led by men embodying the second stage in development, whilst it was men of the first stage who achieved the middle-class revolution in Russia. Since the historic task of the proletariat is to progress from the second to the third stage in development (it is impossible to-day to say when and in what manner this advance will be made), the idealists who embody this third stage play a very important part in the evolutionary process. For despite the many ideological and political mistakes they may make individually these men are the living presentation of its future to the present-day proletariat. It is indeed true that in the future the task of the historian in judging Trotsky will be rendered more difficult by the fact that in 1917 he became formally a member of the Bolshevik Party. Some years later occurred the inevitable break between Trotsky and the Party leaders. Since then Trotsky has maintained that he, and not the rulers of Russia, represents true Bolshevism. This thesis advanced by Trotsky for reasons of political tactics cannot seriously affect the judgement of history.

As early as the Russian Revolution in 1905 and as late as 1917 Trotsky maintained that no truly revolutionary element existed in Russia outside the proletariat. He believed that the Liberal middle class would at once combine with the forces of Tsarism were a radical revolution likely to prove victorious. The *Naródniki* democracy was equally an illusion since its sole support was in the backward and divided peasantry which was incapable of conducting a revolution by itself. Hence there were in Trotsky's opinion only two real political forces in Russia: the Tsar with his feudal and capitalistic supporters and the Socialist working class. And if the latter were successful in overthrowing the former it should not pursue the phantom of a democratic dictatorship and a middle-class revolution but should immediately set up a truly Socialist State in Russia. In an article which he wrote in 1909 Trotsky made clear his attitude towards this problem:

'The Mensheviks have never clearly defined their attitude towards the Russian Revolution as a whole. In common with the Bolsheviks they speak of carrying out the revolution to its conclusion, which both interpret to mean in a purely formal sense the achievement of our minimal programme, after which an epoch should follow of capitalist exploitation under a democratic organization of society. The carrying out of the revolution to its conclusion presupposes the defeat of Tsarism and the seizure of power in the State by a revolutionary class. Which? The Menshevik answer is "the middle-class democracy". The Bolshevik answer is "the proletariat and the peasantry". What is this "middle-class democracy" of which the Mensheviks speak? This is no definite, tangible, and actually existent force. It is a category unknown to history and evolved by journalists by means of deduction and analogy!'

The Menshevik theory would mean in practice that the workers would become the hangers-on of middle-class Liberalism in a revolution and would therefore be incapable of achieving anything. The theory put forward by Lenin was, in Trotsky's opinion, no less mistaken. According to Lenin, the working class was to seize power without making any use of it and to content itself with the achievement of middle-class reforms. Such an act of renunciation on the part of a victorious proletariat Trotsky regarded as an absurdity, and he believed Lenin's ideal of a democratic dictatorship would reveal itself within a few days after the victory of the revolution as impracticable. Strikes would be the immediate consequence of a successful revolution on the part of the Social Democrats. Employers would close their factories and lock out the work-people. Factory-owners would say to themselves: 'Our property is not in danger since it is clear that the proletariat is for the moment bent on setting up a democratic dictatorship and not a Socialist State.' Would a victorious proletariat be content to be shut out from employment? Would it not forcibly open the factories and work them itself to the exclusion of capitalist owners? If, for example, a coalition Government in the sense envisaged by Lenin were established in which democratic representatives of the peasantry sat side by side with Social Democrats, it is clear that the moment the nationalization of industry was proposed a life and death struggle would begin between the workers and the peasants. Either the peasants, and with them the Counter-Revolution, would triumph, or the work-people and Socialism. In no circumstances would Lenin's 'democratic dictatorship of workers and peasants' prove workable.

Trotsky indeed admitted that in a backward agricultural country like Russia the victorious Socialist workers could not alone and permanently maintain themselves in power as against the enormous majority of peasants and lower middle class. From this dilemma only one way of escape remained— the extension of the Socialist revolution to western Europe. If the Socialist Workers' Revolution is confined to a single country, it is doomed; it can only maintain itself by advancing from country to country. That is Trotsky's famous theory of the permanent revolution. In 1909 Trotsky wrote:

'As the result of a victorious revolution power must come to those parties whose support is in the armed populations of the towns—the proletarian militia. On attaining to power Social Democracy finds itself confronted by a profound paradox that is not to be overcome by a simple statement that it is a purely democratic dictatorship. A policy of renunciation on the part of the Workers' Government for the purpose of establishing a republic would be tantamount to a betrayal of the unemployed, of the strikers, and, finally, of the proletariat as a whole. The victorious

revolutionaries will find themselves confronted by definite Socialist tasks whose execution will of necessity bring them at a certain point into conflict with the economic backwardness of the
country. A national revolution provides no way of escape from
this conflict of interests. From the day of its accession to power
the Workers' Government is faced with the task of uniting all its
forces with those of the Socialist proletariat in western Europe.
It is only in this way that its temporary revolutionary rule will
prove to be the prelude to a Socialist dictatorship. The permanent
revolution is necessary in order that the Russian proletariat may
defend itself as a class.'

About the time that Lenin drew up his principles for revolutionary activity in Russia, Trotsky was also formulating his
standpoint. On October 17, 1915, in the Russian newspaper,
Nash Slovo, published in Paris, Trotsky wrote as follows:

'In any debate on the subject of the character of the revolution,
and the tactics to be pursued by the proletariat, the chief historical
question to be discussed is: Is middle-class Democracy in Russia
stronger or weaker than it was in 1905? . . . Our reply is: A
national middle-class revolution is an impossibility in a Russia in
which there is no true revolutionary middle-class democracy. The
age of national revolutions, like that of national wars, is past in
Europe. . . . The longer deceit, enfeeblement, discontent, and
embitterment are permitted to continue among the lower classes of
townsfolk and peasantry, the worse will be the results. That does
not, however, signify that the independent force of revolutionary
democracy would be serviceable alongside the proletariat. Neither
the leaders nor the social material for such a democracy are to
hand. It is, nevertheless, indisputable that the profound discontent of the lower classes will spur on the proletariat in its revolutionary offensive. An ever-increasing discontent exists among the
townspeople and the peasantry. But as a revolutionary force
capable of utilizing this discontent there is only the proletariat—
and in a far higher degree than in 1905. . . . Hence it is not simply
a question of setting up a temporary revolutionary government—
a shapeless block that will at some later date in evolution be given
form—but of establishing a revolutionary Workers' Government
in order to secure power for the proletariat in Russia.'

Ever since 1903 Trotsky had been at variance with other
members of the Bolshevik Party in questions of organization.
Thus he was opposed to the dictatorship of a small circle of
leaders over the workers. Lenin, however, had not adopted

this method out of any love of power, but because it was necessary to effect a coalition of the workers with the lower middle classes in a middle-class democratic revolution. Only a trained and autocratic body of leaders, and not the masses themselves, could carry out so complicated a revolution. Trotsky for his part did not believe in the capacity for revolution of these lower middle classes any more than he believed in the appeal of the ideal of nationality—an ideal that he held to be outworn in an imperialist age. Trotsky is a pure proletarian internationalist. If the workers could carry through their revolution alone and without the help of the peasantry and the inspiration of the national democratic ideal, and solely inspired by their own Socialist ideal, then there would be no need for a dictatorship on the part of their leaders. Trotsky favoured democracy among the workers at the same time as he advocated the suppression of all other classes by the proletariat. Lenin favoured a broad national Russian democracy within the limits considered desirable by the leaders of the governing Bolshevik Party.

Moreover, Lenin and Trotsky were at variance in their opinions as to the position of a revolutionary Russia in the comity of nations. In Trotsky's opinion the Russian Revolution was a failure if the permanent revolution was not a success, and if it was not possible to accomplish a victorious revolution on the part of the western European workers. In event of that failure the revolution in Russia must collapse. Lenin saw a way of escape from the consequences of this eventuality. It is true that a democratic and republican Russia, in the form desired by the Bolsheviks, would have been isolated among the imperialistic Powers and would have been confronted with many difficulties. Nevertheless, there was no *a priori* reason why such a democratic dictatorship of peasants and workers should not be able to maintain itself in a middle-class order of society in the event of the defeat of the world revolution. Thus Lenin was ready with plans for retreat in face of a defeat of the world revolution. Trotsky had none.

THE THIRD INTERNATIONAL

August 1914 to February 1917

AT the time that Lenin parted company from the other Russian Socialists and Democrats he also broke with the Socialist International for similar reasons. In consequence of the rupture of his relations with the International, Lenin sought to inculcate his views into the non-Russian labouring classes in order to obtain sympathizers with the Bolshevik Party beyond the Russian frontiers and to establish a new— Third—International. Throughout the years 1903 to 1914 the existence of the Bolshevik Party within the Second International had only been rendered possible by maintaining the fiction that the leading groups in the International were of as revolutionary a character as were the Bolsheviks. After 1914 this fiction could no longer be maintained.

The so-called break-up of the Second International in 1914 was not indeed due to the fact that the Socialist working class was unable to prevent the outbreak of war. The war would have come even if the Social Democrat Parties in all the eight Great Powers had been led by heroic revolutionaries. For in 1914 there did not exist in Japan, Great Britain, or the United States any great Socialist Parties. In France, Austria-Hungary, and Italy the Socialists formed only a small minority of the population. In Russia, as long as the Tsar maintained his rule the Socialists were powerless. Although the Social Democrats in Germany were supported by a good third of the parliamentary voters, they were powerless when confronted with a middle-class majority supported by the great Prussian military and police system. In not a single one of the eight Great Powers, in July 1914, was a Socialist Government in power, nor were any of the eight Governments dependent for their parliamentary existence upon the Socialist vote. Hence the Socialists were powerless to prevent the war. The International cannot be condemned on this count and its break-up must not be ascribed to its inability to prevent the outbreak of war. Nevertheless, the International was forced in August 1914 to discard the revolutionary mask that it had been wearing, and this action seemed tantamount to its own dissolution.

An organization can only be looked upon as revolutionary when it has for its avowed and sole object the accomplishment of the overthrow of the existing order within a measurable space of time. If judged by this—the only just—criterion, the groups composing the Second International were not revolutionary and their place is in the second category in the classification attempted in the previous chapter. They accepted the existence of the capitalist State and sought to improve the condition of the working class within its limits. In consequence they were forced into a position incompatible with their own beliefs. For the theories of Marx, which they had made their own, called for revolution. There were, indeed, two ways in which they could attempt to evade this contradiction between their professed beliefs and their actions. The first way was an open and sincere confession that Marx's theories must be altered to suit changed circumstances, and that Social Democracy, even possibly in alliance with middle-class opinion and abandoning an ideology dominated by its final aim, must seek to accomplish definite reforms. Those who believed in this course became known as Revisionists (2a). The second way was that of continuing to accord the chief place in agitation and propaganda to the final aim, rejection of reforms, refusal to co-operate in the peaceful promotion of better conditions and to compromise with middle-class political parties and governments. At the same time there was to be no action of a revolutionary nature, and the small successes won for the working class by the 'Reformist' Trade Unions were to be regarded secretly as matters for rejoicing. This course was adopted by the Radicals, who were in general the leaders of the Second International (2b).

There can be no question that up to 1914 the Revisionists had a far better knowledge of actual political and economic conditions than had the so-called Radicals. The Revisionists could accomplish more for the working class and could gain greater influence over Governments by means of their association with non-Socialist Parties. Radicalism, however, afforded the working man comfort and hope in his miserable daily life. It increased his class-consciousness and opened his eyes to the gulf between him and the middle class. Nevertheless, Radicalism of the type 2*b* must of necessity break down at a time of great political crisis; for it could neither act in a revolutionary sense nor pursue a tactical policy of reform. It needed, indeed, the powerful authority of the middle-class State that actually protected it from the consequences of its own 'revolutionary' speeches. A sincere Revisionist could more easily accommodate himself to a difficult situation than could a traditional Radical of this type.

Another contradiction must be examined in considering the differences between Radicals and Revisionists. The Socialists were in the minority in all countries. And it was Radicalism that demanded the seizure of political power. Now the Socialists could only achieve that power by co-operation with a part of the middle class, i.e. by 'Revisionist' tactics. The Radicals by refusing to enter into any compromise postponed the acquisition of power to a time so distant that it ceased to be within the realm of actual politics.

A party in the sense of category 1—Social Democracy as a revolutionary party aiming at completing the middle-class revolution—did not then exist outside the ranks of the Russian Bolsheviks. It would have been Bolshevism, for example, if prior to 1914 the German Social Democrats had proclaimed a revolutionary war against the Hohenzollerns and the Prussian Junkers, if they had set up an illegal organization with its centre in Switzerland, and if they had enthusiastically promoted an alliance with the Catholic Centre and the Liberals against the Prussian Conservatives. In those days, however, nobody in any country outside Russia dreamed of pursuing such strategy and tactics. It is true that Wilhelm Liebknecht played with such ideas from 1866 to 1870 at the time when he laid stress upon the need for a revolutionary struggle with Bismarck and Prussianism, and was prepared to enter into an alliance for that purpose with all middle-class, *grossdeutsche* enemies of Prussia and even with the clerical Particularists. That, however, remained an episode in the history of German Social Democracy without further consequences.

In pre-War Europe there was also to be found the small group of Socialist intellectuals which has been classified under category 3 above. These men were convinced that the age of peaceful Capitalism would shortly be succeeded by one filled with terrible wars and convulsions of society. Hence the necessity in their opinion for the working man to turn his back upon reform and high-sounding phrases and return to the ways of revolution. This revolution could only be a Socialist workmen's revolution in consequence of the tremendous development of modern Capitalism and the destruction of the lower middle class. As has already been pointed out in the previous chapter, this theory met with little support in Poland, Germany, or Holland.

What was the attitude adopted by Bolshevism before 1914 towards the various groups within the International? Apart from the Bolsheviks there were to be found in Russia representatives—naturally in a Russian dress—of all the different tendencies in European Socialism. Thus the Revisionists (2a) were represented in Russia about 1900 by the so-called Economists, who believed that Social Democracy should only occupy itself with the purely economic interests of the working classes, and, after the failure of the revolution in 1905, by the so-called Liquidators, who looked upon the existence of the illegal Social Democrat organizations as superfluous. The Mensheviks were representative of western European Radicalism (2b) and Trotsky of category 3.

In the eyes of Russian working men the Socialist International possessed great authority. They felt themselves strengthened in their desperate conflict with Tsarism and in the persecution which they had to endure at its hands by the feeling of unity with class-conscious workers in all other countries. Thus Lenin was forced to make common cause with those groups—the Radicals—in the International who advocated revolution in their speeches and resolutions. Indeed it would seem that prior to 1914 Lenin looked upon the German Social Democrat Party with its Radical leaders as an organization somewhat resembling Bolshevism. He believed that a Party led by Bebel and whose programme was laid down by Kautsky would at the given moment lead a revolution against Wilhelm II and German Capitalism. Moreover, he noted the strict discipline governing the Party and that a certain group of leaders continuously maintained their authority over it. Nor did complaints against the autocratic methods of the Party Committee escape his notice. Thus he came to believe sincerely that Bebel and his friends were a German counterpart of the dictatorship exercised by the Bolshevik Party over the working men.

That was a grave error. For if in western European Parties and Trade Unions the power of the leaders was great, and at times the Opposition had good reasons for complaining that it was abused, the leaders themselves depended in the last resort upon the suffrages of the members and could not therefore indefinitely maintain themselves in office against the will of the workers who had elected them. If Lenin (as certain of his pre-War utterances would lead one to suppose) really looked upon German Social Democracy as a form of Bolshevism, it was unquestionably a mistake on his part. The fanatical personal hatred with which Lenin pursued Karl Kautsky after August 1914 cannot be explained simply on grounds of differences of opinion. Such hatred can only be entertained by a person who has formerly loved greatly. After 1914 Lenin sought to revenge himself upon Kautsky for having mistakenly admired his ideas and organization for twenty years past.

Although in matters of principle he was for the most part in disagreement with them, Lenin admired Rosa Luxemburg and her followers for their revolutionary enthusiasm. As early as 1903 Rosa Luxemburg had raised her voice in protest against Lenin's theory of revolutionary organization. She refused to accept his conception of a dictatorship over the proletariat and she could only conceive of a great revolution as spontaneous action on the part of the working classes. This notion of spontaneity appeared in Lenin's eyes to be the purest nonsense. Moreover, Rosa Luxemburg rejected Lenin's proposed alliance between the proletariat and the lower middle classes; and she did not agree with Lenin as to the importance to be attached to the problems of the peasantry and nationalism.

In 1912 Rosa Luxemburg's famous book on *The Accumulation of Capital* was published, in which she propounded the theory that Capitalism can only continue to exist for so long as non-capitalist countries and classes remain open to its exploitation. The mad struggle between the imperialistic States for colonies was motivated by the desire to exploit the last remaining non-capitalist territories on the surface of the globe. In a short time the process of dividing up the world among capitalist States would have reached its culmination. Capitalism would find itself faced with destruction. The proletariat would everywhere rise in victorious revolution. Thus in 1912 Rosa Luxemburg already proclaimed the coming world revolution. This revolution, however, was to be a purely Socialist revolution and not the partially middle-class revolution which Lenin was to announce in 1915. Lenin rejected absolutely Rosa Luxemburg's theories of Imperialism. In the essay on Imperialism, which he published in 1915, Lenin praised the book on financial Capitalism written by the Austrian Socialist Hilferding, and did not even mention Rosa Luxemburg's work. The notion that Capitalism would one day automatically break down was in Lenin's opinion a dangerous illusion. Unless the revolution itself overthrew them, the capitalists always had a way of escape from the gravest danger; and the revolution could not be organized according to Rosa Luxemburg's theories of a purely proletarian movement that took no account of the peasants, &c. Rosa Luxemburg and Trotsky were nearer to each other in their ideas than were Rosa Luxemburg and Lenin. In 1903 Trotsky, like Rosa Luxemburg, had emphatically rejected Lenin's theory of the necessity for organization. In 1909 Trotsky published an article in Rosa Luxemburg's Polish newspaper setting forth his ideas on the coming Russian revolution, and in 1915 he agreed with her in insisting that national wars were no longer possible in an imperialistic age.

Then came August 1914. Unable to prevent the outbreak of war, the Socialist Parties in Germany, France, Austria, and Belgium proclaimed their willingness to assist in the defence of their respective countries; and their attitude was defensible from a Marxist standpoint inasmuch as neither Marx nor Engels had denied the idea of nationality. Nevertheless, it was not incumbent upon these Socialist Parties to agree to a political truce in their several countries. They might without risk have maintained the individual position of the proletariat in both political and economic life and have attempted to pursue an independent Socialist and internationalist policy. The moment the Radical groups in the Second International agreed to participate in the defence of their countries they were forced to abandon the attitude of irreconcilability in which they had hitherto persisted. Their freedom of action was lost to them and they became the prisoners of the political truce. To the outside world this seemed tantamount to a complete collapse. The tendencies classified above under categories 2a and 2b became indistinguishable from each other. When, however, the workmen and members of the Socialist movement began to criticize their own actions and those of their leaders, many outstanding personalities among both the Revisionists and the Radicals opposed the official Party Policy of supporting the political truce—thus, for example, in Germany, Bernstein, the formulater of the Revisionist theory, and Kautsky, the adviser of the Party Committee until 1914, both went into opposition to the official Party leaders.

In August 1914 Lenin recognized the non-revolutionary character of the Second International and abandoned it as valueless for his purpose. He hoped, nevertheless, that the convulsion of the World War would result in the creation of new revolutionary groups of workmen in the various European States. As early as November 1, 1914, Lenin demanded the creation of a Third International in an article in which he wrote:

'Opportunism has triumphed over the Second International and it is dead. . . . The Second International accomplished its share of the necessary preliminary work of organizing the proletarian masses throughout the long and peaceful period of cruel capitalistic enslavement and swift capitalistic development in the last third of the nineteenth and the beginning of the twentieth centuries. The Third International is confronted with the task of organizing the proletariat for a revolutionary attack upon capitalist governments, for civil war with the middle class in all countries to achieve political power, and for the victory of Socialism.'

Lenin also endeavoured to find a scientific explanation for the moral collapse of the International and made use for this purpose of his basic principle of Imperialism. He dubbed the policy of support for the middle class on the part of the Socialists in time of war 'Socialist Chauvinism'. Moreover, he maintained the identity of these Socialist Chauvinists with the Opportunists or pre-War Revisionists. Nor could the exclusion of a few individuals affect the validity of this theory. After all Opportunism was a result of Imperialism.

The capitalistic middle class were enabled by the vast profits they made abroad, in colonies, &c., to throw a sop to the working men. This sop took the form of the higher wages paid to skilled workmen. There arose in this manner in America and in Europe a sort of working-class aristocracy composed of work-people who had become identified with the life of the lower middle classes and who felt themselves in sympathy with and dependent upon the economic organiza-tion of their countries. This 'aristocratic' class of work-people dominated the Social Democrat Party organizations in Europe in alliance with a bureaucracy composed of the Party officials and Trade Union officials. The revolutionary spirit and ideal had long ceased to animate them; they were the formulaters and executants of Opportunist and Socialist-Chauvinist policy. The sweated masses of poor and miser-ably paid workmen hated this policy in their hearts. They were radical and revolutionary. At the same time they were not organized because the Party machinery was in the hands of the Opportunists who denied the revolutionary workmen all opportunity for expressing their wishes. Hence the task confronting revolutionary Socialism in every country was to organize the revolutionary masses and lead them in an attack upon the 'aristocratic' workmen and the middle class.

This theory of an aristocracy of working men contained an element of truth. Nevertheless, its universal application was indefensible and had dangerous consequences for the inter-national Labour movement. It is unquestionably true that groups of workers whose incomes far exceed a living wage, and whose habits of life are barely distinguishable from those of the lower or even upper middle class, can only with diffi-culty attain to a proletarian class-consciousness. It is for this reason that even to-day the chief elements in the American working class are opposed to Socialism. Marxism, however, proves that the existence of such elements within the system of wage-labour can only be in the nature of exceptions. It would, for example, be a wild exaggeration to call the standard of life in 1913 of skilled metal-workers in Germany, Austria, and France, non-proletarian. If the restricted living conditions which had been obtained by 1913 for the German metal-workers as the result of protracted struggles on the part of the Trade Unions had sufficed to render them indifferent to real Socialism, then Socialism would have been proved bankrupt both as a political movement and as a conception of the ordering of society. The fact that the raising of wages by a few marks sufficed to turn the workers into counter-revolutionaries and middle-class citizens would have deprived Socialism of all meaning. Revolutionary Socialists would in that case have been forced to watch anxiously for any rise in wages that might send the workmen into the enemy's camp.

Any attempt on the part of Lenin's followers at a future time to found new revolutionary Labour Parties in central and western Europe in accordance with this principle would mean that the poorly paid workers and the unemployed would have to be roused against their skilled and better-paid fellows. This would give rise to mutual hatred and cause a wide gulf to open between the various elements in the proletariat. Any possibility of a successful revolution would thereby be automatically destroyed. The working class on the European continent could only achieve power by gaining a large body of middle-class opinion for their cause. Although Lenin's theory of revolution demanded a popular revolution led by the workers against Imperialism at the time of the World War, it is clear that his theory of a working-class aristocracy implied that skilled turners and carpenters were to be included in the ranks of the enemies of the working class. All employees, officials, and peasants must in that case be looked upon as the enemies of the proletariat. The new Revolutionary Socialist Party would then be nothing more than a sect of the poorest workers, influenced emotionally by the unemployed, filled with hatred for every one who had been more successful, and completely incapable of ever achieving political power.

This profound irreconcilability in the doctrines of Lenin when applied to western Europe did not become evident until after the World War. As early as 1914 Lenin had set different aims before his followers within and without Russia. His followers in Russia were to work for the realization of the middle-class revolution while those in western Europe sought to bring about a Socialist revolution. Out of this difference in aims arose later certain differences within the body of doctrine known as Bolshevism.

It was Lenin's belief that the Socialists could have prevented the catastrophe of 1914 if they had chosen the right moment to exclude from their ranks the Opportunists—the clique of working-class aristocrats and their doctrinaire leaders. In support of his belief Lenin compared conditions in Russia and Italy with those obtaining in Germany, Austria, France, and Belgium. Opportunists and true Socialists were united in the same Party in the four latter countries. On the occurrence of the crisis the Opportunists secured control of the Party organizations. In Russia, on the other hand, the Bolsheviks had separated themselves from the Mensheviks in time; and in consequence the outbreak of war found the Russian proletariat strong and prepared for battle. In Italy in like manner the Opportunists under Bissolati had been excluded from the Social Democrat Party before the World War. Bissolati's ostracism was followed by that of the Socialist-Chauvinist Mussolini soon after the outbreak of war. Hence the Italian Social Democrats were in a position to offer a determined opposition to the militarist policy of their Government.

In truth, however, the Italian Socialists were a typical Second International group composed of a mixture of categories 2a and 2b. They were no more revolutionary than were the German Social Democrats. The difference lay rather in the fact that in Italy, as distinct from Germany and France, in the years 1914 and 1915 national opinion was not solidly in favour of war. A great body of middle-class and lower middle-class opinion was opposed to Italy's allying herself with the Entente. For this reason it was far easier for the

Italian Socialists to oppose a warlike policy on the part of the Italian Government than it was, for example, for the Belgian Socialists. Hence it came about that in 1914–15 Italian Social Democracy appeared more revolutionary than it really was at heart. This illusory condition led to tragic consequences.

The dissatisfaction of Socialists throughout Europe with the policy of maintaining a political truce steadily increased during the first years of the war. Demands were put forward for renewed liberty of action on the part of the Labour Parties, for a policy of opposition to the Governments in power, and for the opening of negotiations for peace. Nevertheless, those who put forward these demands did not contemplate revolutionary action and did not see any prospect of its meeting with success. A general pacification was their principal demand. As a revolutionary Lenin detested this 'middle' group of pacifists and followers of Kautsky as much as he detested the Socialist Chauvinists. For Lenin was not willing to contemplate a peace concluded between imperialistic Governments and resulting in the strengthening of Imperialism. Civil war and not peace was what he desired; and in peace propaganda he saw only a means to the confusion and paralysis of the revolutionary proletariat.

An international conference of Socialist opponents of the policy of a political truce was held at Zimmerwald in Switzerland from September 5 to September 8, 1915, for the purpose of working out a common policy. The Conference was summoned on the initiative of Italian and Swiss Socialists and Germany was represented by ten delegates. Of these, six represented the opinions held by the group that later became known as 'Independent' Social Democrats. These six were led by Ledebour and Adolf Hoffmann. Rosa Luxemburg's Spartacist Union was represented by three delegates. Julian Borchardt came to voice the views of a small private body of opinion. Two delegates came from France. The delegates from England were refused their passports. Other countries represented were Bulgaria, Rumania, Sweden, Norway, and Holland. Russia was represented by the following delegates: Lenin and Zinoviev represented the Bolsheviks; Martov and Axelrod, the Mensheviks; Trotsky, his own group;

two delegates, the Left-Wing Social Revolutionaries; and, finally, Left-Wing Socialists from Poland and Latvia.

It quickly became evident that the majority in the Conference supported Kautsky rather than Lenin. Resolutions were passed denouncing the political truce and demanding the pursuit of a policy of opposition to existing Governments for the purpose of forcing them to make peace. In accordance with the traditions of Socialism in western Europe the Conference rejected all proposals for revolutionary action and refused to recognize the existence of a cleavage of opinion within the ranks of the International. Out of thirty votes Lenin's proposals only received the support of seven. Apart from his own and Zinoviev's, he was supported by the votes of a Lett and a Pole (Radek) as well as by those of the two Scandinavian delegates. (In view of the completely non-revolutionary conditions obtaining in Norway and Sweden the support given by these delegates to a policy of civil war was purely theoretical.) The seventh vote cast for Lenin was that of Borchardt. Even the Spartacists did not vote in his favour. Lenin thus encountered defeat on the platform of the Zimmerwald Conference at the hands of the Opposition among the international Socialists. If the voting is analysed, according to countries, it becomes clear that Lenin had no supporters in France, England, or Italy, and only a few isolated individuals followed his lead in Germany—all these being countries of the utmost importance from a Socialist standpoint. The Bolsheviks indeed did not wax enthusiastic over the Conference in Zimmerwald. In a critical appreciation of its work Zinoviev wrote:

'The Conference only took a first and hesitating step along the path on which we wish to lead international Socialism. The Conference did not above all wish to pass any precise and unmistakable resolution dealing with the crisis. It did not want to declare open war upon Opportunism and hold up, even in theory, the flag of Marxism. Its attitude was perhaps unavoidable in present circumstances. Events move with exceeding slowness; nevertheless they move. . . . It is only necessary to take as an example the question of the Third International. The conveners of the Conference—the majority in the Conference—declared and continue to declare that they will not set up a Third International.

The Italian paper *Avanti* and the *Berner Tagwacht*, the organ of R. Grimm (the leader of the Swiss Socialists), endeavour to prove that the "International Socialist Commission" created by the Conference is not intended in any way to replace the old "International Socialist Bureau" and must indeed result in its resuscitation. Nevertheless there is a logic of events. . . . The day will come when all true Socialists will join with us in crying: "The Second International is dead and was destroyed by the Opportunists. Hurrah for the Third International free from Opportunism!"'

In his own observations on the Conference Lenin admitted the weakness of the Left at the same time that he claimed a 'success' for it. He wrote:

'The success of our policy is unquestionable. It is only necessary to study the facts. In September 1914, when it issued its manifesto, our Central Committee was in a similarly isolated position. In January 1915 the International Women's Conference passed its miserable pacifist resolution. . . . In September 1915 we united to form a single group out of the Left Wing of international Socialism, adopted our own tactics, proclaimed our fundamental principles in a common manifesto, and assisted, despite the opposition of the old Bureau and by means of a manifesto which condemned its policy, in establishing an International Socialist Commission which is in fact a new International Socialist Bureau. . . . As early as 1912–14 an overwhelming majority of the Russian workers already supported our Party and its Central Committee. Their experience of the international Socialist movement will now demonstrate to them that our policy will soon come to have a broader basis and that our principles will be shared by an ever-increasing proportion of the best elements in the international proletariat.'

A very important idea for the first time makes its appearance here: Lenin is determined to show his supporters among the Russian workmen that they have sympathizers and allies outside Russia, and he is prepared to prove this to them by placing a tortuous construction upon events.

The report on the Zimmerwald Conference contained in the illegal 'Spartacus Letter', circulated in November 1915 by Rosa Luxemburg and her followers, is very typical of the attitude then prevailing towards Lenin and his ideas. In a report covering almost four pages of print only a single passing reference is made to Lenin and his supporters. 'An alternative draft for the projected manifesto was put forward by the Russian members of the Central Committee, a Polish delegate, and the Norwegian and Swedish delegates. The great majority of the Conference rejected the draft as a tactical error.' Nothing more. The Spartacists—followers of Karl Liebknecht and Rosa Luxemburg—were then the most extreme Socialists in Europe. It is obvious that they regarded the Bolsheviks as an insignificant minority in the ranks of the international Opposition to the prosecution of the war.

In pre-War days the 'International Socialist Bureau' typified the international solidarity of the Labour movement. The War paralysed its activities. The question therefore became one of what were the aims to be pursued by the opponents of the political truce and the War itself: should they restore the old International or destroy it and found a new one? Those who supported the resuscitation of an International Bureau on the old model were thereby supporting the continued existence of the Second International. The majority in the Zimmerwald Conference were opposed to a cleavage and expressly announced that the new executive organ they had called into being—actually an Italo-Swiss International Commission—was not intended to replace the old Bureau but only to act temporarily as its substitute.

At Easter, 1916, the members of the Zimmerwald Conference met for a second time at Kienthal in Switzerland, the composition of the Conference being little changed from what it had been on the former occasion. Representatives of the movement later known as the USPD, delegates from the Spartacus Union, and a representative—Paul Frölich—of a Left-Wing Radical group in Bremen came from Germany. Russian and Polish, Swiss and Italian delegates were present. France and Serbia were also represented. The Left Wing of the Zimmerwald Conference was represented by the Bolsheviks, their Polish sympathizers, Paul Frölich and a few Swiss delegates. In his attack on pacifism, however, Lenin found himself supported by some members of the majority in the Conference. In the decisive issue of support for the Second or for a Third International, i.e. the establishment of an International Socialist Bureau, the voting led to no conclusive result. Ultimately the Conference passed a noncommittal resolution, in which it declared its resolve not to demand the establishment of the Bureau but left it to the individual Socialist groups to demand it. In other words, the majority of the Conference remained faithful to the Second International. Even after the Kienthal Conference Lenin had no real following in England, France, or Italy, and in Germany his supporters were confined to isolated individuals or small local groups. His views did not gain the support of any one of the great German proletarian movements. This lack of sympathy with Bolshevism outside Russia continued to exist until the triumph of the revolution in Russia.

Zinoviev expressed himself as follows on the subject of the Kienthal Conference:

'The Second [Kienthal] Conference unquestionably marks a step forwards. The influence of the Left Wing was greater than it had been in the Conference at Zimmerwald. Prejudice against the Left has diminished in strength. Is it possible, however, to affirm that the Rubicon has been crossed? Can one say that the Conference has finally decided upon a breach with the official Socialist Parties? Is Kienthal the birth-place of a Third International? No! That cannot conscientiously be maintained. . . . Let there be no illusions! A strong Right Wing exists among the members of the Conference. Nobody can prophesy if it will remain on our side. . . . What then? Fight on for our ideals! Fight on for the cause of Revolutionary Socialist Democracy! Fight on for the Third International!'

Although they themselves were under no illusions, Lenin and Zinoviev upheld for the sake of their Russian supporters the fiction that they were the leaders of a great international proletarian movement. After the Kienthal Conference, however, the 'Spartacus Letters' prove that the resolutions and votes in conferences of Party leaders are worthless and that any great mass movement is of more value than any number of conferences. Nevertheless, these conferences at Zimmerwald and Kienthal saw the birth of the Third International.

The smaller his success in western Europe the greater became Lenin's personal hatred of the working-class aristocracy and its leaders. Ill-success only spurred him on in his fight with them. All who stood in his way became his enemies. He hated the Russian patriotic Socialists as much as pacifists, Kautsky's supporters, and the Right Wing in the Conference. In a word, all Socialists who refused to organize revolution and dissension while condemning the prosecution of the war. In an article written in October 1916, Lenin cited certain sayings of Marx and Engels, in which they had spoken very correctly of the transformation of a part of the English working class of their day into members of the middle class. Lenin proceeded to generalize from their statements. He declared that the appearance of 'middle-class Labour Parties' had become typical of all imperialistic countries— Parties whose members were infected by the virus of Imperialism. Comfortable and lucrative positions had been created for peaceful, patriotic workmen and officials who were content with reforms. In this manner an imperialistic middle class tempted and rewarded supporters of the 'middle-class' Labour movement.

'It is a fact that a middle-class Labour Party has made its appearance as a political factor in all progressive capitalist countries. Hence it is useless to talk of a war against Imperialism, or of Marxism and a Socialist Labour movement, without being prepared for a ruthless struggle with these Parties. . . . Nothing leads us to suppose that these Parties will disappear without a Socialist Revolution.'

Kautsky and his supporters did not indeed constitute an independent movement. Their ideas were rooted neither in the masses nor in the privileged class of those workers who had deserted to the middle class. The danger implicit in Kautsky's programme lay in his attempt to reconcile the proletariat with the middle-class Labour movement in order to increase the authority of the latter movement. 'If we wish to remain Socialists, it is our duty to descend to the true masses. It is for that reason that we wage war on Opportunism.'

It has already been pointed out above what consequences were entailed in this descent to the 'true masses' on the part of Lenin and his followers. A Party might in this fashion be kept in existence. The control of the State machinery could never be won. Of course, it is possible that for the moment Lenin was chiefly concerned to gain supporters in western

Europe for the idea of a world revolution and to put forward any sort of plan in opposition to the programme of the old official Social Democrat Party. Mistakes in tactics and errors in doctrine on the part of these non-Russian revolutionary Parties could later be corrected by the central authority directing the world revolution. Lenin certainly did not over-estimate the rate of progress of the revolutionary Socialist movement in central and western Europe. In a speech which he delivered to young Swiss working men on January 22, 1917, Lenin said: 'We who are already old may perhaps not live to participate in the decisive battle of the coming revolution.' Nevertheless, he hoped that the young European Socialists would prove victorious in the coming proletarian revolution.

Two months later Russian workmen deposed the Tsar.

V

MARCH TO OCTOBER 1917

AFTER two years of war the economic life of Tsarist Russia was completely destroyed, the authority of the ruling caste undermined, and the revolution inevitable. The State finances had been disorganized by the enormous war expenditure and the country was drowning in a flood of paper roubles. Millions of workmen and peasants were continually being withdrawn from their factory benches and fields to make good the wastage in the armies. Food supplies steadily diminished. Rolling stock on the railroads was destroyed through excessive usage and gradually became unobtainable. Despite the assistance received from the Entente Powers, Russian industry was in a far less developed state than that of other countries and was scarcely in a position to keep the armies at the Front supplied with munitions. In the factories, as on the railroads, raw materials were used up carelessly and extravagantly. Shortage of supplies and difficulties of transport brought starvation and lack of fuel to the great cities. The peasantry were war-weary and desperate; and the feeling engendered in the villages gradually infected the millions of peasants composing the army.

The support of the majority of the army had enabled the Tsarist Government in 1905 to stamp out the revolutionary movement. Now hardly a single regiment remained loyal to the Tsar and his Government. The populace was resolved on revolution for the purpose of making an end simultaneously of Tsarism and the war. The propertied middle class were also prepared to revolt for an exactly contrary reason. The middle class recognized that the corrupt and incapable Tsarist régime was leading Russia to a catastrophe. The defeats and set-backs of the first three years of war aroused in them the fear that Russia would collapse entirely if Nicholas II and his courtiers remained in control of affairs. Even the reactionary clique surrounding the Tsar gradually came to see that a continuance of the war meant the destruction of all Conservative and traditional authority in Russia.

From 1916 onwards they strove to achieve a separate peace with Germany.

The Liberal upper middle class refused to contemplate peace. After all the sacrifices which the war had entailed upon Russia it was imperative that her war aims should be fulfilled. Instead of retiring from the contest Russia must hold out until the expected victory of the Entente Powers brought her Constantinople and the Straits. If, however, the Tsar was planning the betrayal of his country for feudal and dynastic reasons, the middle class would rather overthrow the dynasty than give up its hopes of victory.

The ambassadors of the Entente Powers in Petrograd did nothing to oppose a revolution. For a revolution would liberate the middle-class democracies in France and England from their compromising ally, Nicholas II, whose downfall was in any case inevitable. Moreover, the Entente might reasonably hope that a middle-class and Liberal Russia would continue to wage war with renewed energy and without any thoughts of concluding a separate peace. Thus it came about that two revolutionary streams merged in the events of March 1917: from below came the movement of peasants, soldiers, and workers yearning for peace and for bread; from above that of the Liberal middle class seeking victory and conquests. The workmen's revolution in Petrograd was the signal for a revolt of the entire garrison. In a few days the revolution had spread victoriously over the whole country and reached the armies at the Front. The workers and soldiers overthrew the Tsar; the Liberal middle class assumed the reins of government. The fall of the monarchy legally involved that of the Russian Parliament—the Duma—which was elected in accordance with a cleverly devised reactionary franchise. The Liberal members of the Duma, however, set up a Committee that immediately became a rallying-point for the middle-class movement. The victorious workers and soldiers in Petrograd established Soldiers' and Workers' Councils in accordance with the tradition of 1905. The Soviet thus became the rallying-point of the Democrats and Socialists. Hence the struggle between the two contending currents in the revolution took the form of a struggle for power between the Duma Committee and the Workers' and Soldiers' Councils.

In March 1917, Russia was divided politically as follows. The Conservative classes—landowners, nobles, officers, and high officials—were to be found in the ranks of the Liberal middle-class movement. Reactionaries and Liberals were now allies in a battle for the retention of private property and the prosecution of the war to a victorious conclusion. The peasantry and the soldiers, who, being for the most part peasants, shared in their traditions and ideals, supported the *Naródniki*. The Social Revolutionaries were the leading Party in the popular movement. The industrial workers were divided in support of the Mensheviks and Bolsheviks. No mention need be made here of the smaller groups and Parties. The vast majority of the nation, and its physical force in the form of the army, stood behind the Social Revolutionaries. On their right stood the middle class and on their left the Socialist minority. Notwithstanding their power the Social Revolutionaries did not seize the reins of government. Like the Russian Social Democrats, the Social Revolutionaries were convinced that the Russian Revolution must be a middle-class revolution; and for that reason they were prepared to accord the governmental authority to the Liberal middle class. They themselves were content to adopt the role of a friendly Opposition criticizing and controlling the actions of the Government and acting as a propulsive democratic force.

The attitude adopted in this question by the Social Revolutionaries was identical with that adopted in 1905 by the Mensheviks. The Workers' and Soldiers' Councils were to act as a form of democratic control over the actions of the Government and were to be established throughout Russia after the model of the parent Council in Petrograd. Workers' and Soldiers' Councils were to be set up in the towns, Peasants' Councils in the villages, and Soldiers' Councils at the Front.

The identity of views between the Social Revolutionaries and the Mensheviks also extended to cover the all-important question of a continuance of the war. The Russian Republic was to adopt the solution propounded by the majority in the Zimmerwald Conference, as representative of the Socialist Opposition in Europe, namely, a peace by mutual agreement without annexations or war indemnities. Russia was to exert her influence in this sense with the Entente nations, as well as with Germany and Austria, in order to restore peace to the world in alliance with international Socialism. A one-sided and separate peace on the part of Russia was inadmissible. For such a peace would bring in its train the danger that German militarism would overrun Europe. Hence republican Russia must continue to wage war upon William II and his army. The Russian people must defend their revolutionary gains until a general pacification had taken place.

Thus it came about that the majority in the Soviets was composed of the Social Revolutionaries and the Mensheviks. In its capacity as representative of all other Councils the Workers' and Soldiers' Council in Petrograd concluded with the Liberal Duma Committee a compromise that paved the way towards the establishment of a Provisional Government. This Government took the form of a Liberal middle-class Cabinet. Although he did not belong to it as an official representative of the Soviets, Kerensky, the well-known member of the *Naródniki* Party, joined it on personal grounds. Ever since March 1917, the executive authority in Russia had found itself in a remarkable situation. The old police force had everywhere been abolished by the mutinous soldiery. All power was in the hands of armed workers and soldiers under the leadership of the Soviets. Nevertheless, the former bureaucratic administration continued to exist and found itself confronted with the problem of carrying out the terms of the agreement between the new Government and the Soviets. The same situation existed at the Front as between officers and Soldiers' Councils. If the war was to be prosecuted further, then it would be necessary either to restore the authority of the former Tsarist officers as against that of the Councils or to create an entirely new body of officers. The work of reconstruction and of creating a new Russia was left to a Constituent National Assembly in accordance with the ideal striven for by Russian revolutionaries for years past. The dates of the election and assembly of this Constituent Assembly were left open.

What was the attitude of the Bolsheviks to this early stage of the middle-class revolution in Russia? It soon became evident that Lenin had been mistaken in his belief that it would be possible for him to control his supporters in Russia from his exile in Switzerland across a barrier of contending armies. The fateful changes that Lenin had introduced into the old theory of Bolshevism since 1914 had hardly reached the ears of his followers in Russia; and what had come to their knowledge had been by no means acceptable to them. In these days Kamenev was the most important member of the Bolshevik Party in Russia. In common with the Bolshevik deputies in the Duma, Kamenev was sent to Siberia in November 1914, whence he returned to Petrograd after the revolution to edit the Bolshevik newspaper *Pravda*.

Kamenev and his intimate friends still thought in terms of the old Bolshevism that had inspired the Party up to the outbreak of the war. He was utterly opposed to the new theories propounded by Lenin. His aim continued to be the continuance of the revolution in Russia from its initial Liberal middle-class stage to a democratic dictatorship on the part of the workers and peasants. In other words—to the establishment of a 'popular' Socialist Coalition Government whose task would be the realization of the democratic ideal. Since the end of 1914 Lenin had for his part refused to hear of the establishment of such a Coalition Government. Kamenev and his friends still remained in favour of a united front of the entire Russian democracy, and they attached little or no importance to the various attitudes adopted towards the war by the individual democratic Parties. On the other hand, Lenin wanted to use the question of the war as a means to sow dissension among the Russian democracy and was not afraid of single-handed action on the part of the Bolsheviks for this purpose.

It was not until Lenin succeeded in reaching Russia in April 1917 that he secured effective control over the Party and wrested the leadership from Kamenev and his followers after a series of violent debates. These debates and Lenin's leadership of the Party did not, however, make an end to his conflict with the old Bolsheviks. Their polemic continued throughout the entire year 1917 and blazed up again with especial fury at the very moment when the Bolsheviks attained to power. Lenin was on his return to Russia accompanied by Zinoviev. A remarkable change came over their relations the moment Zinoviev once more felt the soil of Russia beneath his feet. This man, who had worked in closest co-operation with Lenin throughout their common exile, who had formulated and elucidated the Bolshevik doctrines in brilliant articles published between 1914 and 1916, now wavered in his allegiance. He deserted Lenin for Kamenev, disapproved of the Bolshevik seizure of power in the State, and conducted a violent opposition to Lenin's policy in October and November 1917. It will presently be shown what reasons induced the ablest and most experienced brains in the Bolshevik Party to turn against Lenin at the very moment of the Party's triumph.

In March 1917, on receiving in Switzerland the first authentic news of the revolution in Russia, Lenin made a fateful discovery. He became convinced that the system of Soldiers' and Workers' Councils—Soviets—was the modern expression of the inevitable Socialist-democratic revolution. If, however, the history of the Bolshevik movement from 1903 onwards be studied, it at once becomes clear that for fourteen years the Soviet system had played no part whatever in its programme. And if one goes still farther back to the arrival of Lenin in St. Petersburg (Petrograd) in 1893, it is true to say that for twenty-four years the Soviet system had not formed an integral part of the Bolshevik doctrine. But Lenin relied consistently upon the teachings of experience both in theory and practice. He never once hesitated to alter his beliefs to conform with new facts. In this Lenin and Marx were in full agreement. For Marx as for Lenin the revolution was not only the realization of the revolutionary doctrine but also the expression of its evolutionary development.

The peculiarity in the situation in Russia in March 1917 that immediately attracted the notice of Lenin was the two-fold character of governmental authority. On the one hand there was the Liberal Provisional Government that was nothing but the customary type of imperialist Government and was only differentiated from similar Governments in England, France, and Germany by the circumstance that it did not control the lesser executive organizations such as the police, &c. On the other hand a new power confronted this middle-class Government—the Soviet. And in the Soviet Lenin recognized the existence in a weak and elementary form of an entirely new type of working-class Government which could only be compared historically with the Paris Commune of 1871. His study of the Soviet convinced Lenin that everything which Marx had said in his famous essay on the constitutional and political aspects of the Paris Commune applied with equal truth to the Russian Soviet in 1917. The typical modern form of the State was a centralized governmental apparatus ruling by force alone. This was the type then prevalent all over Europe and that came into being in England and America during the World War. The imperialistic World War resulted in an enormous increase in the efficiency with which this governmental apparatus worked and in the perfection of its machinery. At the very moment when the apparatus was attaining its maximum efficiency in other countries the Russian people spontaneously began to destroy their own governmental machine. The whole military apparatus of Imperialism came to a standstill in Russia as soon as the soldiers ceased to obey their officers and transferred their allegiance to the Soldiers' Councils. In a similar manner the civil apparatus of government ceased to operate the moment the armed workmen took the place of the police and only obeyed the orders of their Soviets. The essence of the centralized feudal and middle-class State was the separation of the ruling classes from the masses of the nation. The authority of the State was represented on the streets by an armed, uniformed policeman whose behests must be obeyed by the unarmed, civilian population. The manner in which the police discharged their duties in the several States varied greatly, being determined by the differences in the social and legal organization of the States themselves. Thus the police in Tsarist Russia behaved very differently from those in England or France. Nevertheless, the police forces of all countries possessed a common characteristic: their membership of an administrative organization standing apart from the masses of the population and incorporating in their eyes the authority of the State.

In a Communist State police and nation are identical. The

population is armed and responsible to itself alone for the maintenance of law and order. In a similar way the old type of army no longer exists. The armed working classes are themselves the army. Administrative functions in towns and villages are carried out by officials possessing the confidence of the populace. These officials are indistinguishable from the other members of the community in regard to income and manner of life. They are continually under the control of the populace and can be dismissed from their posts at any moment.

A communal system of this type implies the destruction and disappearance of the old form of State. It was the ideal which Marx in common with the Anarchists set before him. On every occasion in history when the populace sought to destroy a feudal or centralized authority ruling by force they did so in seeking to replace it by some such communal organization as, for example, the city communes of the Middle Ages, the Swiss peasant cantons, the early communal type of government in North America, the Paris Commune of 1871, and, finally, the Russian Soviet of 1917. As will presently be demonstrated in detail, the educated (so-called) Soviet Government that has been in power from 1918 to the present day has nothing in common with this type of Government.

Such a 'communal' or 'Soviet' type of Government need not necessarily be Socialist. For example, it would be easy to imagine a system of communal Government by means of People's Councils established in a peasant canton in which the right of private ownership was fully preserved. This extreme form of democracy is, however, according to Marx, the preliminary condition for Socialism inasmuch as Socialism can only be realized in a world enjoying the highest possible measure of individual freedom.

Lenin was convinced that the unique dual system of Government in Russia could not exist for long. If the Provisional Government was successful in asserting its authority, then it would be in a position to acquire control over the whole Executive power. The policeman would make his appearance again in the towns, clad perhaps in a new uniform and with some other title, but identical in principle with the

Tsarist policeman. The nation would once more be disarmed. The old discipline would be re-introduced into the army and the authority of the Soldiers' Councils would be transferred to the officers. If, however, the Soviets were successful in the struggle for supreme power in the State, then they would have to be strong enough to dissolve the former ministries and to remove the higher civil servants and officers from their posts. A consequence of their disappearance would be the downfall of the Provisional Government and the field would thus be left open for the Soviets alone.

This train of reasoning brought Lenin to his solution of the problem confronting Russia: the overthrow of the Provisional Government and the establishment of the Soviets as the sole organs of power. He reasoned somewhat in this fashion: The Russian democracy, as represented in the Soviets and in a political sense by the Social Revolutionary and Social Democrat Parties, desires peace. But the Provisional Government cannot give it peace since it is an imperialistic Government of the upper middle class and bent on conquest. Russian democracy demands liberty. Thanks to the Soviets a large measure of liberty has been accorded to it. Nevertheless, the Provisional Government is opposed to the liberation of the masses of the nation and desires to reconstruct the old governmental machinery. Further, the Russian peasant cries aloud for land and the working man for bread. The Provisional Government is unable to satisfy these demands since it is pledged to defend the right of private ownership, including the ownership of land, and will never tolerate any dictatorial interference with the distribution of food supplies without which famine cannot be overcome. Since the Liberal upper middle class is of necessity unable to fulfil the four great democratic demands for 'Peace, Liberty, Bread, and Land', any toleration of the Provisional Government by the democratic masses of the nation is ridiculous. Russian democracy, i.e. the Soviets, must themselves seize the reins of government.

Here Lenin revealed himself faithful to his political traditions in putting forward not Socialist but only Radical democratic demands. Moreover, his former ideal of a revolutionary democratic Coalition Government again makes its

appearance in a fresh and peculiar guise. For in those days
the Bolsheviks formed only a small minority in the Soviets
and Lenin's cry of 'All Power for the Soviets' meant in the
spring and summer of 1917 a Coalition Government of the
Social Revolutionaries and the Mensheviks. Did not this
contradict Lenin's own solution of the problem—the impossibility of an alliance with Chauvinist democracy—that he had
been preaching to his followers since 1914 without inter-
mission?

It is clear that Lenin distinguished between the active
members of the Social Revolutionary Party and the masses
of the soldiers and peasants who sympathized with the Party
as a matter of tradition. If the official democratic Parties
tolerated an upper middle-class Government, the opposition
among a democratic peasantry hungry for land and a democratic soldiery desirous of peace must grow steadily. If, however, the Soviets obtained control over the State, then the
Government would not be in the hands of the Central Committee of the Social Revolutionary Party but in those of the
nation itself, which was revolutionary in a general sense rather
than the devotee of any special Party tenets.

The Revolution in 1905 had already made the nation
acquainted with revolutionary Soviets. If Lenin's ideal of
'All power for the Soviets' were now to be realized, the
enormous revolutionary force inherent in the nation would be
concentrated in the Soviets and the task of Bolshevism would
become that of adopting the right tactics to secure influence
in the Soviets. Even in 1917 Lenin did not abandon his
principle of a strong Party dictatorship and a centralized
Party organization. In advocating the assumption of the
Government by the Soviets Lenin was very far from assenting
to federalism and the doctrine of the spontaneous will of
the masses. Although he had constructed his own Party
machinery, the Soviets were not his work; they were created
by the nation itself. All that Lenin desired was to use them
in order to destroy Russian Imperialism, which in the situation prevailing in Russia in 1917 could only be overthrown
by the Soviets. In the spring and summer of 1917 Lenin did
not give a thought to the problem of how the centralized and
autocratic Bolshevik system was to be reconciled with the

federalist and anarchist ideal of the Soviets after Russian democracy had won a complete victory over its foes.

In the question of a continuance of the war Lenin was in favour of an immediate rupture with the Entente Powers in pursuance of the ideas which he had held since 1914. The Provisional Government, on the other hand, under cover of the Petrograd Workers' and Soldiers' Council, wished to continue the struggle at the side of its allies. In April 1917, the German General Staff permitted Lenin to return across Germany to Russia in order to strengthen the opposition to the alliance with the Entente. It was a matter of complete indifference to Lenin with whose help he regained Russian soil. If his plans proved successful, Lenin would be a hundred times more dangerous an enemy to Imperial Germany than the existing Government of the Russian Republic. Nevertheless he was forced for some months after his return to endure the reproach that he was an agent of the German General Staff.

Immediately after his arrival in Petrograd Lenin laid down his views on the situation in ten important theses published in *Pravda*. The first thesis showed that, even after the overthrow of the Tsar, the war in which Russia was still a belligerent continued to be an imperialistic war of conquest and that no concession should be made to those who argued that it had become a war of defence. The second thesis demanded that the Revolution having now achieved its first stage must continue to advance towards the second. In theses 3 to 5 Lenin declared:

'No support must be given to the Provisional Government, and their promises, especially those respecting a renunciation of a policy of annexation, must be exposed as the lies that they are. . . . The fact must be recognized that in the majority of Workers' Soviets our Party is in the minority, indeed at the moment in a numerically very small minority, as compared with the block composed of all lower middle-class and Opportunist delegates who are subject to the influence of the middle class and seek to make that influence felt among the proletariat. . . . The masses must be taught to see that the Workers' Soviet is the sole possible form for a revolutionary Government and that therefore our task must, so long as this Government is subject to middle-class influences, be resolute, systematic criticism of its failures and tactics in accordance with the extremely practical demands of the masses. So long as we continue to form the minority we must accompany our criticism by a simultaneous insistence upon the necessity for placing the entire authority of the State in the hands of the Workers' Soviets in order that the masses may learn through experience to avoid their mistakes. Not a Parliamentary Republic —to return to that from the Workers' Soviets would be equivalent to making a retrograde step—but an All Russian Republic of Soviets of Workers, Agricultural Labourers, and Peasants from the lowest to the highest!'

Lenin indeed had little sympathy with the creation of a Constituent National Assembly because he looked upon the system of Soviets as a better expression of democracy than parliamentarism. Nevertheless he did not pronounce himself in 1917 as in principle opposed to a Constituent Assembly, and he doubtless thought that this Assembly might serve as a sort of superstructure in a country organized on the Soviet system.

His sixth thesis demanded the confiscation of the great estates. Theses 7 and 8 ran as follows: 'The incorporation of all banks in a single National Bank to be placed under the control of the Workers' Soviets. Our immediate task is not the "introduction" of Socialism but the acquisition of the control of production and distribution by the Workers' Soviets.' Thus Lenin expressly rejected 'Socialization'. He was prepared to be content for the time being with a control of Capitalism exercised by the working class. He wished to oppose the economic system of Imperialism by one organized in accordance with the interests of the masses and which did not necessarily imply the disappearance of the employer.

His ninth thesis demanded an immediate assembly of the Bolshevik Party Congress for the purpose of altering both the name and the programme of the Party. The alterations which Lenin proposed to introduce into the Party's platform were designed to embody his new beliefs in regard to Imperialism and the State. The name of the Party was to be changed from 'Social Democrat' to 'Communist'. This change was of profound symbolical importance inasmuch as Marx and Engels had styled themselves 'Communists' in the days of the 1848 Revolution. The description 'Social Democrat' had become synonymous with membership of the non-revolutionary Second International. Lenin intended that in future his Party should indicate in their new designation that they had returned to the original Marxism of 1848 and that they no longer had anything in common with the Social Democrats who were prepared to compromise. Lenin's tenth thesis demanded a reorganization of the International.

It was only with difficulty that Lenin induced the Party to accept this programme in the teeth of the opposition of Bolsheviks of the old type like Kamenev. The latter was of the opinion that a Socialist Labour Party which achieved the supreme power in the State by itself and in opposition to every other group could alone carry out a Socialist Revolution. Moreover, he looked upon any attempt to achieve an immediate Socialist Revolution in an agrarian country like Russia as incompatible with the teachings of Bolshevism and highly speculative. For his part Lenin denied resolutely that he wished to introduce Socialism into Russia and he maintained that a revolutionary-democratic dictatorship of workers and peasants already existed in the Soviets and not in some future illusory coalition of the so-called democratic Parties. It was for that reason—he contended—that the Bolsheviks should adopt as their slogan, 'All power for the Soviets!'

The fears entertained by Bolsheviks of the old type were not unfounded and it is significant that Trotsky chose this very moment to join the Bolshevik Party. Although his views on the situation were identical with those of Kamenev, Trotsky drew an exactly contrary deduction: if Lenin was preparing for a second revolution in which the Bolsheviks should seize power to the exclusion of all lesser middle-class and peasant Democrats, this was indeed the aim of Socialism, irrespective of what formulas Lenin might choose to use in his programme. In that case Trotsky was in agreement with Lenin in deed if not in word. Without abandoning his own beliefs in any way, Trotsky felt that he recognized in Lenin's tactics since March 1917 an approach to his own former beliefs, and he therefore felt that he could join the Bolshevik Party without doing violence to his own conscience. Although Trotsky did not bring many supporters with him into the Bolshevik Party, his membership strengthened the Party by the addition of a unique revolutionary personality which was to prove its worth brilliantly in the critical days to come. Moreover, the greater the opposition encountered by Lenin from the side of the Bolshevik Old Guard like Kaménev and Zinoviev, the closer became his friendship with Trotsky, in whose resolute capacity for action he saw his strongest support. In those days Stalin was still a Bolshevik official of quite second-rate capacity. All theoretical differences of opinion between Bolshevism and Trotskyism retreated temporarily into the background to give place to common revolutionary work on the part of Lenin and Trotsky.

The middle-class Liberal Government came into power in March and by May its resources were exhausted. These months served to reveal the weakness of middle-class Liberalism in Russia. Centuries of organic development lay behind the middle class in central and western Europe and a thousand ties bound them both to the lower middle class and to the masses. The middle class in Russia was an excrescence grafted artificially on to the social body of the nation. It was alien to the masses. As long as the peasantry and the lower middle class remained inarticulate and obedient, they continued to be loyal subjects of the Tsar. On attaining to class-consciousness they became 'red' and revolutionary. In no circumstances were they ever Liberal in thought or spirit. Hence middle-class Liberalism was a weak minority in the Russian nation in 1917 and only achieved power because the Socialists and Democrats desired a middle-class Government in fulfilment of their theory of a middle-class revolution. As Lenin had prophesied, however, the political truce concluded between the Government and the Petrograd Soviet proved useless, since Russian Liberalism was incapable of fulfilling the least of the many demands put forward by the masses. The question of peace led to ever sharper protests on the part of the workers and soldiers against the Government, and the desire for peace animating the masses was only strengthened by the Government's policy of a prosecution of the war to victory and territorial conquests.

The growing political tension became acute in May and the Soviet was confronted with the problem of taking over the reins of government itself. The Liberal phase of the revolu-

tion had reached its close. It was now the turn of the Democrats. As the decisive party of the peasantry and the soldiers,
the Social Revolutionaries abandoned their policy of non-
intervention and entered the Government. Would their allies
in the Soviets—the Mensheviks—also accept portfolios?

The traditions animating the Menshevik Party since 1905
forbade their entry into the Government. Nevertheless, they
resolved in May not to dissolve the alliance (with the Social
Revolutionaries) which they had concluded at the beginning
of the revolution. In alliance with the Social Revolutionaries
the Mensheviks were in the majority in all the Soviets and the
two groups together incorporated the Soviet ideal of Russian
democracy. It was their consciousness that they embodied
this ideal that induced the Mensheviks to regard it as their
duty to enter the Government in the altered circumstances
so as to further the democratic cause.

The political picture presented by Russia in May 1917 was
very different from that which it had presented in 1905. The
Mensheviks now formed part of a democratic Coalition
Government and the Bolsheviks were in opposition. Their
decision to enter the Government proved a fateful one for the
Mensheviks and ultimately led to the doom that overtook
them. For it was from the outset clear that the balance of
political power within the Coalition Government would give
the final voice in affairs to the Social Revolutionaries. The
Mensheviks became the prisoners of *Naródniki* tactics. If
they could conquer with them, they could also perish with
them. The Bolsheviks followed an all-Russian policy whereas the Mensheviks pursued only a working-class policy
that could be productive of little result in the special conditions prevalent in Russia. The Bolsheviks would have
been able to maintain themselves in a democratic Coalition
Government as against its other members. The Mensheviks
were drawn down into the abyss by the Social Revolutionaries. If the Mensheviks had not entered the Government in May, they would not in October have been powerless
as a political Party. It is significant that the most important
member of the Menshevik Party, Martov, did not approve of
his Party's entering the Coalition Government. As leader of
a tiny group of Menshevik Internationalists, Martov occupied

in 1917 a sort of intermediary position between the Government and the Bolsheviks. He and his followers, however, never achieved any real influence over the masses. Since a number of Liberals continued to hold office, even after the reconstitution of the Government in May, Russia can be said to have been ruled until October 1917 by a Coalition Government composed of Liberals, Social Revolutionaries, and Mensheviks. This is not the place in which to follow all the domestic changes that occurred within the Government itself from May to October. Power remained in the hands of the Social Revolutionary members of the Cabinet with Kerensky as their leader.

The political bankruptcy of the *Naródniki* movement became manifest in the course of these six months. The criticism levelled by Russian Socialists at the *Naródniki* in the past was now shown to have been fully justified. Although individuals of heroic proportions were to be found among the *Naródniki*, the nebulous romanticism of the movement as a whole collapsed when confronted with stark reality. The *Naródniki* in truth became the prisoners of the imperialistic war. It is undeniable that their attitude towards the problem of peace or war was at least arguable: to work for a general pacification while refusing to conclude a separate peace. It might indeed have been possible to induce the Russian soldier to hold the Front against the attack of the German armies on the ground that by so doing he was defending the Russian Revolution against William II. The Kerensky Government, however, allowed itself to be persuaded by the Entente and former Tsarist Generals into believing that the Russian Revolution must show its strength by taking the offensive. Nevertheless, the decision on the part of the Government in July to order the armies to take the offensive again against the Germans and Austrians was a capital psychological error in view of the opinions and *morale* then prevailing among the armies. Indeed, it was a mistake that in its immensity and its results is only to be compared with that made by the German admirals in October 1918, in ordering the German Fleet to put to sea for the purpose of attacking the British Fleet. The Kerensky Government squandered its moral authority in preparing and carrying out the July offensive, which after a few initial successes ended in complete failure. Its collapse left Russia in ruins.

Kerensky's domestic policy was as great a failure as was his peace policy. The Social Revolutionaries could not bring themselves to deal promptly with the agrarian problem. Month succeeded to month while the peasant waited vainly to see the landowner deprived of his estate. The working man also waited in vain for measures to be taken against famine and the economic crisis in general. Since, moreover, they had no solution for the pressing problems of the day, the Social Revolutionaries committed a second capital mistake in postponing the assemblage of the All-Russian National Assembly. Their fear, indeed, was not that they would suffer defeat at the polls but that their victory would be too great; for a parliamentary election in Russia at that time would have resulted in a decisive majority for the Social Revolutionaries. Supported by a large majority of the nation, the Social Revolutionaries would have been forced to govern Russia by themselves—a possibility from which they recoiled in alarm. Hence, instead of holding an election for a National Assembly, the Government established all possible forms of conferences, committees, commissions, &c., in which all sorts of representatives of middle-class organizations sat side by side with representatives of the Soviets. These artificial creations were utterly lacking in authority. They were, nevertheless, intended to strengthen the hands of the Coalition Government. Moreover, despite the fact that their weakness was patent, the Social Revolutionaries held firmly to their alliance with the Liberals for the purpose of excusing the inefficiency of the Government by the necessity for preserving the Coalition. Of far greater importance than all these Government conferences and commissions was the All-Russian Congress of Soviets, composed of delegates from every Workers', Soldiers', and Peasants' Soviet within the frontiers of Russia. This Congress elected a permanent Executive Committee in which the Social Revolutionaries held the absolute majority throughout the spring and summer of 1917.

The renewal of the offensive succeeded in strengthening the authority of the Tsarist officers in the armies at the Front. In the name of military discipline revolutionary soldiers were punished and even shot. The officers soon felt themselves sufficiently masters of the situation to enable General Kornilov to attempt a counter-revolutionary *coup d'état*. His attempt was defeated by the determined opposition of the Soldiers' Councils. Disaffection became rife throughout the armies. The soldiers believed that Kornilov's rebellion had only been possible because of Kerensky's policy, and their trust in the Government was destroyed. The discontent of the peasantry resulted in outbreaks of disorder of ever-increasing violence in the country districts. The peasantry began to identify the Kerensky Government with the landowners and to lose their faith in the Social Revolutionaries.

Thus the Kerensky Government dug its own grave. Was it inevitable that events should follow the course they did in Russia during the spring and summer months of 1917? After the overthrow of Tsarism, landowners, and the upper middle class, a democratic peasant Republic was inevitable in Russia —not a Socialist Labour Government. The further progress of the Revolution was wholly compatible with a parliamentary Constitution and the retention of the right of private ownership. If the Social Revolutionaries had held elections promptly for a National Assembly, they would thereby have brought into being a powerful and real instrument of government. It must never be forgotten that the Bolshevik October Revolution was not directed against a legal parliamentary democratic Government, but against dictators who had appointed themselves and who had hitherto prevented the assembly of any form of parliament. The motto of the Bolshevik Revolution was not 'Dictatorship of the Proletariat! Down with Democracy!' but was its exact contrary, 'Long live Democracy! Down with Dictators!' When Kerensky finally decided to hold elections for a National Assembly, it was too late. If the Social Revolutionaries had had a National Assembly behind them in the summer of 1917, and had secured from an All-Russian Parliament its assent to the expropriation of landed property, they would in all probability have maintained themselves in power. In those circumstances it might even have been possible to maintain the Front unbroken during the winter of 1917–18.

The failure of the Social Revolutionaries left the way open

for the Bolsheviks to complete the Russian Revolution. Ever since the summer of 1917 it had been clear that the Revolution could only be led by either the *Naródniki* or the Bolsheviks. For neither the Liberals nor the Mensheviks nor any other group exercised sufficient influence over the masses to qualify them for leadership. The Bolsheviks rescued the Revolution after the collapse of the Social Revolutionaries had endangered its existence. If Lenin had failed in the autumn of 1917, Russia would have become a scene of terrible anarchical chaos and not the theatre of a peaceful democratic development. For the vast Russian nation was now in movement. The peasants no longer tolerated the estate-owners; the soldiers refused obedience to their officers; the workmen wished to abolish capitalists. No power on earth could have restrained them in their blind fury once the traditional authority of the Social Revolutionaries had been destroyed. This frenzied chaos would have ended in the break-up of Russia, in pogroms, and in a 'White' Terror. The Bolsheviks rescued the Russian nation from this danger and in doing so saved the Revolution in Russia, notwithstanding their many experiments and failures. The Russian Revolution was not the work of the Bolsheviks. Their service lies in the recognition by Lenin and Trotsky that at midnight a great anarchical revolt would occur. Five minutes before midnight Lenin and Trotsky gave the order for a Bolshevik rebellion and in doing so created the impression that the tremendous occurrence at midnight was their work. It was in this manner that they won for themselves the authority necessary to enable them to govern Russia.

Through their determined opposition to Kerensky's July offensive the Bolshevik Party attracted to themselves the attention of the masses. In Petrograd they demonstrated against the Government. Kerensky proved himself the stronger by bringing reliable bodies of troops into the capital and denouncing the Bolsheviks as German agents and enemies of the Russian Revolution. The Government subjected the Party to a ruthless persecution, arrested its officials, and suppressed its newspapers. Trotsky was imprisoned and Lenin was forced to lead the life of a conspirator. This persecution produced its martyr. Lenin soon appeared before the masses as the sole oppositional force in Russia simply because all other political Parties and groups joined the Government in its anti-Bolshevik policy. The more patent the failure of Kerensky, the Social Revolutionaries, and the Mensheviks, the stronger the conviction in the masses that Lenin was in the right. When Kornilov attempted his counter-revolutionary *Putsch*, Lenin at once called on his supporters to assist the Government against the 'White' General without regard for past differences. The sailors at Cronstadt—the Bolshevik Storm troops—came to Petrograd to support Kerensky in his fight with Kornilov. The Bolsheviks thus revealed themselves as unconditional defenders of the Revolution and regained an appearance of legality. Trotsky was liberated. Lenin, however, was again forced to seek safety in Finland.

The change in public opinion became manifest in September. In Petrograd, Moscow, and many provincial towns, the Bolsheviks gained a majority in the Soviets and the troops went over to them in ever-increasing numbers. The regiments in Petrograd which had enabled Kerensky to occupy the city in July had long since transferred their allegiance to the Bolsheviks. The discontent among the peasants increased from week to week. Nevertheless, an outward appearance of order was still maintained. But Lenin recognized that his hour had struck.

In August and September 1917 Lenin once more defined his theory of Communism and Soviet government in a famous pamphlet entitled *The State and Revolution*. At the same time his mind was preoccupied with the problems arising out of the appalling economic crisis in Russia, where all the evils—famine, failure of transport, diminution in production—inherited by the Republic from Tsarism had only grown worse with the passage of time. In September he published a second pamphlet on *The imminent catastrophe—and how is it to be met?* which contained the economic programme of Bolshevism on the eve of its advent to power. In this pamphlet Lenin regarded the economic situation in Russia from a too optimistic and agitatist standpoint and ascribed the evils from which Russia was suffering in great part to sabotage on the part of employers. While it is undeniable that the radicalization of the Revolution had led to certain acts of sabotage, Lenin nevertheless exaggerated the evil intentions of the capitalists and under-estimated the real factors that brought about the economic crisis. It is because he did so that he was able to advance the opinion that resolute control of production on the part of the masses would render capitalistic profiteering impossible and help to restore Russia to normal economic conditions. Lenin went on to advocate five 'revolutionary-democratic' measures for overcoming the crisis:

1. The union of all Banks in a single organization and State control of their operations, or nationalization of the Banks.
2. Nationalization of Cartels and Syndicates, i.e. the great monopolistic capitalist associations (sugar, naphtha, coal, metal, &c.).
3. The abolition of trade secrecy.
4. A compulsory syndicalization, i.e. compulsory union in associations, of industrialists, traders, and proprietors in general.
5. The compulsory enrolment of the populace in consumers' societies, or the promotion of such societies and their control by the State.

On the subject of the nationalization of the Banks Lenin wrote:

'The blame for the confusion of nationalization of Banks with confiscation of private property lies with the middle-class Press whose interest it is to deceive the reader. The capital with which the Banks operate, and which is concentrated in the Banks, is assured by means of printed and written certificates known as shares, bonds, debentures, bills, receipts, &c., &c.; and not a single one of these certificates is altered in any way or lost in the event of the nationalization of the Banks, i.e. if all Banks are incorporated in a single State Bank. If any one has fifteen roubles to his credit in a Bank, he remains the owner of these fifteen roubles after the nationalization of the Banks. If any one has fifteen million roubles, he will continue to possess them after the nationalization of the Banks either in the form of shares, debentures, bills, or some similar paper.'

Then Lenin goes on to say:

'The gain resulting from a nationalization of the Banks would be very great for the entire nation and not specially for the working man, who has little business with Banks. The gain would be great for the peasantry and small traders. It would mean a great saving in labour and, even if the State retained the services of the present number of Bank employees, it would mark a great step forward in the universal use of Banks, in the increase in the number of their branches, and in the accessibility of their services, &c. The possibility of obtaining credit on easy terms would be enormously increased for the peasants and small business men.'

Thus Lenin was still far removed from the abolition of private property. The platform of the Bolshevik Party on the eve of the October Revolution contained a proposal for 'making the acquisition of credit easier for the small business man'! Such a proposal might have been found in the programme of any middle-class Party.

Lenin took the naphtha industry as an illustration in support of his argument for nationalization of trusts. He said *inter alia*:

'Let us take a glance at the naphtha industry. To an enormous extent it has already been "organized in associations" as a result of the earlier evolution of capitalism. A few naphtha "kings" dispose of millions and hundreds of millions, earn fabulous profits from speculation with a business that on its technical side is already organized like a great city employing hundreds and thousands of workpeople, engineers, &c. . . . In order to achieve positive results it is necessary to substitute democracy for bureaucracy. This must be done in a truly revolutionary manner by declaring war upon the naphtha "kings" and their shareholders, and threatening them with the confiscation of their wealth and imprisonment in the event of their placing hindrances in the way of a nationalization of the industry, concealing profits and tampering with balance-sheets, interfering with production and failing to take measures to increase production. An appeal must be made to the initiative of the workers and employees; they must be at once assembled in conferences and congresses; and they must be made profit-sharers in the industry on condition that they exercise a careful control over the industry and take measures for increasing its productiveness.'

Hence even the naphtha 'kings' were not in principle to have their wealth confiscated, but only in cases where they attempted to interfere with production and the workers' control over the industry.

In support of his argument for the compulsory syndicalization of industry Lenin pointed to German industry during the
World War. He continued:

'It must once more be emphasized that syndicalization does not
in the least affect conditions of ownership and does not deprive the
proprietor of a single penny of his money. It is necessary to lay
great stress upon this fact in consequence of the conduct of the
middle-class Press, which frightens the smaller traders with the
threat that Socialists, and in particular Bolsheviks, desire to
"expropriate" them. From a scientific standpoint this is a false
argument inasmuch as the Socialists do not wish to, could not, and
will not expropriate the small peasantry even in the event of a
purely Socialist revolution. Moreover, we are only discussing the
immediate and inevitable measures that have already been taken
in Western Europe, and that must also be taken at once in Russia
by even a partially logical democracy, in order to combat the
menacing and inescapable catastrophe.'

All the measures proposed by Lenin in the above-mentioned pamphlet are radical and democratic, and in the nature
of State Capitalism. They are not in any way Communist.
In the dreadful condition of want in which Russia found
itself, the masses of the workpeople and employees were to
take an active part in the control of production. It was for
them to know what went on in their factories and Banks and
to see that the common interest was not lost sight of or inter-
fered with. The State was to unite the individual industries
and Banks and compel them to work in accordance with a
rational system. A centralized State Capitalism of this kind
already marked a step on the road to Socialism.

In this connexion Lenin gave a very moderate interpretation of Socialism: 'Socialism is nothing else than the next
step forward from the stage of monopolistic State Capitalism.
Or—alternatively: Socialism is nothing else than a capitalistic
State monopoly worked in the interests of the whole nation
and therefore no longer a capitalist monopoly.' In those days
Lenin did not propose the abolition of private ownership in
Russia, the expropriation of the middle class, but only a
concentration of economic life for the benefit of the nation in
accordance with the principles of State Capitalism. With
such an economic programme Lenin could at that time have

found his associates among Left Wing middle-class politicians in central and western Europe and also in Russia—if his programme had not been bound up with the ideal of an unrestricted political democratization and with the unconditional rule of the armed masses. It was not because of his proposed control of production and his State Capitalism that Lenin was antagonistic to all other political groups in Russia. It was because of his battle-cry, 'All power for the Soviet! The Land for the Peasants! An End to the Imperialist War!'

Lenin embarked on the October Revolution with the firm resolve not only to complete the middle-class revolution but to do so in a radical and logical manner. The masses, however, proved themselves the stronger. They abandoned the Bolshevik economic theory and acted under the impulse of the events of the day. In doing so they justified Kamenev's fears and fulfilled Trotsky's hopes.

THE BOLSHEVIK REVOLUTION AND WAR-TIME COMMUNISM, 1917-21

EVER since September 1917 Lenin had been convinced that the Bolshevik Party must achieve power by a revolution. In October, from his hiding-place in Finland, he bombarded the Central Committee of the Party with letters and articles demanding a revolution, examining every possibility with the greatest care, and suggesting a solution for every difficulty. These letters are unique in their mixture of burning emotion and cold-blooded reflection. His chief concern was lest the Kerensky Government should disappear in an anarchical chaos. For that would mean that the Bolsheviks had missed their opportunity and could never regain it.

Among the Party leaders the followers of Zinoviev and Kamenev were opposed to a revolution which promised to result in the isolation of the Bolsheviks, and which therefore seemed to be no more than an experiment that must end in disaster. Nevertheless, Lenin was successful, with Trotsky's support, in winning over the Party for his plan. On October 10 (23) Lenin attended the secret sitting of the Central Committee at which it was resolved that the sole means of saving Russia and the Revolution lay in a Bolshevik Revolution for the purpose of placing the entire executive authority in the hands of the Soviets. Only two votes were cast against a resolution that bound the Party to a definite course of action.

On October 25 (Old Style; November 7, New Style) the All-Russian Congress of Soviets was to meet in Petrograd, and it was anticipated that the Bolsheviks would have a majority in the Congress in consequence of the change that had come over public opinion during the summer. If the Congress resolved that the whole authority in the State should pass to the Soviets, then it must be prepared to take power into its own hands, i.e. to overthrow the Kerensky Government. Hence October 25 (November 7) would be a decisive day in Russian history. It was clear that it must be the day on which the Bolsheviks raised the standard of revolt.

Both parties made preparations to secure military control of Petrograd on this eventful day. Since the regiments in Petrograd were largely composed of Bolshevik sympathizers, the Government ordered a great number of the troops to entrain for the Front. If this order had been carried out, the Government would have been able to dissolve the Soviet Congress on October 25 (November 7) with the aid of a few companies of storm troops composed of officers. At the instigation of the Bolshevik Party, however, the Petrograd garrison refused to obey the Government's order. The Petrograd Soviet was entirely under the domination of the Bolshevik Party and proceeded to constitute itself a revolutionary military Committee. The entire garrison declared that it would only obey the orders of this Committee and not those of the General Staff. Trotsky was the dominating and energizing personality among the members of the Committee. This decision on the part of the garrison gave the victory to the Bolshevik Revolution in Petrograd before a shot had been fired. On October 24 (November 6) the Committee seized the Central Telephone Exchange in Petrograd, and during the night other public buildings were occupied by their orders. On October 25 (November 7) the seat of the Government in the Winter Palace was seized and the members of the Government arrested, with the exception of Kerensky, who saved himself by flight. On the same day the Soviet Congress held its appointed meeting. On receiving the news of the capture of the Winter Palace the minority who supported the Kerensky Government rose and left the hall. The majority thereupon proclaimed the assumption of governmental power by the Congress in accordance with the Bolshevik plan.

Kerensky made an attempt to collect troops in the neighbourhood of Petrograd and to capture the city by force. He was completely defeated by the Bolshevik troops and left Russia. Within a few weeks the Bolsheviks were masters of Russia and wherever opposition raised its head it was suppressed with ease. Troops, townspeople, and the peasants throughout Russia went over to the Bolshevik cause. It is a fact of considerable importance that the Bolshevik Revolution was able to base itself upon the sole democratic and national representative body, i.e. the Soviet Congress, then existing in Russia. This Congress was really elected by the masses. In comparison with it the artificial bodies created by Kerensky lacked popular support. At the close of his tenure of power Kerensky had finally given orders for the holding of elections for a National Assembly. Since the date of these elections coincided with that of the Bolshevik Revolution, the National Assembly had not come into existence at the critical moment.

The Kamenev-Zinoviev group had opposed the Bolshevik insurrection to the last and they continued to be pessimistic even after its victory. On November 4 (17) Zinoviev and Kamenev resigned their membership of the Central Committee of the Party in order to be free to express their own opinions. They demanded that the Bolsheviks should immediately offer to come to an arrangement with the Social Revolutionaries and the Mensheviks in order to construct a Government composed of all Parties represented in the Soviets. Their proposal was supported by a number of the older members of the Bolshevik Party. Lozovski took their part in an open letter. It is certainly extraordinary that the two men—Lozovski and Zinoviev—who were subsequently to become respectively Chairmen of the Communist International and the Red Trade Union International (whose entire propaganda was founded upon the October Revolution) should have looked upon this very Revolution as a mad adventure at the time of its occurrence.

The situation on November 4 (17) was still obscure. It was still uncertain how the troops at the Front and the country at large would react to events in Petrograd. A general strike of officials put a stop to the activity of the new Bolshevik rulers. Every political Party and group in Russia had declared itself opposed to the Bolshevik insurrection and their ranks were now joined by an influential group composed of former members of the Central Committee of the Bolshevik Party itself. The situation did in fact seem hopeless. Trotsky and Lenin nevertheless refused to retreat a single step. On November 7 (20) the *Pravda* published a remarkable proclamation from the pen of Lenin that ran:

'Shame upon all ye of little faith, doubters, fearful ones! Shame upon all ye who let yourselves be terrified by the middle class and upon all ye who hearken to the warnings brought to you directly and indirectly by their accomplices! No shadow however slight of a weakening in *morale* is discernible in the masses of the workers and soldiers in Petrograd, Moscow, and elsewhere. Our Party stands firm like a sentry at his post and defends the authority of the Soviets and the interests of all toilers and especially of the working men and the poorest peasants.'

The situation cleared up rapidly. The extent of the Bolshevik victory throughout the country became evident, the strike of officials collapsed, and the Zinoviev-Kamenev group returned to the Party fold. The conduct of Zinoviev and Kamenev in these critical weeks reveals clearly how firmly rooted the ideal of a democratic dictatorship of workers and peasants was in the Bolshevik Party. These old Bolsheviks could not conceive of a Russian Revolution as other than a middle-class democratic revolution carried out by a coalition of all democratic and Socialist Parties. It was in the name of this ideal that they rebelled against Lenin in the very days that are among the greatest in Bolshevik history.

His superb common sense induced Lenin to entrust Zinoviev and Kamenev with the most important tasks after their rebellion without ever reproaching them for their vacillations. In a similar manner Lenin looked upon his years of conflict with Trotsky as ended at the moment when Trotsky declared himself ready to support Lenin's policy.

The mass sympathies that lay behind the Bolshevik movement in those days served to prevent its political isolation. The chief enemies of the Bolsheviks—the Social Revolutionaries—split up into two groups and the new Party of the Left Wing Social Revolutionaries rendered Soviet Russia great services in the first six months of its existence. It has already been shown that the masses of the peasants were bitterly disappointed with the Kerensky Government. They had expected from this Social Revolutionary Government that it would dispossess the estate-owners, and it had instead protected them with the authority of the State. The local Social Revolutionary peasant leaders rebelled against the Central Committee of the Party and it was not long before the Opposition was joined by leading Party officials. At the time of the Bolshevik insurrection the Social Revolutionaries split up into a Right Wing that remained faithful to Kerensky and into a Left Wing that demanded the expropriation of the estates and the transference of authority in the State to the Soviets. On October 25 (November 8), when the All-Russian Soviet Congress was confronted with the necessity of declaring itself for or against the Bolshevik insurrection, the Right Wing Social Revolutionaries and the Mensheviks left the hall whilst the Left Wing Social Revolutionaries remained behind with the Bolsheviks and assisted them in building up the new Soviet authority. Certain leaders of the Left Wing Social Revolutionaries subsequently entered the Council of People's Commissars—the new revolutionary Government. It was not until after their breach with the Bolsheviks over the Peace of Brest-Litovsk that the Left Wing Social Revolutionaries dissolved their coalition with the Bolsheviks and went into irreconcilable opposition.

It was thus possible for Lenin at least in the early months of the Soviet Revolution to realize his former programme and to conclude an alliance with a revolutionary and democratic, but not Chauvinist, peasant Party. While the masses of the troops and the workers went over to Bolshevism in the months of July–October 1917, the majority of the peasants remained Social Revolutionaries. Nevertheless, they changed from Social Revolutionaries friendly to the Government into Social Revolutionaries in fanatical opposition to it. It is true that when the various Parties put forward their lists of candidates for the election for the National Assembly, shortly before the October Revolution, the Social Revolutionaries were still undivided and both Right and Left Wing Social Revolutionaries—Kerensky's supporters and Lenin's supporters—appeared together on the same list. The elections for the Constituent Assembly thus led to a singular result. Although he had lost all popularity with the masses of the people, Kerensky obtained a majority of votes. Out of a total of 36 million votes cast in the election the Bolsheviks received 9 millions, the Mensheviks 700,000 without counting the Caucasus and 1,400,000 including the Caucasus, where they enjoyed much popularity among the Georgians, various middle-class Parties 5 millions, and the Social Revolutionaries 21 millions. The vast numbers of peasants who voted for the Social Revolutionary candidates did so because they believed they were voting for expropriation of the estates and not out of sympathy for Kerensky. Since, however, Kerensky's followers almost invariably headed the list of candidates, they obtained their mandates. When the National Assembly met in January 1918, Lenin was determined to oppose it because he did not wish the gains acquired by a successful revolution to be spoilt by a parliamentary majority that did not even truly represent the majority of the nation.

The Soviet Government demanded that the National Assembly should recognize the October Revolution and support the new Government and its policy. On the rejection of this demand by the majority in the National Assembly, the Bolsheviks and Left Wing Social Revolutionaries left the hall. The permanent committee of the All-Russian Soviet Congress—the Central Executive Committee—thereupon ordered the dissolution of the National Assembly and this Rump Parliament was forcibly dispersed. If Lenin had ordered the holding of new elections, there can be no doubt that the Soviet Government would have obtained an overwhelming majority at the polls. He did not do so and in the new Russian Constitution there was no mention of a parliament. Lenin and the Bolsheviks regarded the Soviets as a better expression of democratic government, and to have established a parliament in addition to the All-Russian Soviet Congress would have been superfluous.

The Bolsheviks had promised the Russian nation bread and peace, liberty and land, before their advent to power. They lost no time in seeking to fulfil their promises. The Bolshevik Government dismissed all the former officials and officers and placed the executive power wholly in the hands of the Soviets. Liberty was thus to become an accomplished fact. The new Government placed the factories under the control of the workmen in order to revive production and to supply the towns with food and other necessities of life. They offered to make peace with their external enemies and they authorized the peasants to dispossess the landowners of their estates. How was this programme of the Soviet Government carried out in practice? In the first place Lenin's plan for a supervision of production proved unworkable. Armed work-men intoxicated by their revolutionary victory were not to be kept within the bounds of such a moderate scheme of reform. Instead they took possession themselves of the factories and drove out their employers. Thus Trotsky's prophecy of spontaneous action on the part of the workers was fulfilled to the letter. This spontaneous action on the part of the workers in the towns and industrial areas at once out-distanced the middle-class revolution.

Lenin gradually reconciled himself to the new situation. The 'Declaration of the Rights of Industrial and Exploited Peoples' adopted by the All-Russian Soviet Congress in January 1918, still contains a formula embodying a com-promise:

'The Soviet Law regulating the exercise of control by the workers and the activities of the Supreme National Economic Council is hereby approved as the first step towards the complete acquisition by the Soviet Republic of Workers and Peasants of all factories, works, mines, railways, and other means of production and transport, and towards the establishment of the rule of the industrial workers over their exploiters.'

Thus the 'first step' towards the expropriation of industry was taken on paper at a time when in reality expropriation was already an accomplished fact. And it was not until June 28 (July 11), 1918, that the 'Decree for the Nationaliza-tion of all Heavy Industries' was published. It is interesting for the purposes of comparison to note that the Decree abolishing the right to private ownership on the part of estate-owners had already been published on the very first day of the Revolution, October 26 (November 8), 1917.

In an official Soviet publication entitled *Economic Life and Economic Development in Soviet Russia from 1917 to 1920,* from the pens of Larin and Kritzmann, it is stated that:

'Hardly any one can now be found to argue that the Revolution was organized artificially. It was an irresistible and elemental movement. The moment the political power of the middle class was swept away at the close of 1917, the class feeling of the pro-letariat was no longer to be restrained by forcible measures and found expression in a forcible expulsion of employers and in con-fiscation of the factories. A necessary consequence of this action was the breakdown of the former economic organization and very often the closing down of the factories. The workers who had been appointed by their comrades to manage the factories, and especially those who had been spontaneously placed in authority by their co-workers in the same factory, proved themselves in many cases to be incapable of carrying out their duties for the simple reason that capacity only comes with experience. The work accomplished in the economic sphere by the Soviet authorities consists for the most part in introducing discipline and organization into the spontaneous movement of the proletarian and peasant masses.'

In another place the authors write:

'The proletarian solution [of the industrial problem] consisted in the exercise of a control on the part of the workpeople over the employers in such fashion that the employers could not act before receiving the approval of the Workers' Council for their proposals. The events of November were an attempt to put this solution into practice. The Soviet Decree ordered employers to place their factories under the control of the employees. Meanwhile the system of control by the workers revealed itself to be a half-measure and therefore incapable of execution. The system of control by the workers expressed the growing and at the same time still insufficient authority of the proletariat, i.e. the weakness that had not yet been eradicated from the movement. The employer was not willing to conduct his business merely in order that he should teach it to his workpeople (this was the secret aim underlying control by the workers after the events of November). The workers for their part were filled with a hatred of Capitalism and were unwilling to remain voluntarily as objects for exploitation. It was for these reasons, and notwithstanding insufficient preparations, that it was found necessary to allow the proletariat to take over the conduct of industry even in cases where there nominally existed a system of control by the workers.'

It is clear from this account that the Bolsheviks did not expropriate Russian employers but that it was accomplished as the result of spontaneous action on the part of the workers and against the will of the Bolsheviks. Lenin was thus left with no other alternative than reluctantly to legalize the action of the workers. The Soviet Government then set to work to unite the individual expropriated businesses, to establish economic organs of control and management for the various industries, and to attempt in this way to organize production on a systematic basis.

The Government found itself confronted with enormous difficulties in its work of reconstruction. The economic condition of Russia had been serious in 1917, and by 1918–19 had reached a catastrophic state. The conclusion of a separate peace deprived Russia of the economic support of the Entente Powers and resulted instead in the blockade of her coasts by the Entente fleets and her isolation from the outside world. The Germans occupied the Ukraine in 1918 and Soviet Russia was in consequence cut off from her supplies of coal from the Don Basin and of naphtha from the Caucasus. Lack of raw materials and outworn machinery compelled the majority of Russian industries to close down. Everywhere factories stood idle and factory-hands returned to their native villages. The appalling want of transport and the disorder prevalent throughout the country resulted in a shortage of food-supplies for the towns. The town population of Russia starved from 1918 to 1920. Wealth in the form of valueless paper roubles did not furnish its possessor with the means to improve his condition. All distinctions of class and wealth vanished in the towns. The equality of man was achieved through Communism in starvation. The hopes of an economic restoration of Russia which had found expression in Lenin's pamphlets in the autumn of 1917 had not been realized. But the blame for their failure did not lie with Lenin and his Party: it was a consequence of the World War and the destructive Civil War which succeeded it in Russia.

Four social classes—estate-owners, wealthy peasants or Kulaks, small peasants, and agricultural labourers—inhabited the country districts in Russia at the time of the Bolshevik Revolution. Since the abolition of serfdom, and more especially since the 1905 Revolution, the estate-owners had disposed of a part of their property to the wealthier peasants. As a result there had come into existence a class of well-to-do peasants between the poorer peasants and the nobles. These wealthier peasants also acted as village money-lenders. Agricultural labourers were employed both by the wealthier peasants and by those of the estate-owners who still worked their estates. It is, however, true that the great majority of the estates were not directly cultivated by their owners and were rented in small holdings to poor peasants whose condition— oppressed as they were by all manner of taxes and dues— was miserable in the extreme. It was these small peasants and the agricultural labourers who were the supporters of a social revolution among the country populace. The estate-owners and the wealthier peasants were opposed to revolution. As a result of the Revolution the estates were expropriated without exception and the wealthier peasants were also forced to surrender a large part of their land to the poorer peasants. The agricultural labourers as a whole be- came landed proprietors. Thus two out of the four pre-revolu- tionary classes in the country population disappeared and the two surviving classes—the rich and poor peasants—tended to merge into one another. When about 1919 the results of the agrarian revolution in Russia began to be perceptible, it was seen that the country was now populated by small peasants each owning approximately the same amount of land. These peasants knew that they had cause to be grateful to the Bolshevik Revolution and were prepared to sacrifice their lives in preventing a return to the old conditions. It was the willing assistance of the masses of the peasantry that rendered possible the creation of the Red Army and the victory of the Soviet over the White Army. Nevertheless, the peasants remained faithful to their egotistic standpoint in economic questions. Under the Tsars and throughout the War they had often enough suffered the pangs of hunger. Now they wanted to eat their fill and were only prepared to supply food to the towns in return for adequate compensation. Payment in valueless paper roubles failed to tempt the peasants either to produce or to sell their produce.

The Soviet Government sent all the wares that could be manufactured by the hastily reorganized Russian factories to the country in exchange for the peasants' produce. The supply of bread nevertheless continued inadequate for the needs of the town population. The Government was therefore obliged to resort to requisitioning in order to feed the Red Army and to obtain at least sufficient food for the factory workers. The peasant lost his pleasure in his new possessions through not being able to make an economic use of them.

The lack of money with a fixed value and the absence of free trade prevented him from selling his surplus produce. If, however, he was discovered to be in possession of a surplus, it was forcibly taken from him. Although town and country, peasant and factory-worker, made common cause from 1918 to 1920 against the aristocratic counter-revolution, they were completely separated from each other in a psychological and economic sense; and the Soviet Government was not in a position to bridge the gap.

Immediately after its seizure of power the Bolshevik Government addressed proposals for peace to all the belligerents. The Entente Powers ignored proposals emanating from a 'traitor', while Germany and Austria-Hungary were glad to conclude an armistice with Bolshevik Russia and to open in Brest-Litovsk negotiations for peace. The military helplessness of Russia was clearly shown in the course of these negotiations. Her utterly demoralized army fell to pieces. The peasants hurried home to their villages in order to be present at the distribution of the expropriated lands. The German Supreme Command—the real governing authority in Germany—ruthlessly took advantage of Russia's weakness. A peace was forced upon a defeated Russia that permanently deprived her of the means of existence. The importance of this treaty did not lie in the severance from Russia of Poland, Finland, and her Baltic provinces; it lay in her cession of the entire south of Russia—the Ukraine. The loss of the Ukraine meant the loss of Russia's grain treasury, her most important coal-mines and naphtha springs, and her withdrawal from the Black Sea. The so-called independent Ukraine and all the country up to the Caucasus was occupied by German troops and all that remained to Soviet Russia of territory was shut in on the south and west by German armies. It seemed to be only a matter of time before General Ludendorff gave order for the occupation of Moscow.

A terrible national disaster had thus overwhelmed Russia in the spring of 1918. It is—humanly speaking—not difficult to understand that many influential Bolsheviks and Left Wing Social Revolutionaries preferred to die fighting rather than to put their signatures to such a peace. Nevertheless, Lenin fought with all his authority and strength for the ratification of the Peace of Brest-Litovsk. He was actuated in doing so by the belief that an unarmed man cannot wage war and that theatrical gestures cannot avail to alter facts. Soviet Russia must accept even terms so drastic as were those of the Treaty of Brest-Litovsk in order to gain time. The time so gained must be used to strengthen Russia in an economic and military sense and to enable her to wait for the coming revolution in Germany. Ever since he had pronounced himself in favour of an immediate cessation of the imperialistic war Lenin had been forced to take into his calculations the risk of a peace such as the Peace of Brest-Litovsk. The complete collapse of Russia's defensive resources might confront the new Revolutionary Government with a situation in which they were powerless. It was to avoid a peace like that of Brest-Litovsk that Kerensky and his followers had prosecuted the war and even risked the notorious July offensive. Any one refusing to adopt these methods of defence must be prepared to accept the consequences. Thus Lenin's attitude was completely logical and he succeeded after a heated discussion in persuading the Bolshevik Party that no other policy was possible.

The military defeat of Germany in the summer and autumn of 1918, and the subsequent revolution in November, freed Russia from the German menace. At the same time it increased the danger threatening Soviet Russia from the side of the Entente Powers, who had come to regard the Bolshevik State as their enemy since its conclusion of a separate peace with Germany. The Czechoslovakian Legionaries revolted as early as the summer of 1918. These Legionaries were composed of Czech soldiers who had been captured when fighting in the Austrian armies and who had subsequently been voluntarily formed into regiments by the Tsarist Government. They continued to look upon themselves as a part of the Entente armies and the military weakness of the Soviet Government enabled them to establish themselves along the line of the Volga. Here they began to make preparations for marching on Moscow. By dint of extraordinary efforts the Soviet Government succeeded in raising and equipping a number of trained troops. Trotsky was appointed People's Commissar for War and devoted his entire energy to the creation of a Red Army. In September the Red troops captured Kazan and drove the Czechoslovaks away from the Volga. This was the first success won by the Red Army in serious warfare. After the collapse of Germany the Entente Powers redoubled their endeavours to defeat Russia. Former Tsarist Generals were financed and supplied with munitions of war by England, France, and Japan. From the Black Sea and the White Sea, from the Baltic and the Pacific, White Guards advanced in 1919 with the help of the Entente against Soviet Russia. The most dangerous foes of the Soviet were Admiral Koltchak in the east and General Denikin in the south.

The Civil War was accompanied by the most terrible cruelties. The White Guards endeavoured to intimidate the workers and peasants by mass shootings and terror of all kinds. The Bolsheviks opposed the White Terror with the Red Terror. Wide differences of opinion will always exist as to the forcible methods employed by the Soviet Government —mass shootings, &c.—in the course of the Civil War. From an historical standpoint, and viewed as a whole, the Russian nation was defending itself at that time against a cruel counter-revolution. After a long struggle that lasted until 1920, and in which fortune favoured now one side and now the other, the Red Army was finally victorious on all fronts. The Soviet Government found itself once more in possession of the Asiatic countries which had formed part of the Empire of the Tsars. Its power again extended over the Caucasus, the Ukraine, and the coasts of the Black Sea. Only Finland, Poland, and the Baltic States retained their independence. Moreover, their military successes from 1918 to 1920 gave the Bolshevik Government enormous prestige within Russia itself. The stain of Brest-Litovsk had been wiped out. The Russian workers and peasants could pride themselves that they had successfully repulsed the attack of all the imperialistic Great Powers. From that time onwards 'Bolshevism' and 'Russian Revolution' were identical terms in the mouths of the masses. The Bolsheviks had fought the decisive battle with the Tsarist officers and the landowners to a triumphant end. Trotsky and Lenin had defeated Koltchak and Denikin. All the other political Parties in Russia—Liberals, Mensheviks,

Social Revolutionaries—were ground to pieces between the two belligerents. The Bolsheviks were animated throughout the Civil War by the principle that whoever was not on their side was against them. Moreover, they succeeded in instilling in the masses the conviction that all non-Bolshevik Parties were equally counter-revolutionary.

At the close of the Civil War the Revolution in Russia had triumphed over its enemies. At the same time the Russian nation had lost its newly-won freedom as embodied in the Soviets and its place had been taken by an omnipotent dictatorship of the Bolshevik Party extending from Petrograd to the Pacific.

The events of 1918 had shown that Soviet Russia depended for its existence upon an efficient army. Such an army demands for its successful operation unity of command and strict discipline. No regiment could fight well if its colonel were forced to consult a dozen Soldiers' Councils before giving an order. It was for this reason that Trotsky abolished the Soldiers' Councils in building up the Red Army. A number of former Tsarist officers were given posts of command and placed under the control of Bolshevik Commissars. A young, truly revolutionary body of officers gradually came into being with the passage of time. The first Red troops consisted of volunteers. Subsequently, however, compulsory military service was enforced. The creation of the Red Army was a vital necessity for Russia in those days. Nevertheless, it marked the first definite and decisive breach with the Soviet system. One of the chief benefits of the Soviet system, according to Lenin, was the fact that it abolished the army as a separate entity placed in opposition to the civilian populace. But now there was once more in Russia a centralized standing army isolated from the populace and composed in part of professional soldiers. As early as 1918 the local Soviets in places where detachments of the Red Army were garrisoned or temporarily quartered could not interfere in any way with the dispositions of the regimental commanders. This meant the reconstruction of an important part of the edifice of the authoritarian middle-class State.

It is worthy of mention that this departure from Soviet practice was observed by a great body of Russian opinion and that the creation of the Red Army encountered opposition in the nation itself. In his book entitled *The Birth of the Red Army*, which was published in 1922, Trotsky wrote:

'Left to itself, the peasantry is incapable of creating a centralized army. Nothing is achieved but the formation of local bodies of armed peasants whose primitive "democracy" is customarily used as a cover for the personal dictatorship of their leader. These partisan tendencies reflect peasant nature and found their fullest expression in the Left Wing Social Revolutionaries and Anarchists. At the same time they animated a considerable number of Communists and especially of peasant Communists who had served as soldiers and N.C.O.s. . . . Indignation with the bureaucratic centralization of Tsarist Russia was a principal cause of the Revolution. District administrations, local governments, municipalities, devoted their energies to proving their independence. The ideal of "local government" took on an extraordinarily diverse aspect in the early period [of the Revolution]. The Left Wing Social Revolutionaries and Anarchists associated this ideal with reactionary federalist doctrines. In the broad masses of the people it became an inevitable and healthy reaction against a régime that had been opposed to all initiative. At any rate from a certain moment onwards, and in close association with the counter-revolution and the growing danger from abroad, primitive autonomist tendencies became more and more dangerous both in a political and also—and more especially—in a military sense. This question will unquestionably play a great part in the future in western Europe, and nowhere more so than in France, where prejudices in favour of autonomy and federalism are stronger than in any other country. A speedy liberation from these prejudices on the part of those serving under the banner of revolutionary proletarian centralism is a necessary preliminary to the coming victory over the middle class. . . . The Oppositional and "Left" (in reality intellectual-agrarian) tendencies sought for themselves a universal theoretical formula to cover the creation of the army. A centralized army was declared to be the army of an imperialistic State. In conformity with its character the Revolution must not only break with a war of position (war on definite fronts) but also with a centralized army. The Revolution depends solely upon mobility, clever tactics, and skill in manœuvring. Its striking force is the small independent body of troops composed of soldiers from all arms, acting independently of its base, relying upon the sympathies of the populace, attacking the enemy from the rear, &c. In brief, the tactics of guerrilla warfare are raised to the dignity of revolutionary tactics. The experience of the Civil War quickly made away with these prejudices.'

Trotsky favoured a centralized Red Army both for reasons of military efficiency and because he saw in it a means by which the chaotic masses of the peasantry might be wrought under the leadership of the Socialist proletariat. The enemies of the Red Army were in his eyes 'reactionary federalists', Anarchists, and Left Wing Social Revolutionaries. He forgot that the Commune in 1871 was the work of anarchical Federalists and that the Soviet system of 1917 in its essence was also anarchical, anti-State, and anti-centralist. 'Revolutionary proletarian centralism' may perhaps be necessary in a time of revolution and civil war. Its forebears, however, are the French Terrorists of 1793 and it has nothing in common with the Soviet system.

The reconstruction of the Army was accompanied during the years 1918–20 by a return to State centralization in all departments of public life. The struggle with the conspirators of the Counter-Revolution necessitated the creation of a political police endowed with far-reaching powers and a highly centralized organization. This force was the much-talked-of Cheka that subsequently became known as the GPU. Many wild tales have been told about the activities of this force. It is only necessary here to emphasize the fact that the Cheka has invariably proved itself a trustworthy servant of the centralized State. The Cheka is only an executive organ of the Government, i.e. of the Bolshevik Party. On no single occasion has the Cheka pursued a different political policy from that of the Government, and at no time has it been in possession of a political authority different from that of the Party leaders. The responsibility for the actions— good or evil—of the GPU is borne solely by the Bolshevik Party itself and not by some special secret body.

A centralized economic organization took its place beside the centralized army and centralized police. All three were isolated from the masses of the nation. Every industry, and every branch of an industry, throughout Russia was combined in a Trust for the purpose of systematizing production. In addition to this Trust there were centralized organizations for the control of trade, transport, banking, and the entire economic life of the country. Similarly the civil services, justice, and education were organized on a centralized basis. All important matters were regulated by Government ordinances having the force of law.

In 1917 the local Soviets destroyed the old Tsarist State. Now a new and far more powerful State had risen in their midst and had deprived them of all authority beyond that of a parish council. Was not, however, this mighty centralized Government machinery at least subject to a democratic control exercised by the All-Russian Soviet Congress? Ever since 1918 it was evident that government by Soviets had become an illusion in Russia—an illusion that exists to the present day. It is true that in a formal and constitutional sense the government of Russia is in the hands of the Soviets. The lowest organs of governmental authority are the local Soviets in the villages and towns. The District and Provincial Soviets are composed of delegates chosen by the local Soviets. The supreme power in the State is vested in the All-Russian Soviet Congress, and in the intervals between its sessions that power is delegated to a committee of the Congress—the Central Executive Committee. The Central Executive Committee elects the Council of People's Commissars. The Council of People's Commissars is the Russian Soviet equivalent for a European Cabinet.

This extremely complicated system is in reality only a cloak for the dictatorship of the Bolshevik Party. Free elections are the life-blood of a Soviet system of government. The electorate must be left free to choose between various candidates and these candidates must be given every opportunity for placing their views before the electorate at public meetings and in the press. Electoral freedom gradually disappeared in Russia during the Civil War. The first step taken by the Bolsheviks on attaining to power was to suppress the middle-class Parties as counter-revolutionary. Next came the prohibition of the Kerensky Party, the Right Wing Social Revolutionaries, and the Mensheviks. By the early months of 1918 only two legal political Parties remained in existence in Soviet Russia—the Bolsheviks and the Left Wing Social Revolutionaries. These latter could have secured the support of the revolutionary peasants and organized them into a political force. If that had been done, a two-party system would have been evolved in which the Social Revolutionary Peasant Party would have been a counterweight to a Bolshevik Party composed of the industrial population of the towns. The competition between these two Parties would have kept democracy alive within the Soviets. Unhappily the tragic fate that overtook the whole *Naródniki* movement also overtook the Left Wing Social Revolutionaries. They proved incapable of retaining the strong hold over the peasantry which they had at first possessed and in a short time they had become little more than the camp-followers of the Bolsheviks. After the signature of the Peace of Brest-Litovsk the Left Wing Social Revolutionaries broke up their coalition with the Bolsheviks. After attempted assassinations and revolts on the part of individual Left Wing Social Revolutionaries in the summer of 1918 had failed to achieve the overthrow of the Bolshevik Government, the Party was suppressed and within a short time completely dissolved.

From the summer of 1918 until the present day the Bolshevik Party has been the sole political Party in Russia enjoying a legal existence. This state of affairs has brought about the death of Soviet democracy. In elections for the Soviets the choice of the electors is confined to Bolsheviks or Independents who are pledged to support the Bolshevik Government. Thus all freedom of choice is taken from the elector and he is the prisoner of the Government. Every Bolshevik member of the Soviet is, moreover, pledged to act in strict accordance with the order of his Party leaders. The Bolshevik members of a Soviet constitute a 'Bolshevik Cell' and must invariably vote in conformity with the instructions they receive from the permanent officials of the Party. There are in reality two political edifices in Russia that rise parallel to one another: the Shadow Government of the Soviets; and the *de facto* Government of the Bolshevik Party. The local Party organizations elect the members of the Party Congress. The Party Congress lays down lines of policy and elects the Party Committee. This Party Committee exercises a dictatorial control over the entire Party organization. The overthrow of the Central Committee of the Bolshevik Party would therefore be tantamount to a revolution. Up to the present the Party Congress has never been successful in overthrowing the Central Committee by a vote of want of confidence.

The Central Committee of the Bolshevik Party is the true Russian Government. It takes all important decisions. The Council of People's Commissars is simply the executive agent of the Central Committee. It was thus that the Bolshevik Party was successful within a few months of the October Revolution in excluding the Soviets from the exercise of all real power. In their capacity as organs of the spontaneous will of the masses the Soviets were from the very beginning an unwelcome and extraneous element in Bolshevik doctrine. In 1917 Lenin used the Soviets to destroy Tsarism. Once that had been accomplished he created his own State machinery after the true Bolshevik pattern, i.e. the rule of a small disciplined minority of professional revolutionaries over the great and undisciplined masses. Although from a technical standpoint it would have presented no difficulty, the Bolsheviks nevertheless did not abolish the Soviets and instead retained and used them as the decorative outward symbol of their authority. It was through their symbolic use by the Bolsheviks in 1918 and the succeeding years that the Soviets were first brought into a position irreconcilable with true democracy. There can be no more truly democratic institution than a real and efficiently working Soviet. The Bolshevik Soviets, on the other hand, have been since 1918 no more than symbols of the rule of a small minority over the broad masses of the nation. The same fate overtook the ideal of a 'dictatorship of the proletariat'. The old ideal of a proletarian dictatorship implied the rule of the great majority of the poor and working-class population over the small minority of the rich and the profiteers—an ideal identical with proletarian democracy. Although the Bolsheviks have called their rule in Russia since 1918 a dictatorship of the proletariat, it is in reality a dictatorship of the Bolshevik Party or—better said —of the Central Committee of the Party over the proletariat and the entire nation. Lenin sought to justify this dictatorship of the Bolshevik Party in Russia since 1918 by the existence of the Civil War, and also by the special conditions obtaining in Russia, which rendered it impossible to find any form of compromise between the vast majority of the peasant population and the proletarian minority. Trotsky also excused the policy thus pursued by the Bolsheviks by the necessity for defeating the White Guards and for holding down the peasants.

The membership of the Bolshevik Party in March 1917 did not exceed a few thousands. After the October Revolution the membership rose by hundreds of thousands. The Central Committee consequently took measures to control and to stem the rush of applications for membership. It was clear to them that the great advantages accruing from membership of the dominant Party would cause the influx of many possible rivals. Moreover, Trotsky and Lenin were in full agreement in ascribing a great historical importance to the Party and its work. Their outlooks were nevertheless not entirely identical. Lenin and the older Bolsheviks identified the Party with the 'Old Guard' who were now its rulers. Trotsky saw the 'Party' in the masses of organized workers. This division of opinion was bridged for so long as Lenin with his unrivalled authority stood between the Party machine and the vast body of its members. After his death the conflict became acute.

The Bolsheviks stood to the various Russian nationalities in the same relationship as they stood to the Soviets after their seizure of power. In loyal adherence to his programme Lenin had accorded complete independence to all the various nationalities in Russia in 1917 and 1918. The Ukrainians, the Caucasian races, the inhabitants of Turkistan, &c., all received autonomous government. They were permitted the unrestricted use of their mother tongues and the free development of their national traditions. Nor was any attempt made to 'Russify' them. All these countries became independent Soviet Republics that joined the Greater Russia in forming the Union of Soviet Republics. Nevertheless, the real power in all these Soviet Republics was in the hands of the local Communist organizations. The local Communist Parties in Georgia, Ukraine, &c., were, and continue to be, subject unconditionally to the authority of the Central Committee

of the Bolshevik Party in Moscow. Although the individual
nationalities in Russia retain their cultural independence,
they dare not act in any way contrary to the wishes of the
Central Committee of the Bolshevik Party. In the case of the
various nationalities in Russia democratic self-government
is as much an illusion as it is in Greater Russia itself.

In the years 1918–20 the working class in Russia suffered
from famine. The Civil War imposed terrible burdens and
sacrifices upon them. Soviet democracy had hardly been won
by them before it was lost again. A single gain, however,
compensated them for all their suffering and created in them
a feeling of intense pride. To preserve this gain they were
willing to sacrifice themselves to the uttermost. In the
memory of mankind there had always been poor and rich,
masters and servants. All these distinctions had been
abolished by the common want arising out of the Civil War.
The middle class no longer existed. In the towns scattered
over the face of Russia all men were equal and must contrive
to exist on the same scanty rations. If, indeed, any man
was more favoured than his fellow, it was the workman himself. All notions of value had been destroyed. Money had
become worthless. Although the peasant could indeed boast
in his village that he was the owner of his land, he could in
reality make nothing out of his property. He could neither
buy nor sell and his produce was requisitioned. It was thus
made to appear that Soviet Russia had not only been
socialized in the restricted sense, given to the term by Lenin,
of the nationalization of industries, banks, &c., but that the
highest type of Communism—the equality of rights and
uses, the disappearance of class distinctions, and the abolition of money—had been achieved. That he should have
lived through the greatest revolution in history appeared in
the eyes of the Russian workman like a glorious vision. As
soon as the Civil War and the miseries to which it had given
rise had passed away the road would be open for the free
development of the paradise of a society freed from class
distinctions.

The Communist intoxication of the Russian proletariat
was at once the cause of great strength and great peril to
the rulers of Russia. These enthusiastic workmen could be

relied upon to accomplish any task in their belief in their historic mission. If, however, their illusions were once shattered by the impact of hard facts, then the consequences would indeed be incalculable. Lenin had not foreseen this development in Communism at the time of his accession to power; nor had the transformation of Russian Social Democracy into the Communist Party been motivated by th'e ideas underlying this development. Throughout the years 1918–20 the Soviet Government did indeed emphasize strongly in its official pronouncements its Socialist mission, the destruction of the middle class, and the liberation of the workers. Nevertheless, Lenin himself continued sceptical as as to the positive results that had been achieved. In 1920 Lenin wrote in a critical essay:

'In Russia we are experiencing (in the third year after the downfall of the middle class) the first stage in the change over from Capitalism to Socialism, or to the lowest type of Communism. Class distinctions still exist and will continue to exist for years after the proletariat has achieved power. It is possible that this period will be shorter in England, where there are no peasants— though a class of small-holders exists. The destruction of class distinctions implies not only the abolition of the landowner and the capitalist (we have already achieved their destruction with comparative ease), but also that of the small producers who cannot either be destroyed or suppressed, and with whom one must make a compromise. Then they can and must be changed and educated up to new ideas carefully and slowly.'

Lenin recognized that the millions of small peasants in Russia continued to exist notwithstanding all the forcible measures employed against them by a militarist Communism, and that these small peasants formed part of the middle class and not of the proletarian State. This policy of force directed against the peasants was perhaps necessary in a period of war and famine. It could not be permanently used by the Soviet Government. Lenin was prepared to seek a compromise with the peasants after the restoration of peace. There was, however, throughout the years 1918–20 little hope of a cessation of hostilities. The iron hand of German militarism rested heavily upon Russia. After it had been removed danger threatened from the side of the Entente.

And all the time the Russian Government was confronted in its own country with the presence of millions of untrustworthy peasants. If a great Anglo-French Army were one day to march upon Moscow, would the peasant soldiers in the Red Army be willing to fight?

It was thus that the Bolsheviks were led, contrary to their own plans, to create a Socialist State in Russia after Trotsky's model. In doing so they had to face the consequences foreseen by Trotsky, namely, that a Russian proletarian revolution could only be maintained in existence by a proletarian revolution throughout Europe. During the years 1918–20 Lenin and all the leaders of Bolshevism acted in accordance with Trotsky's theory of the permanent revolution. They devoted all their energies to promoting revolution in central and western Europe in the hope that they would find allies in the victorious revolutionary Governments in Europe who would assist them to save the cause of revolution in Russia. Thus in the years 1918–20 the success of the Third International became a matter of life and death for the Bolsheviks.

THE THIRD INTERNATIONAL AT THE HEIGHT OF ITS REVOLUTIONARY POWER, 1919-21

As early as 1914 Lenin had announced the Third International. Nevertheless, as has already been shown above, the proposal found little acceptance among the working-class masses in Europe until 1917. On the victory of the Bolshevik Revolution the situation underwent a complete change. The middle-class revolution in Russia made little impression upon the European working class. A far deeper impression was made by the fact that the Bolsheviks were the first of all Governments to make peace. And the news of the Socialization of Russia ran through the proletarian masses in all countries like an earth-tremor.

The revolution which had been dreamed of for decades by the working class suddenly became an accomplished fact. Proof was given that it was possible to expropriate the capitalist, to abolish the use of money, and to hand over the factories to the proletariat. Lenin's early ideal—a middle-class revolution in Russia and a Socialist revolution in western Europe—could not have been expected to meet with much sympathy from the European workers. To advise German and English working men to adopt Socialism at the same time that he himself embarked on Capitalism may have been defensible from a theoretical standpoint. It did not provide a platform for a European mass movement. The European working man might very well have replied to Bolshevik agitators that they had better first practise at home the Socialism they preached abroad. It was thanks to the resolute action of the Russian working men who in the winter of 1917-18, and against the will of Lenin, seized the factories, that the ground was made ready for the Third International as a mass movement.

As long as war-time legislation prevented independent action on the part of European working men the profound inward change that had come over the European proletariat was not manifest. After the conclusion of the War it revealed itself with elemental force in the years 1919–20 in the desertion by millions of European workers of their old leaders, traditions, and organizations, and in their turning for guidance to Moscow. Under the immediate influence of the war and the subsequent economic crisis these working men believed in an early break-down of Capitalism and a victorious world revolution. The three categories into which European Socialism was divided. in pre-War days have already been enumerated: on the Right the Revisionist minority (2a), in the Centre the great movement of official Radicalism (2b), and on the Left the small revolutionary groups round Rosa Luxemburg, Gorter, and others (3). The World War resulted in the moral bankruptcy of official Radicalism, and at the same time the supporters of the old Right and Centre had indiscriminately divided themselves between the two new groups of those who supported national defence and those who did not. In the years 1919 and 1920 millions of Socialist workmen joined the ranks of the revolutionary Left. They did not, however, remain constant to the ideals of Rosa Luxemburg but went farther to join the Bolsheviks. Their desire was to serve under Russian leadership and to complete the work of the revolution under the orders of Lenin and Trotsky.

The old leaders of the European Socialist Left Wing recognized the achievement of the Bolsheviks and were prepared to co-operate with them in the cause of revolution. Nevertheless they remained critical in matters of detail. They never lost sight for an instant of the difference between Bolshevik theory and their own ideals. This statement is as true of the Spartacists as of the Dutch Left Wing Socialists. During her imprisonment in the autumn of 1918 Rosa Luxemburg wrote a series of critical articles on the Russian Revolution in which all her old differences of opinion with Lenin once more make their appearance. She pointed out the use made by Lenin of the ideal of nationality and his spoliation of the peasants as well as the destruction in Russia not only of middle-class but also of proletarian democracy. In these circumstances, she argued, Socialism could only be realized by a unique display of energy and spirit on the part of the masses—qualities which could only be developed under conditions of perfect freedom. Rosa Luxemburg added:

'The suppression of all political life throughout Russia must also result in paralysing the activity of the Soviets. Without universal suffrage, liberty of the Press and of public meeting, and freedom of debate, public institutions will atrophy and take on a shadow existence so that powers remain with the bureaucracy alone. Nothing and nobody is exempt from the action of this law. Public life gradually ceases. A few dozen Party leaders possessed of tireless energy and inspired by boundless idealism direct and control everything. In reality a dozen of the most outstanding intellects among them take charge of affairs. A selected number of workmen are from time to time summoned to meetings in order to applaud the speeches of their leaders and to pass unanimously resolutions that are laid before them. In fact it is government by a clique—a dictatorship, and not the dictatorship of the proletariat, but the dictatorship of a handful of politicians, i.e. a middle-class dictatorship like that of the Jacobins.'

It was the middle-class and Jacobin aspects of Bolshevism that specially attracted the attention of Rosa Luxemburg and Gorter and caused them to reject its teachings. On the other hand the broad masses of the people saw only what had been achieved in Russia in the way of Socialism and wanted to copy it in their own countries. Their experience during the War had lessened the fondness of the continental workmen for democracy. The middle-class parliamentary system no longer found acceptance in their eyes and the democratic right to a controlling voice in their own proletarian organizations had proved itself to be of little value. If it would lead to Socialism they were ready to accept a stern dictatorship after the Russian pattern. There can indeed be little question that in the years 1919–20 the majority of Socialist workmen in France and Italy, Germany and the former Austro-Hungarian countries, favoured an alliance with Bolshevism. Strong Bolshevik sympathies also existed in the Balkan States, Scandinavia, Poland, and the Baltic States. The Socialist proletariat saw in the Bolsheviks men called to be their leaders in a successful attempt to organize humanity in accordance with Socialist ideals. They neither saw nor understood the middle-class revolutionary character of Russian Bolshevism.

What was the attitude at that time of the non-Socialist workmen in Europe to the Russian Revolution? The majority of workmen in Spain were followers of the Anarchists and Syndicalists, who also commanded a certain following in Italy and France. Although they were Socialistic in aim, they refused to recognize the authority of the State and the employment of force even when used in the name of Socialism. They rejected parliamentarism and the political Party system. Their ideal was to organize the masses in revolutionary Trade Unions wholly distinct from the Social Democrat Trade Unions. Although the authoritarianism and political Party system characteristic of Soviet Russia was unwelcome to them, they nevertheless sought under the influence of the magnetism exercised by the Russian Revolution to ally themselves with Moscow, and hoped to achieve a compromise with the Bolsheviks over matters of principle.

The great majority of workmen in England up to 1914 were politically supporters of the middle-class Parties. Although millions of English workmen were organized in Trade Unions, only a few small groups professed Socialism before the outbreak of the World War. A great change came over England during the years of the War and the Socialist Labour Party gained millions of members. Lively sympathy was felt by English workmen after 1918 for Soviet Russia. Nevertheless, there was little disposition to adopt a Bolshevik revolutionary policy.

A section of the Christian Socialist and Conservative workmen on the Continent was also borne along on the wave of enthusiasm for Bolshevism. It is only necessary to recall the conduct of the miners in the Mansfeld and Saar districts, in the Ruhr, and in Upper Silesia after 1918.

Another movement of opinion among the working class, in addition to the Marxist-Socialist, Anarchic-Syndicalist, and middle-class tendencies, must be commented upon here. Although this fourth tendency had no organized existence, it nevertheless bore a highly individualized character. It can perhaps be best described under the name of Utopian Radicalism. Its followers were to be found among the very poorest, desperate, and embittered workmen. These men were animated by a passionate hatred not only for middle-class society but for any one more fortunate than themselves. They refused all negotiation and compromise and would only be content with an extreme form of action. A fanatical mistrust of all organization and leaders filled their minds and they felt themselves betrayed by any one who sought to impose discipline upon them or to advise moderation. There was much in common between this Utopian Radicalism and Syndicalism. Nevertheless, the two must be clearly distinguished from each other. It is incontestable that Syndicalism —the question whether its doctrines are false or true does not arise here—is a precise philosophy of life founded upon scientific arguments and pursuing definite aims by means of a formulated policy. On the other hand Utopian Radicalism is a purely emotional state and as such incapable of systematization or coherence. The Utopian Radicals among the workers also turned towards Bolshevism.

The November Revolution in 1918 and the consequent collapse of the militaristic monarchies in Germany and Austria-Hungary appeared to fulfil Bolshevik prophecies. Workers' and Soldiers' Councils established in the seats of the German Kaisers in Berlin and Potsdam now issued orders in their stead. It seemed as if the World War had really set in motion the World Revolution and that the movement which had started in October 1917 in Petrograd was spreading irresistibly from country to country. It was not long, however, before it became clear that notwithstanding Workers' and Soldiers' Councils, the middle-class revolution alone had proved victorious in Germany. The history of the Revolution in Germany clearly proves that the Soviet system is not necessarily identical with Socialism. An attempt on the part of extreme working-class elements to turn the middle-class into a Socialist revolution in Germany led to the disaster of 1919 and the assassination of Karl Liebknecht and Rosa Luxemburg. At the same time it is easy to understand why the Ebert-Scheidemann Government was looked upon in Russia as a sort of German Kerensky Government and the same fate prophesied for it that befell Kerensky and his followers. Moreover, Italy found herself involved in a serious domestic crisis, disturbance was rife in all the Succession States, in the Balkans, in the Baltic States; and in France and England extremist tendencies were openly manifesting themselves in the proletarian masses of the

population. The spring of 1919 saw the temporary establishment of Soviet Republics in Hungary and Bavaria. Thus the
ground was prepared for giving practical expression to the
ideal of a Third International.

The Third International was formally established in March
1919 at a meeting held in Moscow for that purpose. The
difficulties then attendant upon a journey to Russia prevented
the arrival of more than a few foreign delegates. This first
World Congress was only a beginning. The second World
Congress in July-August 1920 was thoroughly representative
of the majority of European workmen and also included
important delegations from other parts of the world. At this
Congress the Communist International was for the first time
given a definite programme and a definite political stamp.

From the very outset the Socialist Parties in Italy—filled
with pride for the loyal adherence to their principles throughout the War—had joined the Third International to a man.
The majority of the Socialist Parties in France were also
prepared to co-operate in its work. Among German Socialists
the first to join the Third International was the Spartacist
Union, which had changed its title towards the end of 1918
into that of German Communist Party (KPD). In the days
of the World War the small group of Marxist leaders centred
round Rosa Luxemburg in the Spartacist Union had been
opposed by a membership that was largely Utopian Radical
in its opinions. It was contrary to the wishes of Rosa Luxemburg that the Party had been compelled as the result of a
poll of its members to take part in the unsuccessful fighting
in January 1919. After the deaths of Rosa Luxemburg and
Karl Liebknecht, Paul Levi took over the leadership of the
KPD. At a Party Congress held in Heidelberg Levi resolutely
carried out the exclusion from the Spartacist Union of the
Utopian Radical workmen. As a result his Party was reduced
heavily in numbers. The ostracized workmen in common
with a number of doctrinaires holding Syndicalist views
founded the German Communist Labour Party (KAPD). Its
members formed only a small minority of the German proletariat.

The majority of the German Socialist workmen in 1920
were members of the German Independent Social Democrat

Party (USPD). This Party won greater and greater successes in its struggle with the old Majority Socialists. While the Majority Socialists wished for the time being to content themselves with a middle-class democratic Republic, the USPD demanded the establishment of a Socialist State. The USPD was prepared to join the Third International. The KAPD did not wish to sever its relations with Moscow.

The majority of workmen in the Balkan States, in Czechoslovakia, and in Norway were also in sympathy with the Third International. There was indeed hardly a country in the world in which a more or less powerful Communist Party had not been established. The Second International was completely disorganized and the leadership of the world proletariat seemed to have passed finally into the hands of the Bolshevik Party in Moscow. Lenin and the Bolsheviks, however, were little concerned in 1920 with securing the moral support of the international proletariat. That could be of little use to them. Their aim was to direct a Socialist Revolution to victory as speedily as possible in one or more of the greater States of Europe. If they succeeded in achieving their aim, the encirclement of Soviet Russia by the capitalist Powers would be broken; and the Bolsheviks would receive from the new Labour Governments in Europe the economic, moral, and, perhaps, even military assistance that was necessary to enable them to defend Socialism in Russia against the attack of the peasants. A successful working-class revolution seemed easiest of achievement in Germany and Italy, where the majority of the proletariat had openly declared themselves in support of the Third International and the existing middle-class organization of society was manifestly crumbling to pieces. If Soviet Republics could be established in Germany and Italy, the victory of Communism would be assured in the countries that lay between them and Russia—Poland, the Baltic States, the Succession States, and the Balkan States. The Union of Soviet Republics would then extend from Russia to the Rhine and the Alps.

The task confronting the Communist Parties, especially in Germany and Italy, would in this eventuality be no light one. Indeed, it would be a task of exceptional difficulty inasmuch as trained revolutionary Parties like those in Russia did not exist in Europe. Lenin was fully cognizant of these difficulties. He had, however, no time to lose. Communist Parties must be set up in all the more important European countries as quickly as possible and must be thrown into the battle. From the moment when Lenin seriously resolved upon the preparation of a working-class revolution in Europe he abandoned all purely agitatist catchwords and occupied himself with a sober calculation of facts and forces. A preliminary to victory was that the revolutionary Communist Party should in each country win the support of all or almost all the proletariat. Such a proceeding was obviously irreconcilable with the theory of the existence of a working-class aristocracy. Although Lenin remained faithful in theory to a conception that he had evolved during the War, he abandoned it in practice. In 1920 he wrote:

'Socialism inevitably inherits from Capitalism on the one hand the old differences between the workers (differences that arose out of those between the various trades and handicrafts and that have evolved through centuries) and on the other hand associations of Trade Unions that have slowly and after many years developed— and are continuing to develop—into broader industrial associations less reminiscent of guilds and embracing not merely trades, crafts, and professions but entire industries. Thanks to these industrial associations the Trade Unions will further develop into organizations for abolishing division of labour and for educating and training all-round men and women—men and women capable of undertaking any task. This is the goal towards which Communism is striving and to which it will attain only after the lapse of many years. To attempt to-day to anticipate the achievements of a perfected and mature Communism is like attempting to teach higher mathematics to a four-year-old child. We can and must begin to build up the edifice of Socialism with the materials left to us by Capitalism and not with some human compound that is our own special discovery. This will unquestionably be very "difficult". All other solutions to the problem are nevertheless so vain that they are not worthy of discussion.'

Lenin here admits after sober reflection the existence of differences between the various types of European workmen. It does not, however, follow that the poorest workmen should therefore attack and destroy their more fortunate fellows.

On the contrary they should build up Socialism together under the leadership of the Communist Party. The great majority of the skilled workers in Europe are organized in Trade Unions. Hence if the Communist Party desires to secure control over the masses, it must, according to Lenin, obtain a foothold in the existing Trade Unions. Nor must it allow itself to be influenced by the consideration that the leaders of these Trade Unions are for the most part 'Reactionaries'—enemies of the revolution and the Third International. In no circumstances must the Communists abandon their activities in the Trade Unions. For if they withdraw with revolutionary speeches from reactionary associations, they surrender their chances of winning over the masses and of leading the revolution to victory. Thus Lenin was led to refuse categorically any co-operation with Utopian Radicalism and any recognition for certain Syndicalist ideals. The Trade Union question is indeed one of the most fateful problems confronting modern Labour. It constitutes the acid test of whether a Party is really prepared to lead the proletariat or whether it is no more than a sect content with pseudo-radical doctrines. In placing before the Communists, as one of their chief tasks, the seizure of control over the Trade Unions, Lenin showed his recognition of the importance of the skilled and better-paid workman for the proletariat as a whole; and he thereby refused to build up the Communist Party solely out of the unemployed and the very poorest class of workpeople. Nor did Lenin in those days contemplate this seizure of control over the Trade Unions by the Communists as a long process of careful organization extending over many years. There was indeed no time to spare. He foresaw instead a violent change in the character of the old Social Democrat Trade Unions as a result of a revolution.

In 1920 Lenin published a pamphlet specially devoted to an attack on Utopian Radicalism and Syndicalism. In this pamphlet, entitled *Communism and the Infantile Disease of Radicalism*, Lenin demanded categorically that Communists should participate in parliamentary elections and in political life generally, and, above all, that they should define their attitude as a political Party to all political issues arising in

their country. The Communist Party was to refrain from
a reckless policy and from rushing wildly at its objective.
It must learn to conclude alliances and compromises, and
even to retreat if the occasion demanded it. This pamphlet
was written with the deliberate intention of provoking and
alienating Utopian Radicals. Lenin was well aware that an
unrestrained, emotional Radicalism on the part of the proletariat could only lead to anarchy, and that it could not be
used for constructive and practical purposes. Every movement animated by the spirit of Utopian Radicalism was at
once deprived of all serious political purpose and aroused
mistrust in the broad masses of the people. Thus, for example,
Lenin would rather have lost the support of fifty thousand
working-class members of the KAPD than risk losing that of
the five million members of the USPD through shaping his
policy to accord with the views of the fifty thousand. The
attack led by Paul Levi in 1919 against the KAPD was fully
in accord with Lenin's own views. If, however, the KAPD
and the Syndicalists were to recognize the error of their ways,
then they should be welcomed back to the fold. Their ideals
must, nevertheless, meet with no response in the Communist
International.

The Communists in Europe were not only to obtain control
over the proletariat but also over the peasants and lower
middle classes. If they could not win these latter over to
their side, they were at least to avoid rousing their hostility.
Neither in the towns nor in the country was the property
of these classes to be expropriated. A Socialist Revolution
in Europe was conceived by Lenin in 1920 solely as the
nationalization of the great monopolies and as the expropriation by the working-class State of the great Trusts, Companies, and Banks. Lenin remained faithful to his principle
of State Capitalism and economic centralization as realized
in the World War and was content to remove the handful of
plutocratic capitalists from all control over this centralized
economic system. A revolution of this type would indeed
have been possible in Europe in 1920 in an era of distress,
crises, and conflicts. There is not the slightest exaggeration
in the analysis of world conditions made by Lenin in
those days.

At the first session of the second World Congress of the Communist International (July 1920) Lenin delivered a speech in which he adapted his theory of Imperialism to the new conditions obtaining in the world. Once again he spoke of a small number of parasitic imperialistic nations living by the spoliation of other peoples. Among these exploited colonial areas Lenin reckoned also countries like China or the South American States, which enjoyed a nominal independence. A principal result of the World War, in Lenin's opinion, was the reduction of Germany and the States formerly comprising Austria-Hungary to the level of protectorates exploited by the victorious Powers. The Entente had intended to mete out the same fate to Russia. Who derived profit from the appalling misery of the world? Lenin calculated as follows: The United States has a population of 100 millions, Japan of 50 millions, and England also of 50 millions. If to these figures there be added those of the smaller neutral States who grew rich through the World War, the total will amount to some 250 million people. Since France and Italy were at that time indebted to America and England, Lenin did not reckon these two Powers among the real victors of the World War. The picture of the world as it presented itself to Lenin's eyes was that of 1,500 million people driven desperate through exploitation at the hands of 250 million. Nor do the 250 millions of the so-called victors constitute an entity. In these countries, as elsewhere, the vast mass of the population was subject to a small group of financial magnates. Since, however, impoverishment and indebtedness on a vast scale had overwhelmed the whole world, the victorious Powers could not find a market for their products; and thus unemployment and a rise in prices occurred within their own frontiers. Debts and the devalorization of money had caused the complete break-down of the machinery of the capitalist system throughout the world.

Nevertheless, Lenin refused to abandon his belief that it was impossible to expect an automatic collapse of Capitalism. Unless they were overthrown by a deliberate and organized revolution on the part of the oppressed peoples, the Imperialists would still be able to find a way of escape from their present dilemma. And this revolution must be prepared by a collaboration between the exploited peoples and the proletariat. 'In this Congress the revolutionary proletariat from highly-developed capitalist States meets together with the revolutionary peoples of those countries in which there is no, or virtually no, proletariat—the inhabitants of the exploited countries of the East.' Indians and Chinese would rise against Imperialism. The problem was one of finding a footing for Communism in the non-capitalist countries. 'Here there will be no Workers' Councils. There will be Peasants' Councils or Councils of active individuals.' The World Revolution then as always was, in Lenin's eyes, not solely an affair of the proletariat but a democratic rising of humanity against Imperialism.

The great revolutions in Asia and Africa that would have brought relief to Soviet Russia were certainly not likely to occur in the immediate future. Help could only come quickly through an extension of the revolution to central Europe. Lenin advised the German working class in 1920 in the event of a successful revolution to accept temporarily the Treaty of Versailles, after the fashion in which Russia had been forced to submit to the Peace of Brest-Litovsk. A Soviet Germany would thus secure a breathing-space in which to carry on its work of domestic reconstruction. The Italian workmen should ally themselves with the small peasantry and lease-holders in order to achieve power. In the event of a successful revolution on the part of the Italian workers and peasants, Lenin reckoned on a blockade of Italy by France and England. At the same time he believed himself to be in a position to assure Soviet Italy reliable assistance—probably by an advance on the part of the Red Army through Hungary to the Adriatic.

In England Lenin did not expect a Communist revolution in the immediate future. He anticipated a Socialist victory at the polls and the advent to power of a Labour Government in a constitutional manner. The various tiny Communist groups in England must unite to form a single Party and support the Labour Party in its struggle with the middle-class Parties in Parliament. The Communists would not take the place now occupied by the Labour Party until a much later stage of development had been reached. Lenin was also right in assuming as he did that the existence of a Socialist Labour Government in England would make the international situation of Russia easier.

An attempt has been made above to describe the way in which workmen belonging to all Parties in Europe turned in the years 1919 and 1920 towards the Third International. By the side of these workmen, inspired by a belief in the necessity for a speedy Communist revolution led by Bolsheviks, stood the Utopian Radicals whom Lenin so bitterly opposed. And in addition to this danger threatening the revolution from the Left there also existed what Lenin considered to be an even greater danger coming from the Right.

The World War made an end of the old official Radicalism of the Second International. A Radicalism that did not bind its followers to revolutionary action was no longer possible in Parties which had voted war-credits and least of all in an International which could serve as a platform for this type of 'reform'. Officials and leaders of the Labour Movement as well as many European workmen were, nevertheless, desirous not to abandon the old traditional, radical form of speech, the irreconcilability and aversion to compromise, and the concentration in thought and speech upon the goal lying ahead. At the same time they were far from any thoughts of realizing Socialism through revolution. These men sought in 1919–20 for a new faith and believed themselves to have found it in Bolshevism. Here was revolutionary action on an heroic scale. Here was the realization of Socialism, and here an unbridgeable breach with Capitalism. Entry into the Third International made a workman free of all these achievements. The 'disgrace' of 1914 was wiped out and the organizing work of pre-War Radicalism could be resumed and continued towards the ultimate goal. Italy became the scene of a typical development of this kind.

The chance and superficial causes that led the entire Italian Socialist Party to refuse to vote war-credits have been described above. This Party had thus avoided committing the 'sin' of 1914 and could take part as a whole in the Third International. Pre-War traditions were thus preserved unaltered in a post-War Italy, where the extraordinary situation arose in which not only the entire pre-War Radicals (2b) but also the Revisionists (2a) became members of the Third International.

The European supporters of the Third International presented a kaleidoscopic picture in their conflicting tendencies and beliefs. Revisionists and Radicals of the official pre-War type stood side by side with experienced revolutionaries determined to realize Bolshevism in their own countries, with Utopian Radicals, with Syndicalists, and with the supporters of Rosa Luxemburg. Only the exercise of democratic self-criticism and actual experience on the part of the masses could have gradually created a single unified Party out of these diverse elements represented in the new Communist Parties in Europe. And there was no time to spare for such an organic development. Instead it was essential to create as quickly as possible Communist Parties in all the leading European States capable of revolutionary action in the near future. According to Bolshevik opinion the foundation of an efficient combative Party was to be found in its possession of a strong Party Committee animated by a resolute fighting spirit. In order to obtain this desideratum the control of the Party must be purged of all who might be suspected of weakness and indecision in a time of revolution. It was for this reason that Lenin demanded of the former Socialist, now Communist, Party in Italy that it should exclude from its ranks the old group of Revisionists led by Turati. His demand resulted in the break-up of the Italian Communist Party into three groups: a Right Wing led by Turati; a Left Wing which supported Lenin's demand; and a broad Centre group, approximating to the pre-War Radicals, led by Serrati. Although this latter group was strongly opposed to the attitude adopted by the Right Wing, Serrati hesitated to provoke a cleavage in the Italian Labour Movement by insisting upon the exclusion of Turati and his followers. He preferred to resign from the Party himself with all his supporters.

On the subject of the situation in Italy Lenin wrote in a manner highly characteristic of his own personality:

'Serrati failed to understand the peculiar conditions obtaining in a period of transition such as that through which Italy is now passing. As is generally recognized, Italy is now moving towards a decisive conflict between the proletariat and the middle class for the control of the State. The exclusion of the Mensheviks, Reformists, and of Turati and his followers, from the Party is in such a moment not only inevitable and necessary but it may even be necessary to remove sincere and able Communists from all important posts if they show signs of indecision and especially of inclining towards an "agreement" with the Reformists.'

Lenin went on to say that he would cite an apt example of what he meant. Immediately before and after the October Revolution in Russia a number of outstanding Communists made a mistake 'which we now hesitate to mention'. And Lenin went on to describe the hesitations displayed by the Zinoviev-Kamenev Group at the time of the October Revolution. He depicted these men resigning from the Party Committee at the decisive hour. Their resignation, however, was not a misfortune. For

'on the eve of the Revolution and in the midst of a violent struggle for victory the slightest hesitation within the Party itself might have cost us the victory, destroyed the Revolution, and taken power from the hands of the proletariat—a power that is not secure inasmuch as its possession is still hotly contested. If hesitant leaders disappear at such a moment, their departure strengthens rather than weakens the Party, the Labour Movement, and the Revolution. Such a moment has now come in Italy.'

In addition to ostracizing Turati and his friends, the Communist Party in Italy was also to allow Serrati and his followers to go their own way peacefully. The Party would only find itself the stronger for their absence in the hour of revolution. After the victory of the Revolution the honourable men among those who had abandoned the Party in the moment of crisis would admit their mistake and return. On this subject Lenin wrote:

'A part of the Italian Mensheviks and followers of Turati would most probably return after the crisis of the revolution was over and be received again into the Party in the same manner (we have lived through three critical years since the Revolution) in which a number of the Mensheviks and Social Revolutionaries have returned to us after fighting on the other side of the barricades in 1917–18.'

It is clear from these sentences that Lenin did not at that time contemplate a state of things in which in every country in Europe a 'pure' Communist Party and an 'impure' Social Democrat Party would be in permanent opposition to one another. He was concerned solely with the acute stage in the revolution. The masses were desirous of fighting and were waiting for a resolute leader to give them the signal to engage the battle. It was not of importance how many members a Communist Party possessed at the outbreak of a revolution. Two conditions alone were of importance: the Party must carry the masses with it; and the Party Committee must not contain any faint-hearted member who would seek to hinder the revolution. The Party should dispense with the support of a few thousand Left Wing Radicals if by doing so it retained control over millions of workmen. With the same equanimity it should exclude doubters from its leadership, or refuse to accept them, even if by so doing it should lose members. Those who remained faithful to the Party would all the more certainly prove victorious in a time of revolution while the workmen and Party officials who had temporarily stood aside would then return to the fold of the Communist Party. This purge was not an end in itself, but only a tactical means for rendering easier the conduct of a revolution; and the aim remained the reunion of the working class and of the leaders who were truly in sympathy with the proletariat.

Lenin's attempt in 1919–20 to organize a revolution in Europe was a magnificent experiment. There were, however, gigantic difficulties to be overcome before it could succeed. The tradition of the working class in Europe was without exception democratic in the sense that Labour policy could only be decided upon in accordance with the free exercise of the right to self-determination on the part of the masses. The conversion of the proletariat from a policy of reform to one of revolution seemed only possible if the masses altered their opinions first and subsequently discovered a suitable means of giving expression to them. Now the exactly contrary process was to be embarked upon with all possible rapidity. A revolutionary Party Committee was to be set up in every country and endowed with dictatorial powers over the members of the Party, and with an unquestioned authority over the masses, and this Party Committee was to carry out a revolution. Although in the Promised Land of professional revolutionaries—Russia—it was possible to create such a central authority, there was nobody in Europe capable of undertaking such a task. And if, indeed, a revolutionary of this type was concealed somewhere in Europe in the editor of a Labour newspaper, or a Trade Union official—how was he quickly to be discovered? Even in Russia and under Lenin's direction the Central Committee of the Bolshevik Party had only gradually gained the confidence of the masses after years of work. How was an improvised Central Committee of the KPD or Communist Party in Italy to win over the majority of the nation to its cause? The creation of a Central Committee of European Communists could only be accomplished through the persistent use of dictatorial methods. For the time being the only way of knowing whether any particular person was a good revolutionary or not was by his voluntary acceptance or rejection of resolutions emanating from Russia. Hence twenty-one conditions were formulated for the acceptance of any Party desirous of joining the Third International. The seventh condition read as follows:

'Parties desirous of belonging to the Communist International are pledged to recognize the complete cleavage with Reformism and the policy of the Centre and to propagate this cleavage as widely as possible among their members. Unless that is done there can be no consistent Communist policy. The Communist International unconditionally and absolutely demands the carrying out of this cleavage in the shortest possible space of time. The Communist International will never be prepared to agree that notorious Opportunists such as Turati, Kautsky, Hilferding, Hillquit, Longuet, MacDonald, Modigliani, &c., shall have the right to pass as members of the Third International; for that would only lead to making the Third International closely resemble the Second International that came to a disastrous end.'

By 'Centre' is meant the middle or moderate tendency in Socialism. The twentieth and twenty-first conditions ran:

'Those Parties anxious to join the Third International whose policy has not already undergone a radical change must before their entry into the Communist International take measures to see that not less than two-thirds of the members of their Central Committees and all other central executive organs are comrades who unmistakably and openly advocated entry into the Third

International before the assemblage of the Second Congress of the Communist International. Exceptions may be made with the approval of the Executive of the Third International. The Executive of the Communist International possesses the right to make exceptions for the representatives of the Centre named in paragraph 7.

'Members of Parties who refuse in principle to accept the conditions and theses propounded by the Communist International shall be expelled from the Party.

'The above has special application to delegates to extraordinary meetings of the Party.'

Thus confidence was automatically placed in European leaders who had never performed any revolutionary action but who had announced their adherence to the Third International before a given date. In the same manner entry to the Third International was denied to certain persons mentioned by name who had during the War belonged to Kautsky's group. These were the men upon whom Lenin had already declared war at the time of the Zimmerwald Conference—the 'Centrals'—who stood between him and the so-called Social Patriots. Although the executive of the Third International could make an exception in favour of individuals among these men, the principle was not thereby altered in any way. Any one refusing to agree to the twenty-first condition was excluded from membership. If, for example, the Party Congress of the USPD put the question of membership of the Third International to the vote, and if the majority were in favour of accepting the Twenty-One Conditions, then the delegates composing the minority were automatically excluded from the new Communist Party by the mere fact of their voting.

The employment of such methods in European Labour Parties must inevitably result in creating an atmosphere of sectarianism and heresy-hunting. Valuable members would be rejected merely because they refused their support for certain theses and not because they had proved themselves useless in revolutionary work. Moreover, the question remained to be answered whether those who assented to these propositions would in the event lead the revolution to victory. The truth is that Lenin was then the prisoner of circumstances. In order to preserve Socialism in Russia revolution must be propagated in Europe as quickly as possible. And if organized and developed revolutionary Parties and Party committees did not already exist in Europe, then they had to be in some way—good or bad—created.

The passing of the Twenty-One Conditions was the most important achievement of the Second World Congress. These conditions reveal the spirit animating the Communist International in the very brief period—they ceased to exist by 1921—in which this organization was the real leader of the international Socialist revolution. Although this spirit was characterized by a stony one-sidedness, it also revealed a mighty revolutionary will-power. The first of the Twenty-One Conditions demanded that every Party should conduct truly Communist propaganda and agitation and, above all, hold up the ideal of a dictatorship of the proletariat before the eyes of the masses. The second demanded the removal of all Reformists and supporters of the Centre from responsible posts at the disposal of the Party. The third demanded that each Party should create an illegal, in addition to its legal, organization because in practically all American and European countries class warfare emerged at some stage in a civil war. At such a moment the legal status of a Party was not sufficient to enable it to carry on its work. The fourth condition demanded the pursuit of a systematic Communist propaganda in the armies. The fifth condition was of importance as defining the relationship between the working class and the peasantry. It ran:

'A regular and systematic agitation must be carried on in the country districts. The working class cannot achieve victory unless it is supported by the country proletariat and at least a part of the poorest peasantry, and unless it has assured itself by its policy of the neutrality of a proportion of the remaining inhabitants of the villages. At the present time Communist activity in the country districts is of the utmost importance. It must be pursued through the co-operation of revolutionary Communist workmen who have friends and relations among the peasantry. An abandonment of this activity or the entrusting of it to unreliable and not truly revolutionary workers would be tantamount to an abandonment of the proletarian revolution.'

The sixth condition required the disavowal of the 'sham of Social Pacifism'. The seventh condition has already been given above. The eighth required that all Communist Parties should work for the liberation of all colonial peoples and for the independence of the colonies belonging to their own countries. The ninth condition contained a rejection of Utopian Radicalism and Syndicalism in the Trade Union question. It ran:

'Every Party desirous of joining the Communist International must develop Communist activities in a systematic and resolute manner in the Trade Unions, Labour councils, factory committees, consumers' associations and other mass working-class organizations. Communist cells must be organized within these organizations for the purpose of winning the Trade Unions, &c., for Communism through determined and persistent propaganda. These cells are to expose the treason of the Social Patriots and the fickleness of the "Centre" on all possible occasions. The Communist cells must be completely subordinated to the Party.'

The tenth condition is ambiguous. In every country the Communists are to pursue their work zealously in the Social Democrat Trade Unions. If, however, the Central Committee of the Trade Unions in any country becomes Communist, then these Trade Unions are to desert the old Social Democrat Trade Union International—the so-called Amsterdam International—and to join a new International of Red Trade Unions. As the revolution passes rapidly from country to country, the capture by the Communists of the Central Committees of the Trade Unions in the individual countries must automatically follow, and the creation of the new Trade Union International progress parallel with the growth of the Communist International. If, however, the revolution is delayed, then violent controversies will arise within the individual Trade Unions—for example, the German Metal Workers' Association—over the question of union with Moscow or Amsterdam. This controversy might easily result in the emergence of the danger of a cleavage notwithstanding the activity of the Communist Party within the Trade Unions. The Trade Union question has from 1920 to the present day remained one of the gravest difficulties confronting the Communist International.

The eleventh condition dealt with parliamentary activity. In opposition to the Syndicalists it approved parliamentary activity before the advent of the revolution. At the same time the Communist members of Parliament were to be completely subordinate to the Central Committee of the Party and to carry on truly revolutionary propaganda and agitation at all times.

The twelfth to the nineteenth conditions are concerned with organization. All Communist Parties are to be organized after the Bolshevik model. The Central Committee of the Party is to be entrusted with the 'fullest power and authority, and with far-reaching rights'. 'Iron discipline' is required of the members. All these demands are founded upon the necessity for an absolutely unanimous leadership of a revolutionary Party in time of civil war. This form of organization is given the name of 'democratic centralization' in view of the fact that the authority of the Central Committee of the Party should rest upon the confidence reposed in it by the members. Any opposition group within the Party would be at a disadvantage in comparison with such an autocratic Central Committee. The Central Committee is empowered to appoint all the Party officials, control all Party newspapers, and to expel from the Party undesirable members. Hence the Central Committee can make its preparations beforehand for the Party Congress and assure itself of the vote of confidence necessary to enable it to continue in office until the next Party Congress. The Central Committee of a Party is subordinated to the Executive Committee of the Communist International in an exactly similar manner to that in which the Party members and local groups are subordinated to it. The World Congress elects the Executive Committee. The majority of its members are non-Russians. Nevertheless, the real policy of the Communist International is laid down by the representatives of the Russian Communist Party. All decisions of the Executive Committee are binding upon all Communist Parties. An opposition group within a Communist Party can never in normal circumstances overthrow the Central Committee. It is, however, master of the situation at the moment when it succeeds in gaining the ears of the Executive Committee, i.e. the leaders of the Russian Bolshevik

Party. In that case the Central Committee succumbs to an attack on two fronts and its opponents take its place in the control of the Party with the approval of the Executive Committee.

It is undeniable that such an organization of an international Labour movement was only tolerable in an age of civil warfare. Even then it is necessary to ask if a great popular revolution can be conducted on military lines. In peaceful times the organization of the Communist International would inevitably lead to grave disputes among European workmen. Zinoviev was chosen as Chairman of the Communist International, and Lozovski was entrusted with the management of the International of Red Trade Unions. Both men sought to wipe out the memory of their indecision in the autumn of 1917 by an increased display of revolutionary energy.

The immediate problem was that of giving effect in Europe to the decisions of the Second World Congress. The remarkable Party Congress of the USPD which was to decide for or against acceptance of the Twenty-one Conditions was held in Halle. Zinoviev appeared in person. He delivered a speech that lasted for four hours in which he explained the Bolshevik point of view with brilliant ingenuity. The majority of the delegates accepted the Twenty-one Conditions; and the majority of the USPD thereupon united with the old KPD (Spartacist Union) to form a great new United German Communist Party. In France the majority at the Socialist Party Congress accepted the Twenty-one Conditions and founded the French Communist Party. In Italy, however, the Twenty-one Conditions were rejected both by Turati's supporters and by those of Serrati. It was therefore only a minority of the old Italian Socialist Party that founded the Italian Communist Party. The various tiny groups in England who had declared themselves in favour of the decisions of the Second World Congress united to form the English Communist Party.

The establishment of Communist Parties in the sense desired by the Second World Congress had thus been achieved in all important European countries. It is true, however, that this was done at the cost of serious cleavages and the alienation of large numbers of former Socialist and Syndicalist workmen. The author of the Twenty-one Conditions had from the first reckoned with these losses. Moreover, it was of no importance in 1920 whether the Communist Party in a particular country was supported by 20, 30, or 40 per cent. of the electorate, nor what percentage of workmen in a country were already organized. All that was of decisive importance was whether the Communists would be successful in securing the support of the majority of the people for revolution. Whether the European Communist Parties would be able to organize a successful revolution so quickly that Socialist Russia would be freed from her cares, and whether Soviet Russia in her dangerous condition of domestic crisis would be able to wait and hold out until the revolution made itself perceptible in Europe—these were the all-important questions of the day

THE GREAT CHANGE

NEP and the Third World Congress, 1921

THE winter of 1920–1 was an especially hard and difficult one for Soviet Russia. The Civil War had been terminated in 1920 by the defeat of the White General, Wrangel, and the expulsion from Russia of the last counter-revolutionary troops. Peace had also been concluded with Poland after a series of successes and defeats. The cessation of warfare did not result in any improvement in the condition of the Russian nation. The year 1920 had with all its other evils brought a bad harvest. Famine reigned in the villages as well as in the towns. The passive opposition and dislike of the peasants for Communism increased, and in the towns factories were for the most part idle. Civil War had not helped to restore the disorganized system of transport. Freezing and starving workmen became desperate. The Russian proletariat had been called upon to defeat the White and Polish armies and to restore productivity to the factories. In his hope of peace at home and in his belief in the progress of the World Revolution, the Russian workman had accomplished heroic deeds. Peace had come. But the sacrifices required of him only became heavier. Doubts began to be entertained as to the permanence of the existing system. In any case the Government was expected to take action to overcome the misery of the masses of the nation.

The tense atmosphere surrounding the Bolshevik Party discharged itself towards the close of the year in the form of a curious debate. Its subject was the Trade Union question. At this time the membership of the Russian Communist Party was about 600,000. Nevertheless, it was impossible to open the ranks of the ruling Party in a State containing 130 million inhabitants to professional revolutionaries alone. Necessity had turned Lenin's Bolshevik Party into a mass organization. At the same time care was taken to preserve the Bolshevik tradition by maintaining the authority of the

Party leaders and insisting upon the strictest discipline on the part of the members. New members were only admitted with the greatest caution. The ruling Party was only a minority of the Russian proletariat as well as a tiny fraction of the Russian nation. An entirely different picture was presented by the organization of the Russian Trade Unions. Membership of a Trade Union was obligatory upon all workmen, employees, and civil servants. The Trade Unions in 1920 comprised 6 million members. Of these 6 millions, however, only 1 million were actually factory-workers. All Russians who could in the widest possible interpretation of the term be called proletarian were members of the Trade Unions. The management of the Trade Unions, like the control of the Soviets, lay in the hands of the Communists. Nevertheless, the Communists employed in the management of the Trade Unions held different views in many individual questions, notwithstanding the strict Party discipline, from those held by fellow members who, for example, were employed in the Commissariat for Foreign Affairs or in the Red Army. The Communist officials of the Trade Unions were forced to listen daily to the complaints and demands of the members and were thus involuntarily turned into mouthpieces for conveying the grievances of the workmen to the Party leaders.

The worse the condition of the Russian workmen the greater the depression in the Trade Unions and the stronger the conviction among many workmen that they would be given more food and fuel if the Trade Unions had a greater voice in the government of the country. The most fundamental of all the problems of Soviet Russia was thus brought into prominence. The dictatorship of the proletariat—it was said—existed in Russia. The State was a working-class State. Was it not therefore absurd that the workman as a member of a Trade Union should make accusations and bring complaints against his own State? Absurd or not— the fact remains that the Russian workman felt himself to be placed at a disadvantage in comparison with the soldier or peasant through mistakes on the part of the governing bureaucracy. It thus came about that towards the end of 1920 the complaints of the Trade Unions raised the question of the nature of the Soviet State and its relationship to the working man.

Discontent with existing conditions was rife. Change might be achieved in two ways. The Trade Unions could defend the interests of their members without regard for the general political life of the State and the theories of the ruling bureaucracy. (If the Trade Unions adopted this policy it would be tantamount at least to an indirect admission that Soviet Russia was not a working-class State.) Or the exact contrary would occur and the Trade Unions be incorporated in the machinery of government. This would amount to a fresh proof that Russia could not and must not be anything else than a working-class State. Trotsky recommended the adoption of the latter policy. He hoped to overcome the existing crisis by mobilizing the whole strength of the proletariat. The Trade Unions should be amalgamated with the civil administration. Although Trotsky showed great caution in formulating his proposals in detail, his purpose was clear: the restoration in Russia of working-class democracy by means of the Trade Unions. If 6 million Trade Unionists seized control of production and economic life in general (the ideal of productive democracy here makes its appearance), there would be an end to the dictatorship of the higher officials of the Communist Party.

Lenin promptly saw through Trotsky's disguised attack on the Bolshevik system of organization and energetically took up the cudgels in its defence. He openly told the Opposition that Soviet Russia was a Workers' and Peasants' State and not a Workers' State alone. For this reason the Trade Unions must be allowed to put forward complaints and demands directed against State officials. Phrases like 'productive democracy' could only result in undermining the dictatorship of the Bolshevik Party and in endangering the revolution. His immense prestige with the Party enabled Lenin to secure the rejection of Trotsky's proposals. In this discussion of the Trade Union problem the leading men in Soviet Russia refrained from calling things by their true names. They contented themselves with vague allusions to avoid arousing a feeling of panic in the nation. But Trotsky's aim was clear: no concessions to the peasants and therefore the development of working-class democracy. On the other hand Lenin was opposed to any weakening of the dictatorship, but in case of necessity was ready to make concessions to the peasants, and it would appear that as early as the winter of 1920–1 he had developed the fundamental principles of his subsequent so-called 'New Economic Policy'.

Despite his defeat Trotsky remained at the head of the Red Army and continued to take a leading part in the work of the Central Committee of the Bolshevik Party. Lenin entertained no thoughts of dispensing with Trotsky's services merely on account of a difference of opinion with him in the Trade Union question. Trotsky indeed realized during the winter of 1920–1 that he was not in a position to win over the Bolshevik Party to his ideas. Although for years past it had seemed as if Bolshevism had become coloured with 'Trotskyism', this impression now revealed itself as false. Moreover, Trotsky was incapable of conceiving the notion of mobilizing against the Party the non-Bolshevik masses with whom he had helped to make the revolution. For the time being Trotsky submitted to Lenin and the majority in the Party and in 1921 he offered no opposition to the fateful decision to embark on a new economic policy.

Trotsky's caution was not shared by other members of the Communist Party in Russia. A radical Opposition grew up in the Party during the debate over the Trade Union question. This Opposition was led by two former metal-workers and highly respected and long-standing members of the Party—Shlyapnikov and Lutovinov. Among their demands was the following: 'The organization of the administration of the national resources and production is placed under the control of the All-Russian Conference of Producers united in trade associations. This Conference shall elect a central committee to administer the entire economic life of the Republic.' Framed in these dry words, this amounted to a demand for the exclusion of the Bolshevik Party and its replacement by self-government on the part of the producers among the population. Lenin designated these proposals of the working men's Opposition as an anarcho-Syndicalist heresy. Nevertheless, Shlyapnikov and his supporters in reality only desired a return to the Soviet democracy of 1917 in the form in which it had been put forward by Lenin in his pamphlet on *State and Revolution*. Shlyapnikov and his supporters contented themselves with carrying on a legal propaganda within the Bolshevik Party and its affiliations. Other workmen and the soldier sons of peasants were less restrained, and, in March 1921, a rebellion broke out in Cronstadt. The island-fortress of Cronstadt, lying at the gates of Petrograd, was and is the main base of the Russian Baltic Fleet. The Russian Navy was a hot-bed of revolution as early as 1905 and in 1917 the Cronstadt sailors furnished the Bolsheviks with their staunchest troops. Of this 'Old Guard' many had since fallen on the battle-fields of the Civil War or been sent to other posts by the Soviet Government. The great traditions of the Revolution continued, nevertheless, to be associated with Cronstadt. And it was in this very place of sacred revolutionary memories that in March 1921 the soldiers and sailors revolted against the Soviet Government and took authority into their own hands. A Provisional Revolutionary Committee of Soldiers, Sailors, and Workmen took over the administration of Cronstadt. The programme of the revolutionaries contained among other points the following:

'Out of regard for the fact that the present Soviets no longer reflect the state of opinion among the workers and peasants, new Soviets should at once be elected by a secret ballot and with free electioneering facilities for all workers and peasants. Liberty of the Press and of Speech for Workers and Peasants, for Anarchists and the Left Wing Socialist Parties! Liberty for the Trade Unions and Peasants Unions! Liberation of all imprisoned Socialists and of all workers.and peasants arrested for pursuing the aims of their several movements! The abolition of all Communist propaganda sections in the Army in order that no single Party shall have the advantage over others in propaganda and receive funds from the State for its prosecution! Equal rations for all engaged in work! Freedom for the peasants to dispose of the land which they cannot cultivate themselves!'

This is virtually tantamount to the demand put forward by the Workers' Opposition: Overthrow of Party dictatorship and return to Soviet Democracy. It is unquestionable that the exiled enemies of the Soviet Government greeted the Cronstadt rebellion with enthusiasm, sought to support the rebels, and even to some extent subscribed to their battle-cry of 'Soviets without Communists'. The Soviet Government made use of this knowledge in its propaganda against the rebellion and laid special emphasis upon the sympathy displayed by the White Guards for the Cronstadt rebels. At the same time Lenin never regarded the Cronstadt rebellion as an ordinary White Guard rising of the type led by Denikin and Wrangel. He looked upon it as the symptom of the deep enmity between the Bolsheviks and the masses of the Russian nation.

The Soviet Government did all that lay in its power to prevent the movement from spreading to other districts. Picked regiments of the Red Army were sent across the frozen waters of the Baltic and stormed the fortress after heavy losses. Its capture did not put an end to the grave menace. What had happened to-day in Cronstadt might take place to-morrow in twenty other districts in Russia. The Revolution had given the masses Communism and in addition famine and servitude. If they must starve, they were at least determined to starve in freedom. Although it was Trotsky's Red Army which stormed Cronstadt, his views on the Trade Union question found their support in the Cronstadt rebellion and the demands put forward by the Workers' Opposition.

Lenin recognized the need for swift action in these terrible weeks. Although he was resolved not to give democracy to the masses, Lenin was anxious to provide them with bread even at the cost of sacrificing Communist ideals. All hopes of a speedy salvation for Soviet Russia through revolution in Europe had been proved to be illusory. On the subject of the emotions animating the leading men in Russia at the time of the First and Second World Congresses of 1919 and 1920 Trotsky, in 1921, wrote as follows:

'The First Congress met at a time when Communism was in its infancy as a European movement and when there seemed to be some probability that the almost spontaneous rising of the working classes would destroy the middle class before it had had time to find its bearings and establish itself firmly after the War. . . . And the rising was in truth spontaneous. The losses were enormous. Nevertheless, the middle class withstood this first assault and in consequence was strengthened in its self-confidence.'—'The Second

Congress met in 1920 at a decisive hour and at a time when it was already realized that the middle class could not be overthrown in the course of a few weeks or months, but that for this to be accomplished deliberate and careful political and other preparations were necessary. At that time the situation was critical. It will be remembered that the Red Army was marching on Warsaw. In view of the revolutionary condition of Germany, Italy, and other countries, it was believed that in its function as a force additional to and strengthening the forces in operation in Europe, this military blow (which was of no importance by itself) might serve to dislodge the avalanche of revolution from the ledge on which it had come to rest. This did not happen. We were driven back.'

In the summer of 1920 the Russian armies, after winning a series of battles against the Poles, wildly pursued their retreating enemy up to the gates of Warsaw. From a military standpoint this was a hazardous action and one that exposed the numerically weak and ill-equipped Red Army to the risk of meeting with a decisive defeat. This offensive was a desperate political experiment on the part of Lenin, who wished to see if the advance of the Red Army into the Polish Corridor would cause the outbreak of a working-class revolution in Germany. Germany, however, remained quiet and the Red Army was forced to retreat.

In September 1920 Italian workmen seized possession of the factories without their action resulting in a political revolution. In March 1921 armed conflicts occurred at Mansfeld in central Germany between Communist miners and the police. The Central Committee of the KPD wanted to support the miners by proclaiming a general strike. Since, however, only a small proportion of working men obeyed the Communist order to strike, the 'general strike' was a complete fiasco. There seemed indeed to be no likelihood of the outbreak of a working-class revolution in Germany or Italy— not to mention any other countries—in the near future. Since the Communists in Germany and Italy were unable to accomplish what had been expected of them by the Second World Congress, Soviet Russia was forced to rely upon itself. Lenin had embarked on the October Revolution in 1917 with a very cautious Socialist programme. He had never promised the masses to introduce Communism into Russia. The war-time Communism of the years 1918 to 1920 came into existence through the force of circumstances and not by the desire of Lenin or as a result of Bolshevik ideas. Even in these years Lenin remained sceptical of the extent of what had been achieved in the way of Socialism. He did not believe it possible to abolish the millions of tiny peasant proprietors by a stroke of the pen.

In the spring of 1921 Lenin embarked upon his retreat from war-time Communism to the 'New Economic Policy' (known as NEP). The confiscation of grain from the peasants ceased and instead the peasant was required to deliver a certain proportion of his harvest to the State as a tax in kind. The rest was left to him to dispose of as he wished and he was free to sell it when and how he chose. Thus the right of private ownership that had been disguised by war-time Communism with a network of requisitions was restored at a single stroke. Simultaneously free trade was restored and retail trade and small industries started again. As a result there followed a return to the employment of currency after the fashion of foreign countries. War-time Communism had been at pains to do away with currency, and therefore the re-stabilization of the rouble was now necessary. The State retained control over big industry, railways, banks, and also reserved the monopoly of foreign trade. Private ownership once more came into existence beside and beneath this State control.

The NEP did away with the equality of mankind in the form in which it had existed under war-time Communism— the equality imposed by a common lack of food. Once more a minority of workers stood beside a majority of peasants and other members of the middle class. Moreover, the economic condition of the landowning peasant was far better than that of the factory-worker in the towns. In addition there existed a Red Army with professional officers and N.C.O.s, an army of State and Party officials of all kinds, employees and technicians in all industries, teachers, doctors, writers, and artists. All these professions revived the moment their followers received a living wage in hard cash. The grey monotony of war-time Communism changed under the NEP into a brilliant kaleidoscope of classes and professions in

which—truth compels the admission—the factory-worker
occupied the lowest rank. It was left to the further development of the NEP in the succeeding years to show how this
social condition would fit in with the so-called political
dictatorship of the proletariat.

The new economic system that came into being through
the NEP was called by Lenin 'State Capitalism'. At the
Third World Congress of the Communist International in
July 1921, Lenin delivered a speech on this subject in which
he said *inter alia*:

'Taxes in kind obviously imply freedom of trade. The peasant
has the right after payment of his taxes in kind to exchange the
remainder of his corn. This freedom of exchange implies freedom
of Capitalism. We make no secret of that and I repeat it. We
make no secret of it whatsoever. We should indeed be degraded
if we attempted to make a secret of it. Free trade means freedom
for Capitalism—for a new form of Capitalism; a Capitalism that
we shall build up anew in certain aspects. We are doing that
openly. It is State Capitalism. State Capitalism in a land in
which Capital is the governing authority, and State Capitalism
in a proletarian State, are two very different things. State Capitalism in a capitalistic State means Capitalism recognized and
controlled by the State for the benefit of the middle class as
opposed to the proletariat. In a proletarian State this process
benefits the working class and enables it to defend itself against a
middle class that is still too powerful.'

Thus Socialism still possessed for Lenin the same narrow
and moderate interpretation that it had had in 1917. Lenin
termed factories belonging to a working-class State, or to a
working-class and peasant State, Socialist undertakings; and
he held that Socialist factories of this description could also
exist within the limits of a system of State Capitalism. Even
after the October Revolution Lenin considered a system of
State Capitalism in Russia to denote an advance on the
existing backward condition of the country.

'The development of Capitalism,' he wrote, 'under the control
and regulation of a proletarian State (that is to say, in the sense
attached to the term "State Capitalism"), is good and absolutely
necessary in an exceptionally poor and backward country of small
peasants (only of course up to a certain degree, and in so far as its
development is capable of hastening an immediate improvement

in the agricultural system of the peasants). If the State retains control of the chief factors in economic life such as foreign trade, heavy industry, railways, and banks, then it will be in a position to control and regulate the private Capitalism that would develop in the country and in the middle class.'

Of great assistance to the State in its regulation of retail trade, in Lenin's opinion, was the co-operative association. In one of his last articles in May 1923, Lenin expressed the view that the cultural level of the Russian peasant should be raised to the point at which he was ready for membership of a co-operative society in a civilized State. Russia would have attained Socialism, in Lenin's view, when the organization of these societies had been perfected throughout the land. Lenin wrote:

'A society consisting of the educated members of an association for common ownership of the means of production and based on the class victory of the proletariat over the middle class—that is the Socialist order of society. . . . We now have the right to say that the simple growth of co-operative societies (under the above-mentioned "small" reservation) is in our eyes identical with the growth of Socialism. We must, however, admit simultaneously that we have fundamentally altered our conception of Socialism. This fundamental change consists in the fact that formerly we laid, and were forced to lay, the greatest emphasis upon political warfare, upon the revolution, and upon the seizure of power. Now the chief emphasis must be laid upon peaceful, organizing, "cultural" work. . . . Only this cultural revolution is wanting for Russia to become a completely Socialist country. This cultural revolution, however, makes unheard-of demands both of a purely cultural (overcoming illiteracy) and of a material nature, since in order that we may turn into a civilized country it is necessary to have a certain material basis and to promote a certain development of the material means of production.'

Something more will be said subsequently about the remarkable doctrinal consequences that resulted from Lenin's theory of co-operative associations. In the Russia of 1921–3 such an organization of the peasantry into co-operative societies could only be an ideal for the future. The immediate problems were the isolated peasant industries and State Capitalism. It was because Lenin decided upon the transition from war-time Communism to State Capitalism

that he resolutely refused to make any concession whatever to any form of democracy. The working-class minority
in Russia could only maintain itself as against the great
majority of small owners, especially in the new capitalist
conditions, by means of a relentless dictatorship. For the
same reason the Communist Party must be the undisputed
leader of the proletariat and must itself maintain the strictest
discipline and unanimity.

Lenin's change over to the NEP brought the desired results
in the succeeding years. The Bolshevik dictatorship maintained itself in power. Discontent among the masses vanished
with the disappearance of famine. After seven years of depression and unemployment Russian industry experienced
an upward movement. A radical change came over the relations between the Bolsheviks and foreign States and workers.
A Russia organized on a basis of State Capitalism was no
longer dependent upon the irresistible advance of the world
revolution. It could exist peacefully within a capitalist
world. From 1921 Lenin sought to obtain foreign capital
for the reconstruction of Russia. Foreign investors might
rent ground, mines, forests, &c. They were permitted to
start industries from whose profits a part went to the Soviet
Government as rent or tax and the remainder was left at the
free disposition of the investors. Lenin saw nothing irreconcilable with his system of State Capitalism in the presence
in Russia of these great foreign capitalist undertakings.
Despite the endeavours of the Soviet Government since 1921
the number of concessions granted to foreign capitalists has
been relatively small.

After 1921 Soviet Russia was formally recognized by a
large number of foreign Powers. Others entered into relations
with her without giving her Government formal recognition.
Soviet Russia made her appearance as a buyer and seller on
the capitalistic world market. Soviet ambassadors and trade
delegations took up their residence in foreign capitals. Both
Parties—Soviet Russia and the capitalist States—grew
accustomed to each other and began to take each other into
their calculations. Lloyd George endeavoured to get the
Soviet Government to co-operate in his plans for reconstruct-
ing Europe and was responsible for the invitation sent to the

Soviet Government to take part in the Genoa Conference in 1922. It was at this Conference that Soviet Russia and the middle-class German Republic concluded the Treaty of Rapallo. A glaring light was thrown upon the changed attitude towards the international situation adopted in Moscow since the spring of 1921 at the Third World Congress of the Communist International in July 1921. The resolutions concerning the world situation passed by the Third Congress on the proposal of the Russian Communist Party first defined a four-year period of revolution dating from March 1917 (Overthrow of the Tsar) to March 1921 (Miners' Strike in central Germany). It was then laid down that 'This great wave failed to pass over and bear away with it Capitalism either in Europe or in the world at large'. The resolution goes on to declare:

'The years elapsing between the Second and Third Congresses of the Communist International saw a number of insurrections and struggles on the part of the working class which in many cases ended in defeat. (The offensive undertaken by the Red Army against Warsaw in August 1920, the proletarian movement in Italy in September 1920, the insurrection of German workmen in March 1921.) The first period of revolution after the War appears virtually to have reached its conclusion. It was characterized by an elemental offensive force, a lack of system in methods and aims, and by the tremendous panic which it induced in the ruling classes. The self-confidence of the middle class as a class and the apparent strength of their State organizations unquestionably increased and fear of Communism lessened if it did not wholly disappear. The leaders of the middle class armed themselves with the power of their State apparatus and have in all countries taken the offensive against the working-class masses both on the economic and on the political front.'

A victorious world revolution was once more held up as the ideal and a complete recovery of Capitalism declared to be impossible. At present the proletariat was forced to adopt the defensive. It could not wage war for supreme power in the State and must therefore content itself with lesser conflicts and more moderate demands of an economic nature. The resolutions of the Third Congress on this subject run:

'All agitation and propaganda and the entire work of the Communist Parties must be animated by the consciousness that no lasting improvement in the condition of the masses of the proletariat is possible within the capitalist order of society, and that only the overthrow of the middle class and the destruction of the capitalist States affords the possibility of commencing the work of improving the state of the working classes and of rebuilding the economic system destroyed by Capitalism. This consciousness must not, however, find expression in an abandonment of the struggle for the daily necessities of life required by the proletariat before it is capable of securing them for itself by establishing its own dictatorship. . . . All objections to making such partial demands, all complaints on the part of Reformists against participation in this semi-warfare, are symptoms of the same incapacity to comprehend the essential nature of revolutionary action that manifested itself in the opposition of individual Communist groups to participation in the Trade Unions and in parliamentary life. It is not enough to proclaim to the proletariat the aim to be striven for without intensifying the everyday struggle that is alone capable of leading the proletariat towards the battle for the final objective.'

The interest of the debates in the Third Congress centred round the insurrection of the German workers in March—the so-called 'March Action'. It has already been mentioned above that local disputes in central Germany resulted in conflicts between police and workmen, and that the KPD then attempted to support their Party colleagues in central Germany by means of a general strike throughout the country. In this connexion the so-called 'offensive theory' made its appearance in the ranks of the KPD—a theory according to which a revolutionary Party must resolutely and permanently continue the offensive for the purpose of achieving power without regard for unfavourable circumstances. This theory sounds fantastic and dangerous. In order to understand it properly it is necessary to recall the resolutions passed by the Second World Congress in the summer of 1920. These were: 'The proletariat of the world is confronted with its final struggle. The age in which we are now living is an age of actual civil warfare. The decisive hour approaches. In almost every land in which there is a Labour movement of any importance the working class is confronted with a succession of fierce armed conflicts.' If the Second World Congress was in the right, then countries like

Italy and Germany were already in a state of open civil warfare. In civil warfare, however, as Marx, Engels, and Lenin repeatedly insisted, a ruthless and clever offensive is the sole possible weapon for use by insurrectionaries. The mistake made by the KPD in March 1921 is in reality the mistake made by the Second World Congress in taking an exaggerated view of the tenseness of the situation in Europe. In the resolutions passed by the Third World Congress no mention is made of this error on the part of the International—also on the part of Lenin and Zinoviev—and the failure of the 'March Action' is laid wholly at the door of the KPD. The resolutions of the Third Congress on this subject ran:

'The March Action was forced upon the VKPD (United German Communist Party) by the Government's attack upon the Central German proletariat.

'In this first great struggle since its foundation the VKPD made a number of mistakes, of which the most important is to be found in its failure to emphasize the defensive nature of the struggle and in its designating it an offensive action. The VKPD thereby laid itself open to the accusation on the part of the unscrupulous enemies of the proletariat—the middle class, the SPD, and the USPD—of fomenting insurrections by the proletariat. The effect of its failure was only increased by a number of members of the Party who declared an offensive to be the chief weapon in the armoury of the VKPD in present circumstances.'

The criticism made by Lenin and other leading members of the Congress in the debates was sharper. The European working class must be convinced by the members of the Congress that the Communist International regarded all idea of an armed revolution in the immediate future as wildly adventurous and that a return must be made to the pre-War policy of unarmed economic struggle. The resolutions of the Third Congress are open to the gravest objections in regard both to their appraisal of facts and to their logic. The notion of an epoch of world revolution developed by Lenin in his great speech to the Second Congress was still valid. The revolt of subject peoples against Imperialism was still in progress in countries outside Europe. At the same time the inner contradictions in the capitalist system revealed themselves with increasing clearness in Europe and the United States—indebtedness, the results of the Peace Treaties of 1919, depreciation of currencies, and unemployment. All these factors were as much in evidence in 1920 as in 1921 and 1932. The fundamental characteristics of an epoch of world revolution had undergone no change in the interval between the Second and Third World Congresses. Moreover, no important change had taken place between the summer of 1920 and that of 1921 in the leading European States. Severe as was the suffering caused by the loss of life in the March Action in 1921 for mourning working-class families, the Action itself was only an unimportant episode in the post-War history of Germany and not to be compared with events such as the Kapp Putsch in 1920 and the economic crisis in 1923. Of all the problems crowding upon Germany not a single one had been solved in 1921. Indeed, the Franco-German tension, the Reparations question, and the depreciation of the mark and growing industrial distress were threatening to produce a new crisis in the immediate future— the crisis that actually came in 1923.

Lenin had truly prophesied the advent to power of a Labour Government as the first step in a revolutionary development in England. This opinion was as sound in 1920 as in 1921. The situation had undergone no change. Moreover, the political and social condition of France had remained unaltered during the same year. The growth of Fascism in Italy had brought about a state of actual civil war in that country. Nevertheless nothing of a decisive nature had occurred in Italy. Thus the situation in Europe and that of the world at large had not altered in any way between the Second and the Third World Congress. Soviet Russia alone had changed. In the summer of 1920 Lenin hoped, by forcibly hastening on the revolution in countries like Germany and Italy, to establish Labour Governments in those States that would be friendly to Soviet Russia. This is the explanation of the fervour displayed in the resolutions of the Second World Congress. By the summer of 1921 Russia had withdrawn into herself and come to rely upon her own resources. She adapted herself to life without the world revolution. Lenin ceased to believe in a speedy and successful working-class revolution in Europe. Hence the symbolic importance of the March Action in Germany for the Third World Congress. It was falsely taken to indicate the close of that period of active revolutionary movement among the European working class that had begun in the World War. In truth, its importance for the Communist International lay simply in the fact that it practically coincided with the change over to the NEP. The Third World Congress seized the opportunity to demonstrate in the March Action the mistakes of its former policy.

It would indeed have been only right if the Third Congress had corrected certain exaggerations on the part of the Second Congress in its estimation of the universal extent of a state of civil war. Instead it went to the other extreme. Since Lenin no longer believed in the possibility of a revolution in Europe in the immediate future, he overlooked the tense revolutionary condition of Italy and Germany. It was still within the bounds of possibility that the Italian workmen would defeat the Fascists and achieve power, and that the disordered social and economic condition of Germany might lead to the establishment of a Socialist Labour Government. It is true that the resolutions passed by the Third Congress held forth the victory of the united Italian proletariat over the Fascists, and of Communism in Germany as objectives to be pursued. At the same time, however, these resolutions announced a defensive policy on the part of the proletariat and directed the eyes of workmen towards the pursuit of predominantly economic aims. It is indeed in the highest degree questionable whether political Parties artificially organized from above, as were the Communist Parties in central and western Europe, were capable at all of revolutionary action. And in so far as the capacity for revolution existed the decisions of the Third Congress paralysed it.

The majority of European workmen supported the Third International during the years 1919 and 1920. As a result of dissensions, and their rejection of large sections of the working class, the Communists found themselves once more in the minority. The SPD, strengthened by the addition of a part of the USPD which had not gone over to the Third International, had a far greater membership than the Communist Party in Germany. The Social Democrats in 1921 were once more supported by a clear majority of the workmen in England and Italy, Sweden and Denmark, Holland and Belgium, Austria and Switzerland. Only in France, Czechoslovakia, and Norway were the Communists in 1921 supported by the majority of organized workmen. Communism was forcibly suppressed by the Governments in the Baltic and Balkan States, Poland, and Hungary. The Syndicalists, who were supported by the majority of the Spanish workmen, left the Third International; and their example was followed in Germany by the small KAPD (German Communist Labour Party). Communism hardly existed in non-European countries.

In the years following upon 1921 it would have been possible in these circumstances to reconstruct the Socialist International to include the majority of the working class. The Communists were in the minority from an international standpoint. In the course of a great revolutionary movement an active minority can become the majority of the nation. This was shown by the change that came over Russia in 1917. The Third International now demanded of the Communists that they should win over the majority of the working class in all countries by means of a skilful and successful leadership of the proletarian struggle for the daily necessities of life. This task proved incapable of accomplishment. The Social Democrats possessed a long and successful tradition of leadership in the proletarian economic struggle and especially in the Trade Unions. The Communists might at the most excel the Social Democrats in the conduct of revolution; they could never do so in the matter of wages. The Communists had gained for themselves the support of great numbers of European workmen by summoning them from the peaceful daily struggle for existence to engage in an armed struggle for political power. Now, however, the Communists were to lead back the workmen to this daily struggle, i.e. to invade a sphere from which the trained and experienced Social Democrats could not be driven. Moreover, if there were in Europe a permanent Social Democrat majority opposed to a Communist minority of workmen, if both pursued the same aims in the daily struggle, if both worked together in the

Trade Unions, then the question in Europe at the close of the Third World Congress would become one of deciding what reasons there were for the separate existence of Communist Parties. Up to the meeting of the Third World Congress there had been a distinct and unmistakable difference between Social Democrats and Communists. The Communists proclaimed the necessity for an immediate armed working-class revolution; the Social Democrats denied the possibility of such a revolution in existing circumstances. Now the Communists declared that this aim could only be realized in some far-distant future. They did, indeed, promise the workmen that they should one day participate in a revolution and that on that occasion the Social Democrats would again be found wanting. A permanent cleavage in the working class could not be justified by this promise of something that was to happen in a conditional future.

The contradictory and ambiguous nature of the resolutions passed by the Third World Congress are to be explained by the fact that Lenin and all the leading Bolsheviks were perplexed as to the future of the Communist International. If a great wave of revolution was one day to come again the Communist Parties would once more be able to take the lead. For the moment the only alternative before them was an alliance with the Social Democrats. In October 1921 the Executive of the Communist International proposed to the Social Democrat Parties and Trade Unions the building of a 'United Front' for the purpose of carrying on the struggle for the daily necessities of the proletariat.

The opinions entertained on the subject of the Third World Congress by the most critical minds in the European Labour movement found their ablest expression in the writings of the brilliant Dutch Marxist, Hermann Gorter, who wrote immediately after the conclusion of the Third World Congress as follows:

'The Third Congress of the Moscow, or Russian, International has decided the fate of the world revolution for the present. The trend of opinion that seriously desired world revolution—that is to say German, English, and western European revolutions in the first place—has been expelled from the Russian International. The Communist Parties in western Europe and throughout the

world that retain their membership of the Russian International
will become nothing more than a means to preserve the Russian
Revolution and the Soviet Republic. The western European
revolution and the world revolution are pushed into the background in order to enable the Russian Revolution to live a little
longer. Thus the world revolution is condemned to disappear for
years to come.

'The Russian Revolution was only superficially a proletarian
and Communist revolution. In reality it was far too little proletarian and Communist and far too greatly peasant and democratic. . . . Out of this partially concealed contradiction arose the
domestic policy of the Soviet Republic and the Communist Party
—the dictatorship of the Party leaders, the rigid discipline, over-
centralization, &c.

'At the head of the Third International stands a Party which
is compelled, and will be still more compelled, to pay more regard
to peasant and middle-class democracy than to the proletariat,
and that forces, and in the future will still further force, the International to follow its example. It is a Party that with the one hand
supports English and German Capitalism by foreign trade and
concessions, and with the other hand supports the German and
English proletariat. The tactics pursued by this Third—Russian
—International are of the same ambiguous nature in the case
of all countries and all Parties. In other words, a third International forced by world Capitalism and Russian democracy to
adopt a policy of compromise and opportunism and in which
revolution will become more and more a matter of phrases possibly
alternated with insurrections.'

These sentences of Gorter's contain exaggerations and are
coloured by the personal sympathy entertained by the writer
for the German 'Communist Labour Party'. But he has
correctly defined the fundamental problem: whether after
1921 the Government of a Soviet Russia organized in accordance with the principles of State Capitalism would be capable
of directing the proletariat of the world in its struggle with
Capitalism.

LENIN'S TESTAMENT, 1922–4

AN apoplectic stroke in 1922 brought to a close Lenin's active life. Although his condition improved towards the close of 1922 and again early in 1923 sufficiently to enable him to deliver a few speeches and write some articles, it soon became worse again and he died in January 1924. After carrying out the Russian Revolution Lenin had assured peace for his fellow countrymen by making an end of both the Civil War and the war with Russia's external enemies. Through the adoption of the NEP he overcame famine and restored a quiet daily life to towns and villages. As ruler of Russia Lenin kept up the same modest and simple habits of life which he had pursued in his furnished room in Zürich. His life-work was characterized throughout by an unvarying regard for reality and he never once permitted himself to be swayed by personal feelings. In the eyes of the nation Lenin was a simple son of Russia who shared the anxieties of his compatriots and was accessible to every one. He abhorred all theatricality because it was unnecessary for his purpose. Hegel said: 'Robespierre declared virtue to be the greatest of all moral qualities and it can with truth be said that he practised what he preached.' The same may be said of Lenin. In the last years of his life Lenin enjoyed unbounded respect among the Russian nation. His body was embalmed and placed in a public mausoleum in the Red Square in Moscow. People come there daily to gaze upon the features of the 'Saint of the Russian Revolution'. No one would have been more astonished than Lenin himself if this posthumous reverence had been prophesied to him. His realism and modesty, nevertheless, did not avail to prevent his becoming the embodiment of all that was mystic in the Russian Revolution.

The great motivating force in Lenin's life was his passionate desire to liberate Russia from the thraldom of the Tsars. Marxism provided him with a weapon ready to his hand. Although his life-work was accomplished on Russian soil, Lenin saw the Russian Revolution against the background of the greater World Revolution. Throughout the thirty years of his political activity Lenin remained faithful to himself and despite tactical changes in matters of detail he never changed his opinions on matters of principle. Thus it would be a mistake to see in the NEP an admission on Lenin's part that his Socialist ideal was shattered. On the contrary, the NEP belonged organically to the body of opinion formed by Lenin before 1917 on the subject of the Russian Revolution and the economic future of Russia. The war-time Communism of 1918-20 was not Lenin's work, but was a temporary change of plan which circumstances forced him to make. Lenin never denied, at least in theory, during the years 1918-20 his fundamental principle of State Capitalism.

Lenin bequeathed to the Bolshevik Party the task of holding together the Russian peasants and workmen. An economic link necessary for this purpose was to be forged between the State administration of heavy industry, transport, banks, and foreign trade on the one hand and private interests in the form of peasant ownership of land and retail trade on the other. Conditions in Russia had been stabilized by the NEP to such an extent that no great disturbance occurred during Lenin's illness and the Bolshevik Party could continue to rule Russia unopposed after his death. The most important economic consequence of the NEP was the return of Soviet Russia to a stabilized currency. After lengthy preparations inflation was successfully overcome and a new and stabilized rouble placed in circulation by 1924. At the same time the State monopoly of foreign trade enabled the Government to maintain a careful control over Russia's international trade balance. Soviet Russia only bought from abroad goods payment for which could be covered by the proceeds of its own export trade. The Soviet Government punctually discharged its obligations to foreign suppliers and never contracted debts beyond its capacity to pay. It was thus able to prevent foreign speculators from tampering with the Russian rouble. The circulation of money within Russia itself was in 1924 brought into relation with the volume of trade, and arbitrary printing of new notes ceased. Naturally Russia suffered after 1924 from the distresses attendant upon this process of deflation. Strictest economy was enforced upon Government offices and all undertakings. State industry was to be made to pay its way. The various State trusts were enjoined to take the greatest care in making their calculations; the working capacity of the workmen was to be increased as far as possible; and wages were to be brought into relation with profits.

The reconstruction of Russian industry went on apace after the adoption of the NEP. In 1920 the output of Russian industry was only 15 per cent. of its pre-War output. This figure had increased by 1924 to 45 per cent. It must not, however, be forgotten that even in 1924 Russian industry was still in a backward condition from a technical standpoint. Money and material were wanting to modernize the older factories. In consequence the rate of production was slow and the cost of production unduly great. The number of workers employed in factories rose from 1,200,000 in 1922 to 1,600,000 in 1924. After enormous difficulties had been overcome the railway system was reorganized during these years and a reliable service of trains put into operation.

A bad harvest in 1921 retarded improvement in Russian agriculture. After that year, however, its progress was rapid. The light taxes imposed upon the Russian peasant were at first payable in produce and only after 1924 in money. Since 1920 ownership of land had been put on an ordered footing and no further State interference took place. It is true that new social distinctions gradually grew up in the country districts. The restoration of Free Trade and money payments brought into existence a new and well-to-do class of big peasant proprietors who carried on the traditions of the Kulaks. The poor peasants had no land to spare for their younger sons, who therefore emigrated to the towns, flooded the Labour market and contributed to the unemployment so typical of Russia under the NEP. In 1924 there were already one million unemployed in Russia. With the assistance of a small dole from the State they endeavoured to make a living by doing casual labour. A new class of agricultural labourers also came into existence.

The social equality characteristic of the period of war-time Communism disappeared completely in the early years of the NEP. Money had again become an influential factor. People

began once more to distinguish themselves from their neighbours by the amount and manner of their earnings. At the
head of the social scale came the small governing clique of
Bolshevik Party leaders. Next came the millions of public
servants and officials employed by the Soviets, the Bolshevik Party, Trade Unions, and co-operative societies, office-
workers of all descriptions, engineers, and technicians in
State industries, teachers in higher and lower schools, officers
and N.C.O.s of the Red Army. Rykov, a leading member
of the Soviet Government and Chairman of the Council of
People's Commissars in succession to Lenin, said in 1924 on
the subject of the State administration:

'The Soviet administration is of the greatest importance for our
work. It employs many hundreds of thousands of officials of whom
the overwhelming majority were educated in and imbibed the
traditions of the former Government. These characteristics are
brought by them into their new work of construction. These
Soviet officials, who are for the greater part indifferent to the vital
concerns of the Party and the working class, have neither the
planning capacity nor the unwearying resolution in its execution
that are required for a swift discharge of the tasks which the Party
has set before them. Bureaucratic and lower middle-class strikes
and bureaucratic divergences are inevitable in the Soviet administration in these circumstances.'

Lenin himself wrote in May 1923 on the subject of 'the
great and epoch-making task of reorganizing our practically
worthless administrative apparatus that has been taken over
in its entirety from a previous age. We have not, and could
not, achieve anything worthy of mention during the five
years of warfare.' The State machinery of Soviet Russia is
nevertheless far better than the Tsarist bureaucracy and if
circumstances be taken into account can be compared not
unfavourably with administrations in other countries. The
violent criticism of the Soviet administration voiced by
leading Bolsheviks like Lenin, Rykov, and others, is to be
explained by the fact that these men found in it a foreign
element, i.e. the middle-class ideal as opposed to the proletarian ideal of the State. The Soviet administration cannot
be other than it is as long as the Government uses it as an
instrument for maintaining its dictatorship over the nation.

The choice is either true democracy in the form of effective government by the Soviets or bureaucracy in the form of government by the State apparatus. A third alternative was and is impossible in Russia. Moreover, it is no less inevitable that in the course of years these Government officials will take on the appearance of a new middle-class society through being the more educated and materially secure upper class of brain-workers controlling the administration of the State and of the means of production.

Beside this great army of State officials in the widest sense of the term there stood in Russia in 1924 the richer and poorer peasants, merchants, and manual workers, the professional classes (doctors, artists, writers, &c.), and—finally—the factory-workers. Nor was the proletariat in 1924 any longer an entity. Instead there existed a long scale of wages graded according to occupation and qualification. A million unemployed formed the base of this social pyramid.

The dreams of Communist equality that had haunted the minds of Russian workmen for years past were thus dissolved, and it was no easy matter to effect an intellectual change in the Russian proletariat without running the risk of endangering the existence of the Soviet State. This change was rendered possible by the fact that, even after 1921, Lenin continued to reiterate that he regarded the Soviet system of government as a dictatorship of the proletariat. It bears that name to the present day. The Government and the Bolshevik Party continually assure the Russian workers that the existing State is their State—not, indeed, a State organized in accordance with the chance interests of individual workmen but the State of the working class as a whole. Further, they sought to maintain that all that happened in Russia was done in the interests of proletarian government. Compromises, apparent injustices in individual instances, the sacrifices that were continually being demanded of the workers—all these were necessitated by the demands of the proletarian State. Nevertheless, it was difficult for the ordinary factory worker to persuade himself that he exercised a class dictatorship over his technical manager, for the tram-conductor to feel that he was master of the well-paid official whose fare he collected, and for an unemployed man to imagine himself the ruler of the owner of the provision store before whose window he stood and gazed hungrily. Ever since 1921 Lenin's Russia was in truth a compound of State Capitalism with a proletarian myth. The most extraordinary aspect of the situation was that no special attempt was made to conceal the real state of affairs. Lenin and his successors have always sincerely and openly discussed the true facts. If, however, the complicated existing governmental system is depicted as a dictatorship of the proletariat, the picture will belong to the realm of fantasy and not of truth.

The beginnings of the proletarian myth stretch back to 1918, to the time when Soviet democracy was replaced in Russia by a Party dictatorship, although no attempt was made to change the name of the State from that of a Soviet State, and the fiction was maintained that everything that was done in Russia was done in the name of and by the self-governing Soviets. The real roots of the Bolshevik myth of the proletariat are, nevertheless, to be found in the works of Marx and Engels. According to Marx it was for Communism to point the right path to the proletariat, and the actions of the Communists are those of the proletariat as a class in the historical sense of the term, even though any number of 'backward' workmen protest against them. It is not for the proletariat to seek to improve the condition of the individual workman. Its great mission is the liberation of mankind. And in executing this mission it will be called upon to make greater sacrifices than the other classes. This was the interpretation placed by Marx and Engels upon their policy—for example, in the *Neue Rheinische Zeitung*—in styling it a proletarian policy; and in a similar manner Lenin and the Bolshevik Party leaders could claim that their State was a proletarian State and all their actions were acts done in the name of the proletariat.

The completion of the middle-class revolution, the liberation of the peasants, and the restoration of liberty to oppressed peoples, &c., are in Marx's and Engels's view tasks to be fulfilled by the working class. These, however, are simple and obvious matters of fact. The fable first appeared in the moment in which the proletariat falsely identified the completed phase of middle-class evolution with the coming

proletarian and Socialist phase. The dictatorship of the
proletariat is simultaneously the realization of Socialism.
Nevertheless, Lenin had always admitted that Soviet Russia
was not a purely Socialist State but a form of State Capitalism
in which both middle-class and Socialist elements were
present. The fable here conflicts glaringly with the truth. In
his famous essay in 1923 on the organization of co-operative
societies, however, Lenin had pointed out a way by which
this conflict might one day be resolved: Socialism would be
realized when once the cultural level of the Russian peasants
had been raised and they had been united in co-operative
societies. At the same time no effort must be spared to
enlarge the State-controlled industries, to place them on a
higher technical level, and to increase the number of workmen employed by them. A State-controlled industry of
greater productivity and efficiency—Lenin was specially
interested in plans for the electrification of Russia—should
form the foundation for the peasant co-operative societies
and engage with them in an exchange of commodities. The
result would be Socialism.

Such was the testament in an economic sense left by Lenin
to his Party and the Russian nation. If Lenin was right, the
Russia certainly was not a Socialist State in the years 1921-4,
but it could become one if the difficulties arising out of
deflation and currency stabilization had once been overcome;
and become one in a few years without any specially dramatic
events and, above all, by an organized evolutionary process
in Russia itself that paid no regard to the progress of world
revolution.

'Socialism' is capable of many interpretations. The term
is defenceless against those who misuse it. Lenin laid a strict
interpretation upon it in the sense of Marxism and his whole
attitude to Socialism can only be criticized by bearing in
mind Marx's definition. The meaning attached by Marx to
Socialism in an economic sense can be discerned quite clearly
in his *Capital* and other works. Marx distinguished between
three phases: a primitive phase in which the producers—
manual workers and peasants—are also owners of the means
of production; a second phase—Capitalism—in which the
working man finds himself severed from the means of pro-

duction that are now the property of a minority in whose interest the dispossessed working man must labour; and a third phase—Socialism—in which the working man recovers his control over the means of production. The spoiler is now himself despoiled. Nevertheless, there is no return to the primitive phase, and no fresh division of the means of production among small proprietors, but instead centralized production is maintained—this time in the interests of all. In a Socialist organization of society barter in the barest necessities of life would replace trading in goods with its exploitation of markets, striving after profits and accumulations of unwanted goods.

The Russian Revolution in 1917 destroyed agriculture on a large scale. It also resulted in the return to a system of small ownership and small farms. This was a development that had nothing in common with Socialism and that did not take on a more Socialist character merely through the incorporation of ten or a hundred peasant proprietors in a co-operative society. For such a society produced goods, made and accumulated profits, and would be a middle-class organization in a middle-class monetary system. Indeed Lenin's theory of the peasant co-operative societies as a form of Socialism is irreconcilable with Marxian economics. Nevertheless, Lenin had received absolution in anticipation of his 'sin against Marxism' from the hands of no less a person than Marx himself.

During the last years of his life Marx had followed with intense interest the revolutionary movement in Russia that led to the assassination of Alexander II. It has already been stated that the *Naródniki* were in those days the leaders of revolution—intellectuals inspired with the ideal of liberating the Russian peasants. The industrial proletariat at that time played no political part in Russia. The *Naródniki* persuaded themselves that certain remains of communal property still to be found in Russian villages were capable of further development and that a peasant Socialism based on village councils would one day replace the Tsars. In this manner Russia would avoid passing through the phase in the evolution of western Europe characterized by fully developed industrial Capitalism and proletarian Socialism, and would pass direct from Tsarist feudalism to a nationalist Russian peasant Socialism. During these last years Marx was often asked by Russian revolutionaries for his opinion on this question. If Marx had been nothing more than a Socialist *doctrinaire*, he would have been forced to reply to the *Naródniki* that their ideas had nothing in common with his. Marx, however, was a revolutionary first and foremost, and a theoretical economist only in the second place. Hence it was that he hailed the *Naródniki* movement with enthusiasm and made possible a reconciliation between their ideals and his own theories. A Russian translation of the Communist Manifesto appeared in 1882 with a preface by Marx and Engels, in which they say:

'The purpose of the Communist Manifesto was to proclaim the inescapable and approaching disappearance of the present system of middle-class ownership. In Russia, however, in addition to a feverish development of Capitalism and the beginnings of middle-class property ownership, the greater part of the land is to be found in the communal possession of the peasants. The problem is: Can the Russian village community—an already much dilapidated relic of the primitive communal ownership of land—develop directly into a higher Communist type of landownership, or must it undergo the same dissolution that took place in the historical evolution of the West? The only possible answer to-day to this question is: If the Russian Revolution is the signal for a workers' revolution in the West, and if these complement one another, then the present-day system of communal ownership in Russia can serve as the starting-point for a Communist development.'

The *Naródniki* grossly exaggerated the extent cf communal ownership in Russia. It had completely vanished by the outbreak of the Russian Revolution. It is of importance, however, to find that in 1882 Marx assented to the existence of peasant Socialism in Russia at the side of proletarian Socialism in western Europe. Moreover, if the victory of the Revolution over the Tsar could be accomplished in no other way, then Marx was also prepared to concede to Russia a separate national development on a peasant basis. It is true that Marx only considered peasant Communism possible in Russia if the true Socialist Workers' Revolution had simultaneously proved victorious in western Europe—if, in other words, an agrarian Socialist Russia could find its support in a proletarian Socialist western Europe. Thus, when Lenin found a new way to Socialism for Russia in 1923 through peasant co-operative societies, he was able to link up his ideas with those of Marx. At the same time his ideas implied a return to *Naródniki* theories. There is indeed an element of tragedy in the fact that after fighting a ruthless political battle with the Social Revolutionaries for thirty years Lenin was forced at the close of his life to bring his system into some sort of agreement with their ideals. The force of social evolution is indeed stronger than the will of any Party organization. When the Russian Revolution destroyed feudalism together with the bigger private capitalists, and when it could not be carried on by the industrial proletariat alone, then it was forced of necessity to seek a middle path that led it by way of State Capitalism and peasant co-operative societies to a nationalist Russian 'Socialism' wearing *Naródniki* colours. In his old age Lenin was prepared to tread this path. Stalin has followed it.

Marx, as a western European, could only conceive of a *Naródniki* revolution in Russia as parallel to and in alliance with the workers' revolution in the West. On the other hand Lenin was forced after 1921 to content himself with a Russian revolution in the midst of a world that had remained capitalist. If the last speeches and writings of Lenin are read with care, it will be seen how he came to concentrate his thoughts wholly upon Russia and how he was determined to achieve what he called Socialism in Russia alone. International connexions are only of importance for Russia in so far as they are able to protect her from foreign invasion. There is no longer any mention of Russia's receiving definite support from a world revolution. All justification for the existence of the Third International was therewith destroyed and it only remains to ask why Lenin and his successors maintained it. Enemies of Bolshevism frequently declare that Soviet Russia makes use of the Third International in the interests of its foreign policy or that it is used as a magnet to attract the attention of foreign workers to Russia. An impartial study reveals both views to be false. It would indeed be serviceable from the standpoint of Russian foreign policy if a Communist Party dependent upon Russia were to become the Government of a foreign country. Since 1921, however, Communists have not achieved power in any non-Russian country; they never had any hope of doing so; and they have nowhere exercised any real influence upon the existing Government. If it is to be successful, Russian foreign policy must be prepared to treat with existing Governments and Parties. The existence of Communist Parties in the countries themselves, far from lightening only helped to render more difficult Russia's relations with Mussolini, Kemal Pasha, Germany, England, &c. Russian diplomacy would work better and be more fruitful of results if it was not compromised by the existence of the Third International. Russian diplomacy and foreign trade are wholly independent of the Third International, even though they both have a common base in the Central Committee of the Communist Party in Moscow. Nevertheless, the rulers of Russia are well aware that if they wish their foreign policy to be successful they must not identify it with the Communist International.

Moreover, Soviet Russia is deeply concerned to gain the friendship of the working class throughout the world. Now the majority of the international proletariat since 1921 has once more belonged to the Social Democrat Party and the continual attacks made by Communists on Social Democrat Party officials have not been calculated to promote feelings of friendship for Russia. It is in spite of and not because of the local Communist Party that a Social Democrat remains friendly to Soviet Russia. The path leading to the friendship of the majority of European and American workmen is closed and not opened to Soviet Russia by the activities of the Communist International. It will be shown below that the existence of the Third International has exercised a prejudicial effect even upon the relations between Soviet Russia and the Asiatic peoples engaged in a struggle against Imperialism. Moreover, the Communist Parties in foreign lands can be of little real assistance to Soviet Russia in its upward path and only do harm to its international position. For all these reasons it appears all the more extraordinary that the Soviet Government should not have long ago cast off the Third International. As a matter of fact two attempts have been

made by the Bolshevik rulers of Russia in the past decade to
dissolve the Communist International: the policy of a united
front on the part of the international proletariat that was
pursued from 1921 to 1923, and the attempt to achieve the
unification of the Trade Unions in an international sense that
was made from 1925 to 1927. Both these attempts ended in
failure because they were pursued by Moscow in a hesitant
and contradictory manner.

What is the mysterious force that has time and again
bound together Soviet Russia and the Communist International during the past decade? It is the proletarian and
Socialist fable which even Russian Bolshevism cannot dispense with and whose importance for Russian domestic policy
has grown even greater since 1928. If a dictatorship of
the proletariat really existed in Russia, the fact would be
recognized by the international proletariat or at least by
its revolutionary element. If all the international Labour
organizations were to certify that Soviet Russia is a middle-
class State, their testimony would not overthrow the Soviet
Government but would certainly prejudice its relations with
the Russian proletariat. The recognition and moral support
of international opinion has always been of great importance
to Russian revolutionaries. The fact of least importance was
that Russian exiles received money or other assistance from
citizens of the countries in which they found an asylum.
What was of extreme importance was that the revolutionaries
became convinced that they formed a part of the great international movement for the liberation of mankind. This was
the reason that led the *Naródniki* in the seventies and
eighties of the last century to seek the blessing of Marx and
Engels for their work. This was the reason why the Russian
Social Democrats in pre-War days were enthusiastic members
of the Second International. This was the reason why Lenin
at the time of the World War sought to find in the Zimmerwald movement a moral support for the coming revolution in
Russia. In the years 1918–20 the Bolsheviks expected their
material salvation to come to them directly from the hands
of the Third International. It was of decisive importance
during the Cronstadt rebellion in 1921 not only that all White
Guards and Monarchists in foreign countries supported the

rebels but that the entire revolutionary working class in Europe stood behind the Soviet Government.

The Third World Congress in the summer of 1921 and the Fourth World Congress towards the close of 1922 expressly approved the NEP in Russia and declared its adoption to be necessary in the interests of the international proletariat and Socialism. Lenin and his successors were sincerely convinced that the Russian Revolution in 1917 was a great historical achievement of the world proletariat and that workers in every country were under an obligation to recognize and support Soviet Russia. The Social Democrats in Europe very naturally sought to defend themselves against the continuous Bolshevik attacks by criticizing Soviet Russia and by adopting the views of exiled Menshevik leaders. The rulers of Soviet Russia were therefore anxious to find some thoroughly reliable means of combating Menshevism and anti-Bolshevism in Social Democracy throughout the world. The first demand made by the Bolsheviks of every Communist Party abroad was its recognition of the proletarian and Socialist character of the Soviet State. The Communist International was therefore not to lay stress in its propaganda on the State capitalist character of the Soviet State with its system of compromises but rather on the revolutionary and proletarian legend. A classic witness to the existence of this Soviet Russian legend is to be found in the resolution passed by the Third World Congress in July 1921 on the subject of the tactics to be pursued by the Russian Communist Party. The resolution ran:

'The Third World Congress of the Communist International looks back in admiration upon almost four years of struggle by the Russian proletariat for the capture and retention of political power. The Congress unanimously approves the policy pursued by the Russian Communist Party, which from the outset has accurately judged the dangers implicit in each situation as it occurred and, true to the principles of revolutionary Marxism, has always found ways and means to overcome them; and which—after the temporary conclusion of the Civil War—by its policy towards the peasants, and in the questions of concessions and industrial reconstruction, has concentrated under its leadership all the energy of the proletariat upon maintaining its dictatorship in Russia until the proletariat in western Europe shall be able to come to the assistance of their brothers.

'In thus giving expression to its conviction that it is only
thanks to this resolute and purposeful policy on the part of the
Russian Communist Party that Soviet Russia will continue to be
regarded as the first and most important fortress of the world
revolution, the World Congress brands as treachery the conduct
of the Mensheviks in all countries who by their attacks upon
Soviet Russia and the policy of the Russian Communist Party
have strengthened the hands of the capitalist reactionaries in
their war against Russia, and have attempted to delay the coming
of the Socialist Revolution throughout the world. The World
Congress calls upon the proletariat in all countries to place itself
unanimously at the side of Russian workmen and peasants and to
make the October Revolution a reality throughout the whole
world. Long live the war for the dictatorship of the proletariat!
Long live the Socialist Revolution!'

A marked contradiction thus came into existence in the
years 1921-3 between the Russian revolutionary manner of
speech of the Communist International and its Revisionist
actions. Communist policy in these years was inspired by the
idea of the united front. The argument ran somewhat as
follows: Communists and Social Democrats are not agreed
in their aims. But the international proletariat is confronted with urgent problems of the day. The workmen must
defend their political freedom, hours of work, social gains, and
wages, against the attack of their employers. The Communist
workman is as much interested in these matters as is the
Social Democrat, Christian Socialist, or non-Party workman.
And this great struggle for daily needs cannot be led by the
Communist minority among the workers alone but must be
waged by the proletariat as a whole. For this reason Communists should go to the Social Democrats and the Trade
Unions and say to them that, even if agreement did not
exist in the question of the dictatorship of the proletariat, it
existed in that of the daily bread of the working class, and
that they should therefore join together in the struggle for
'the price of bread'.

Even in the days when it was pursuing this policy of a
united front the Communist International sought to find a
revolutionary alibi by demonstrating that the Social Democrat leaders were incapable of fighting for the smallest social
reforms. Common action would result in bringing the entire

proletariat under the control of the Communists, and out of
the lesser struggle for economic objects there would slowly
evolve again the revolutionary struggle for power. These
arguments, nevertheless, failed to alter the fact that a systematic pursuit of the policy of a united front must result
in the disappearance of the Communist Parties. It is indeed
possible for a Party to ally itself with another for a definite
time without losing its individuality. It is not possible for a
Party to change its principles to suit those of another for a
long period of time; nor can it declare that the other Party
merely exists to formulate a policy which it will itself carry
out. What has been the effect of the pursuit of a policy of a
united front with the Conservatives upon the English Liberal
Party since the World War? What doom awaits the German
National and German Peoples' Parties in consequence of their
pursuance of a similar policy with the National Socialists in
the years 1930–2? It was obvious that the Communists must
be the sufferers as a result of the pursuit of a common platform with the Social Democrats in Europe; for they were the
weaker party in the alliance and the policy to be followed by
the 'United Front' would be a Social Democrat and not a
Communist policy. The leaders of the Communist International also found a political excuse for the economic aspect
of their policy of a united front in the existence of a Labour
Government. In association with Social Democrats, Communists were to try to capture a majority in Parliament and
then form a Coalition Government with them.

The following definition of a Labour Government was
formulated at Leipzig in 1923 at the Congress of the German
Communist Party: 'It [a Labour Government] is neither the
dictatorship of the proletariat nor a constitutional approach
to it. It denotes an attempt on the part of the working class
within the framework and employing the methods of middle-
class democracy to pursue a Labour policy with the support
of proletarian institutions and a proletarian mass movement.'
This was in effect the translation to the Continent of the
policy which Lenin had recommended in 1920 for adoption in
England. A Labour Government that attains to power by
peaceful and legal means can only govern within the framework of the middle-class social and political order. The

economic policy of a Government of this type cannot be Socialist. It must consist in a middle-class Radical financial policy combined with participation by the State in great industrial undertakings—the so-called theory of real values. The existence of a Labour Government even within the limits of a middle-class democratic State is an important victory for the working class. The history of Labour Government in England witnesses to the truth of this statement. When, however, the Communists came forward with proposals of this nature, they immediately abandoned their claim to be looked upon as a separate Party; for a parliamentary Labour Government is in its essentials entirely a Social Democrat institution. Even the distinction between Communists and Social Democrats—that the Social Democrats were prepared to enter a coalition with the middle-class Parties whereas the Communists were only prepared to coalesce within the boundaries of Socialism—did not continue to operate. For the policy of a united front in Germany was extended to cover the Christian Socialist workmen and thus a completely representative German Labour Government would have included leaders of the Christian Trade Unions under the influence of the Centre Party. And when the Executive of the Communist International extended the term 'Labour' Government to cover the Workers' and Peasants' Government that was the ideal to be pursued in every land— then, indeed, the theoretical possibilities of coalitions became indefinite. What could not be comprised under the term 'Peasant Party' in central and western Europe?

At this distance of time it is a cause for astonishment that the same members of the Communist International who in 1919-20 were animated by the ideal of insurrection and world revolution accepted Communist Revisionism in 1921-3. It must not, however, be forgotten that after the World War the Communist International became the meeting-place of all workmen and officials who were desirous of carrying on the formal pre-War Radicalism. The reconstructed post-War Social Democrat International pursued a Revisionist policy. The result was that the Social Democrat Parties did not always display sufficient energy in keeping their policy free from middle-class capitalist ideas. An important advance had been made, nevertheless, by the abandonment of the superficially Radical phraseology of pre-War days. On the other hand the Communist International after 1921 returned to the official pre-War Radicalism characterized by political passivity, camouflaged Reformist practices, and intoxication with the ultimate aim. The ideal State pictured by Radical workmen before 1914 had now been realized in Soviet Russia. The vision of Soviet Russia as it revealed itself to the eyes of these workmen afforded them consolation in their daily cares and embodied their hopes of a better future. And they consoled themselves for the compromise and tactical manœuvres of Soviet Russia and the Communist International by saying: The Bolsheviks are the leaders of the world revolution. What they do cannot be inspired by motives of expediency. One must trust them, even if one cannot always understand their policy, and one must time and again seek inspiration in the Russian Revolution.

After 1921 the Communist International was thus permeated simultaneously from above and below by a belief in the revolutionary proletarian legend. This is the secret of its existence. It is a singular and yet comprehensible paradox that the Communist International at one and the same time sharply criticizes the Second International in its pre-War form and continues its work. For the Communist criticism of the Second International washes away the 'sin' of 1914, and thus makes ready the path for the continued use of the old phraseology, whilst the post-War Socialist International must in some form or other accept the responsibility for the 'sin' of 1914 and cannot therefore continue to use the old pseudo-Radical catchwords. It was precisely its combination of non-revolutionary, Revisionist action with a pseudo-Radical habit of speech that had for its subject Soviet Russia that enabled the Communist International, even after 1921, to retain a large proportion of its supporters. This combination was successful in satisfying not only the workers desirous of carrying on pre-War Radicalism but also up to a certain degree the Utopian Radical proletarian who found in it a means of ventilating his vague hopes of revolution and his hatred of State and Society and Social Democrats. Nevertheless, it is impossible for a great Labour movement to

subsist, in the present stirring and truly revolutionary condition of the world, upon a legend alone. The crisis would come
in the same moment that the hard hailstones of actual facts
fell upon the glass-house of the Communist International
and compelled at least a part of its members and officials to
think for themselves.

The Communist International subsisted upon a mixture of
Russian revolutionary theories and Reformist practice. And
the International would collapse the moment either of these
elements was taken seriously. If a Communist was sincerely
convinced that the working class could strive for reform and
not revolution in the existing state of the world, then the
phrases emanating from the Russian Revolution must be
unwelcome in his ears and he must become aware of the
existence of Reformist practice in Soviet Russia itself. He
would be forced to ask himself the question whether there
was any justification for a separate existence of a Communist Party beside the Social Democrat Party. If, however,
a Communist believed seriously in the revolutionary phrases,
and wished to bring about a revolution in his own country,
then he must speedily be brought to the recognition of the
fact that the Executive of the Communist International with
its policy of a united front was an obstacle in the way of
revolution. Thus he would be led to see through the contradictions inherent in the Communist International and to
discover their cause in the system of State Capitalism in
Russia that concealed itself beneath the cloak of a dictatorship of the proletariat. These two trends of Communist
opinion resulted in the development after 1921 of a 'Left' and
a 'Right' Wing group within the Communist International
in distinction to the loyal 'Centre'. Each trend had its own
starting-point and they only came together in their common
matter-of-fact Marxian criticism of conditions in Soviet
Russia. The leaders of the Communist International saw in
these two trends of opinion nothing more nor less than the
invasion of their domains by anti-Bolshevism and they sought
to strangle this opposition by all the means available to them.

The iron discipline imposed upon the Communists for the
purpose of the Civil War was now used to crush subversive
opinion in their own ranks. The rulers of Russia feared in

even the slightest divergence from the official tenets the
beginning of the end—namely, the growth of a doubt as to the
proletarian-Socialist character of the Soviet State. For this
reason they have branded every form of opposition both in
the Communist International as well as in Russia itself since
1921 as counter-revolutionary and anti-Bolshevik, and as
something to be destroyed by all the means that lay in their
power. Ever since 1921 all independent critical thought has
been stifled by official persecution both in Soviet Russia and
in the Communist International. The Bolshevik Empire
resembles the empire ruled over by the Emperor in Andersen's
immortal fairy-tale. The Emperor can walk about naked
because every one who fails to see his supposititious clothes
is a moral outcast. Similarly the Emperor walks through the
Bolshevik Empire and to his right and left go Party officials
driving away every one who dares to cry aloud 'The Emperor
is naked!' Thus in 1921 Paul Levi and his friends were
expelled from the German Communist Party. Levi was one
of the very few German Socialists who had given Lenin his
unconditional support before the Bolshevik Party came into
power. He began as early as the winter of 1920-1 to entertain
doubts about the imminence of a proletarian revolution in
Germany and in doing so anticipated the decisions taken by
the Third World Congress. In the days of the March Action
in 1921 Levi was no longer Chairman of the Party but he was
one of its outstanding leaders and a member of the Reichstag.
He strongly disapproved of the March Action and wrote a
pamphlet in which is to be found everything that was subsequently said in criticism of the March Action by Lenin and
other important Bolsheviks at the Third World Congress.

It might have been expected that as a result the Executive
of the Communist International would have ceremoniously
invested Paul Levi after the World Congress with the leadership of the German Communist Party as being the outstanding Bolshevik in Germany. Instead Levi was expelled from
both the Party and the International. The explanation was
that, in addition to pointing out the mistakes of the German
Communist Party, Levi had gone on to depict the mistakes
of the Executive and to tell the truth about the condition
of Soviet Russia. Moreover, he refused to be a party to

the traditional veneration for anything and everything that happened in Russia. His presence could therefore no longer be tolerated in the Communist International. Paul Levi subsequently returned to the Social Democrat Party. The greater number of members of the KPD had also strongly opposed Levi's action owing to a fundamental political difference of opinion. In opposition to Levi these members still believed in the imminence of a German working-class revolution and wished to promote it by every means available to them. The trend of opinion in the Communist International which rejected the Revisionist policy of the Executive since 1921, and which was opposed to a united front and Labour Governments, constituted the so-called Left. This Left comprised practically the whole Italian Communist Party led by Bordiga, who was noted for his high character and his keen ideological mind. The circles in Italy upon whose support the Executive might have counted in its pursuit of the new policy had already fallen away under the leadership of Serrati. It is noteworthy that Serrati rejoined the International in its changed condition. The Executive devoted all its energies to driving Bordiga out of the Italian Communist Party and to establishing a Central Committee that would be subservient to it. Meanwhile the Fascists marched from victory to victory. In 1922 Mussolini became dictator of Italy.

In Germany the Central Committee of the KPD, under the chairmanship of Brandler, sought to carry out punctiliously the policy laid down by the Executive and the World Congresses. Although, in 1923, under the influence of the occupation of the Ruhr and inflation, the disintegration political and economic of middle-class Germany proceeded apace, the Central Committee of the KPD forbade propaganda in favour of a dictatorship of the proletariat and the Socialist revolution. It remained faithful to the policy of a united front and Labour Government. And this policy led to practical results in Saxony and Thuringia, where Social Democrat Governments came into power and maintained themselves with the help of the Communist votes in the Landtag. In October the Communists themselves accepted several portfolios. For the first time a Labour Government in the sense

preached by the Communists had come into existence. The
Central Committee hoped to see this system of government
extended from Saxony and Thuringia to cover all Germany.
The Left Wing in the KPD, supported by the Party organization in Hamburg and Berlin, refused to support this policy, in
the belief that it would destroy all possibility of a revolution
in Germany. Although the Left complained to Moscow, the
rulers of Soviet Russia remained true to their Revisionist
policy; and it was not until August 1923 that a change in
opinion made itself apparent in Russia. Meanwhile, the
Soviet Government watched the steadily increasing discontent in Germany, especially after a general strike had resulted
in the fall of Cuno's middle-class and Conservative Government. Stresemann succeeded Cuno at the head of a Coalition
Government of Social Democrats and the Centre. The
French were firmly established in the Ruhr and the Rhine-
land. The Kahr-Hitler Putsch was in preparation in Bavaria.
The mark became valueless. Germany was threatened with a
dissolution of the Reich and civil war.

The Bolsheviks now began to believe once more in the
possibility of a German proletarian revolution and demanded
that the KPD should lead it. Nevertheless, Soviet Russia in
1923 was no longer vitally interested in the victory of a proletarian revolution in Germany, since the conclusion of the
Treaty of Rapallo rendered possible friendly relations with
a middle-class German Government. At the same time if
revolution should break out in Germany the Third International did not wish to lose an opportunity for refurbishing
its revolutionary laurels. But it was soon shown that the
Communist International was no longer capable of leading a
revolution. The Central Committee of the KPD continued
even after August 1923 its Revisionist, non-revolutionary
agitation for the establishment of a Labour Government, &c.;
and simultaneously made secret preparations for revolution
in the form of a conspiracy without the co-operation of the
great masses of the proletariat. This led to the presence in
the Communist secret organizations of all possible types of
adventurers and spies. When, however, in October 1923,
open warfare was to begin, the Central Committee realized
its unfitness for the struggle and the whole preparations

exploded like a toy balloon. In Saxony and Thuringia the
Government of the Reich dissolved the Labour Governments
with the help of the Reichswehr and without meeting with
any opposition. In consequence of a misunderstanding
several hundreds of Communist workmen in Hamburg took
up arms. They were defeated after a sanguinary battle with
the police. Nothing of a political or military nature occurred
anywhere else in Germany. After the cessation of the Ruhr
conflict and the stabilization of the mark the German middle-
class was able in the winter of 1923-4 to strengthen its hold
on the government of Germany.

The collapse of the revolutionary movement in Germany
in October 1923 was the second—this time decisive—defeat
sustained by the Communist International. The first was
Mussolini's accession to power in Italy. Nor was the fact that
a proletarian revolution had proved unsuccessful in Germany
the most depressing aspect of this second defeat. It is possible to hold very various opinions on the subject of whether
a revolution of this type would have been possible in Germany
in 1923 and in what manner it should have been carried
out. The most discouraging aspect was the inefficiency and
weakness displayed by the Communists in their tactics and
strategy. For two long years no opportunity for revolution in
Germany had presented itself to the rulers of Russia. Then
suddenly they discovered the imminence of a German revolution, and instead of a great popular movement they produced a conspiracy. The bureaucratic officials of the German
Communist Party kept their eyes obediently turned on
Russia. They never permitted themselves an independent
idea and their sole desire was to follow precisely the policy
laid down for them by the Executive. That such a mechanical
body of subservient Party officials could not lead a revolution
is obvious. Ever since the Parties composing the Communist
International have served solely as disseminators of Soviet
Russian legends they have ceased to be capable of real
political activity. After October 1923 the Communist International refrained from any further attempts to promote
revolution in Europe.

The members of the KPD were embittered as a result of the
failure of their Party's policy. They supported the Left Wing

Opposition that had sharply criticized the conduct of the Central Committee from 1921 onwards. The Executive of the Communist International also attempted to beat a retreat by admitting some mistakes on their own part at the same time as they placed the principal share in the responsibility for the defeat in October upon the shoulders of Brandler. Yet Brandler had never for an instant deviated from the instructions given by the Executive, and his policy was approved by the leading men in Russia up to the very last. These men now hoped by unjustly blaming Brandler and by effecting a compromise with the Left to retain the working-class members of the KPD within the Third International. For the complete break-up of the KPD was possible at the close of 1923 and the beginning of 1924, and would have been followed by that of the Third International.

Owing to his illness Lenin had no share in the detailed work of the leaders of the Third International in 1923-4. Nevertheless, the course followed by the Third International that led to defeat and paralysis was laid down by Lenin himself at the Third World Congress. The downfall and break-up of the Third International is no less the work of Lenin than was the resuscitation of Soviet Russia as a result of the NEP.

STALIN *VERSUS* TROTSKY, 1924-7

THE question of the succession to Lenin became actual in 1922 in consequence of his long illness. It was obvious that his work could not be carried on by any particular individual or individuals, but that his heir must be the Bolshevik Party as a whole. In practice this would mean the government of the 'Old Guard', who in the years succeeding to 1903 had built up the Party in common with Lenin. Lenin's cloak thus fell upon the shoulders of Zinoviev and Kamenev. Since, however, they were both politicians and ideologues, they needed the assistance of a practical organizer. Such a one was found in Stalin. Stalin had for years been a member of the Party and was a Georgian, or Grusian (as they called themselves), from the Caucasus. The Georgians have contributed a whole series of brilliant men to the Russian revolutionary and Socialist movement. There were many Georgians among the influential Mensheviks in 1917. In the revolutionary movement in the days of the Tsars nationality played no part and Great Russians, Ukrainians, Jews, Poles, Letts, and Georgians worked together with no thought save of the common cause.

Stalin is an educated Russian revolutionary of the pre-War type. The fact that he belonged by blood to the small nation of Georgians was at the most responsible for his special interest in the problem of Socialism and Nationalism. It is an exaggeration to connect Stalin in any way with Circassian romances. In February 1913, in a letter written from Galicia to Maxim Gorki, Lenin said that he agreed with his opinion that it was essential to take Nationalism seriously. Lenin continued: 'We have here a fine type of Grusian' working on a great study of the question of nationalities for which he has collected the entire Austrian material. The 'Grusian' was Stalin, who had just succeeded in escaping from Siberia and who lived for a time in Cracow and Vienna. After 1917 Stalin gradually became more and more prominent as an organizer. In the spring of 1917 he still belonged to the moderate group led by Kamenev and it was only by slow degrees that he became a supporter of Lenin's policy. As Secretary-General of the Bolshevik Party in 1922 Stalin exercised supreme control over the Party machinery. A Committee of Three—Zinoviev, Kamenev, Stalin—ruled Russia from 1922 to 1925. No constitutional existence was given to this 'Committee' and the Central Committee of the Communist Party continued as before to take all important decisions. In every important matter, however, these three men made common cause after previously consulting with each other. Any proposal they made was at once accepted by the Central Committee, or its smaller sub-committee, the Political Bureau.

This government by old-time Bolsheviks meant the exclusion of Trotsky from the conduct of affairs. True, he remained a member of the Central Committee and People's Commissar for War, but his advice was not asked by the three ruling personalities before they decided upon any important action. Although Trotsky enjoyed great authority among the masses of the nation, the clique of old-time Bolsheviks always looked upon him as an interloper. It was known that Trotsky was not in agreement with these old-time Bolsheviks in important matters of policy and organization. As long as Lenin was well, and controlled the Party himself, he had contrived to bridge the gulf separating these old-time Bolsheviks from Trotsky, but the moment Lenin fell ill the chasm was reopened. Towards the close of 1923 Trotsky openly came forward in opposition to the three rulers of Russia. He showed that a small bureaucratic clique had seized power; that the members of the Party no longer possessed their right of self-determination; and that the new leaders of the International were involving it in defeat after defeat. It was hardly astonishing that the German Revolution should have collapsed so pitifully in 1923 if the Bolshevik Party and the International were led by the very men who had in 1917 threatened to ruin the revolution in Russia. In conjunction with Lenin, Trotsky had in 1917 led the revolution to victory, despite the opposition of the 'Opportunists' Zinoviev and Kamenev. What moral right then had this so-called Old Guard autocratically to lead the Party and the International proletarian movement? Although an old group of leaders may have rendered services that will live on in history, there is always the danger that they will grow stiff and bloodless in the same manner as the Social Democrat leaders before the World War. Democratic control on the part of the members and the recruitment of new members from the coming generations could alone save the Russian Communist Party from destruction.

It is obvious that these arguments of Trotsky's attacked the very essence of Bolshevism, namely, the hierarchic construction of the Party from below upwards, and the traditional authority of the old Bolshevik Central Committee. If, however, the dictatorship within the Party were destroyed, then the dictatorship of the Party itself over the Russian peoples could no longer be maintained in its present form. Of necessity the one involved the other. At the end of 1923 and the beginning of 1924 an animated discussion took place within the Party on the subject of Trotsky's opposition. His views were enthusiastically supported by the younger members and especially by the educated proletarian students in the working-class universities. The entire Party machine was, however, opposed to him—and the machine ruled the members. Hence the Party Congress in 1924 declared itself unanimously against Trotsky and for the three rulers of Russia. Trotsky was dismissed from the Commissariat of War and withdrew, temporarily, from all active participation in politics. The Party dictatorship and the NEP continued without further opposition.

The membership of the Russian Communist Party rose by the beginning of 1927 to a total of 1,200,000. Of these, about 600,000 were employees and officials of all kinds. Among these employees were a quarter of a million former workmen and 150,000 ex-peasants. The membership of the Party also included 150,000 peasants still engaged in agriculture and 450,000 workers in factories. Thus the employees (agents of the governmental machine) and peasants together composed almost two-thirds of the total membership of the Party and the actual factory workers only just over one-third.

The governmental apparatus in Russia continually renewed itself from the ranks of clever ex-workers and ex-peasants.

In itself this is a sound principle of utilizing the best forces
in the nation. A genuine dictatorship of the proletariat
could not dispense with able officials. These officials, however, would in such a case be subject to a continuous democratic control exercised by the masses and would thus maintain connexion with the masses. In the Russian dictatorship,
on the contrary, the official ruled the masses with the aid of
Party and State discipline. Hence the ex-proletarian under
this system, on entering the service of the governmental
machine, ceased psychologically and actually to be a member
of the working class.

The numerical proportion of workers to non-workers
among the members of the Russian Communist Party is
typical and significant. But it is less the proportion among
the ordinary members than among the members of the Party
administrative apparatus that is of decisive importance. It
was estimated in 1927 that in the Party committees charged
with the taking of decisions—not only in the Central Committee itself, but also in the local administrative bodies
throughout the country—only a tenth of the membership
consisted of actual factory workers. The State capitalistic
governmental machine had thus come to be independent of
the productive classes in the nation.

The reconstruction of Russian industry made great strides
from 1924 onwards. In 1927 the pre-War rate of production
had almost been restored and the total of actual factory
hands at work amounted in that year to 2,300,000. The
industrialization of Russia has indeed been in progress ever
since 1921 and not only in recent years. The achievement of
the six years 1921–7, in which there was little or nothing in
the way of material from which to build, is even more deserv-
ing of praise than the results obtained in more recent years,
when a firm foundation had already been laid. Moreover,
the careful advance calculations and planning of economic
development for many years to come is as old as Soviet
Russia itself, and not a sensational new discovery of the past
five years.

The real wages of the Russian workman rose considerably
up to 1925, sank in 1926, and rose again in 1927. It is true
that the workmen complain of the power wielded by the

factory management in whose hands lie in reality the engagement and dismissal of workmen. In the event of disputes between the workmen and the management the State Economic Council decides the issue in a dictatorial fashion by means of compulsory arbitration.

Production also increased in the country districts between 1924 and 1927—years in which Russia was free from famine. Those were years in which every one could purchase food-supplies of the best quality in the shops to the limit of his purchasing capacity. Industrial products were scarce and much dearer than in Europe. Increased prosperity brought social distinctions back to life among the peasants. It is incontestable that the typical Russian form of agrarian middle class, the Kulaks, the village money-lenders, and wealthier peasants, increased in number and influence. There are no figures available to show what percentage of the Russian peasants then belonged to the Kulak class; for the characteristic of the Kulak is less his possession of a large farm than of money for speculative purposes, and hence the difficulty of arriving at any precise statistical estimation of the number of Kulaks. In addition to this difficulty the Russian Government and the Opposition were then engaged in a controversy as to the nature and number of Kulaks. The one side continually reproached the other with under- or over-estimating the danger from the Kulaks, with the result that agrarian statistics were made to serve the purpose of this dispute within the Communist Party itself. Nevertheless, the number of agricultural labourers affords a means of ascertaining the social differences existing in the Russian villages. These agricultural labourers were said, in 1927, to have numbered 1,600,000. Their state was deplorable. Only 20 per cent. of their number were members of Trade Unions. Their real wages were less than before the War, and their daily hours of work were seldom less than ten. Indeed, no limitations were set to their hours of work in the majority of cases, and their wages were paid irregularly and often after months of waiting.

The Kulaks were the sole employers of agricultural labour. The small peasants and even those with moderate-sized farms employed no labourers. It may reasonably be supposed that

in 1927, in Russia, the number of agricultural labourers far
exceeded the number of Kulaks. There can, of course, be no
doubt that there existed many hundreds of thousands of
farmers of the Kulak type. When, in 1928, the Government
resolved to place a super-tax upon the Kulaks, it determined
to tax 2–3 per cent. of all peasant holdings. The total number
of peasant farms in Russia was estimated to be 20 millions,
and thus the number of Kulaks about half a million. The
increase in the number of Kulaks during the years 1925–7
produced an extraordinary state of affairs in regard to land
tenure. Many poor peasants were unable to cultivate their
land properly for lack of farm implements and oxen for
ploughing. Hence they were forced to let their land to the
Kulak, who then cultivated it with the aid of his horses and
ploughs. The rent received by the peasant consisted of a
moderate share in the harvest. This singular procedure was
adopted because the direct purchase of land by the well-to-do
was attended by difficulties under the Soviet legal system.
In contrast to the customary type of land tenure there thus
arose in Russia an extraordinary type in which the rich and
not the poor were the tenants. Impartial observers have
described the relationship of the poor peasant and the
agricultural labourer to the Kulaks in many parts of Russia
as a form of serfdom. Although the percentage of agricultural
labourers as of Kulaks was small in proportion to the total
agricultural population of 100 millions in Russia, the emergence of these two classes beside the poor peasants and small
farmers was symptomatic of the trend in economic development. It was nothing less than a tragedy that ten years after
the victorious October Revolution the spoliation of millions
of agricultural labourers and small peasants should be
possible.

The unemployed sons of the small peasants migrated to
the towns and thus helped to increase the total of unemployment in Russia, until in 1927 it reached a figure of 2 millions.
Class enmity increased during the years 1924–7 beneath
the cover of the so-called proletarian dictatorship. If the
number of industrial workmen engaged in work increased,
the number of unemployed also grew larger. Although the
real wages of the workmen improved, the profits made by

Kulaks and traders simultaneously rose; and in the so-called NEP class of traders there were not a few millionaires. For example, there were persons who worked under the cover of a so-called co-operative society. A buying society was established for purchasing textiles from poor home-workers at miserable prices. This 'society' concealed a successful millionaire speculator. The ruling Party bureaucracy in Russia was therefore confronted with the task of restoring the balance between all these contending forces in the social life of Russia. The time had come for the rulers of Russia to decide whither their policy was leading them.

After 1924 Stalin developed certain original ideas on the subject of the future of Russia that speedily involved him in a fierce conflict with his two colleagues. The most important of Stalin's theories, and the one that has become the fundamental doctrine of Bolshevism since 1924, is the theory of the possibility of realizing Socialism in a single country. It has already been pointed out above that this theory is to be found as early as 1923, in Lenin's last writings and speeches. It is true that Lenin did not precisely formulate the theory and place its execution in the forefront of the Party's activities. He contented himself with giving it indirect expression in his works. It was Stalin who for the first time clearly formulated the theory and made it the basis of Bolshevism. As late as April 1924, Stalin propounded this old and truly Marxian doctrine in a pamphlet in which he wrote:

'An effort on the part of a single country is sufficient to overthrow the middle class. This is shown by the history of our own Revolution. An effort on the part of a single country, especially a peasant country like Russia, is not sufficient to achieve the final victory of Socialism and the Socialist organization of production. The efforts of the proletariat in several highly developed countries will be necessary for that purpose.'

In December 1924, Stalin repudiated his theories and declared that they must be improved upon. He now divided up the problem into two parts: First, can it be said that there is a complete guarantee against the restoration of a middle-class order of society in Russia? Such a guarantee would imply that for the future all military intervention of no matter what kind on the part of foreign Powers in Russia would be

impossible. In order that this guarantee may become a real
one—Stalin now admits—the victory of a proletarian revolution will be necessary in at least several highly-developed
countries. Second, can it be said that the creation of a completely Socialist order of society is possible in a single
country? Stalin now unhesitatingly answers this question
in the affirmative. The path leading to Socialism is the one
already pointed out by Lenin in 1923: the increased industrialization of Russia and the simultaneous organization of
the peasants into co-operative societies. The pursuit of the
right policy on the part of the Party could result in winning
over a decisive majority of the peasants for Socialism.

The Russian peasants are not, in Stalin's opinion, the same
as European peasants. The peasants in Europe received their
land at the hands of a Liberal middle class in the course of
its struggle with feudalism. Thus the European peasants
have become a source of strength for the middle class. In
contrast to the European the Russian peasants received land
and peace at the hands of the proletariat, and have thus
become a source of strength for the proletariat. Moreover,
agriculture in Europe continues to develop within the limits
of Capitalism and to the accompaniment of all the crises
attendant upon Capitalism, and the steadily increasing
impoverishment of larger and larger classes among the agricultural population. In Russia, on the contrary, the Soviet
Government closes the path to the growth of Capitalism and
consequently the peasants are progressing towards Socialism.
If, indeed, as Stalin believes, the economic organization of
Russia is leading to the complete realization of Socialism,
then it can no longer be termed 'State Capitalism'. Stalin
admits that in 1921, at the time of the introduction of the
NEP, Lenin rightly described the conditions obtaining in
Russia as a system of State Capitalism. The growth of
Socialism in Russia, however, had as early as 1923 rendered
the description 'State Capitalism' inapplicable, and it was
now meaningless. Stalin's theory resulted in an extraordinary
and illusory fashion in resolving the contradiction between
legend and reality in Soviet Russia. A proletarian dictatorship existed in Russia, which was only reconcilable with
complete Socialism. Therefore this complete Socialism would

now be established in Russia by abolishing entirely all traces of Capitalism. The temporary abandonment of Socialism which Lenin was compelled to make in 1921 had come to an end. The dream of a Socialist order of society that had inspired the Russian workman for so long would at last become a reality. This great aim can obviously only be achieved by Stalin after the manner of Lenin in 1923 by giving Marxist economic doctrines a *Naródnik* interpretation. Stalin's theory of a Russian peasant that is no ordinary peasant, but a Socialist in embryo, is a purely *Naródnik* notion. The peasant member of a co-operative society remains a peasant and a producer of food-supplies. The Russian workman is still the slave of a dictatorship of semi-middle-class Government officials, even in a State organized in accordance with the Socialist doctrines of Stalin. Thus Stalin failed to resolve the fundamental contradiction inherent in Soviet Russia. All he had done was to place it on another footing. Since 1925 the Soviet myth consists in the fact that the official Bolshevik doctrines declare nationalist Russian Socialism to be the only true Marxian Socialism.

Nevertheless, the theory put forward by Stalin marks, from a middle-class nationalist standpoint, a great step forward in the development of the Russian nation. Up to the year 1925 there existed a continual danger that Utopian-Communist aspirations on the part of the Russian proletariat might paralyse all practical constructive work and drive the State into making the wildest experiments. Unless a revolution in Europe brought relief, and there was little likelihood of its occurrence, the opposition between the idealistic demands of the working class and the actual state of the country must destroy the Russian Revolution. At this juncture Stalin held up before the workers an ideal difficult of attainment and demanding sacrifices—but still an ideal capable of being attained. Although only after great opposition has been overcome the peasantry can, by Stalin's method, be made an organic part of the Soviet economy. It would not be necessary for Russia either to sink into a chaos produced by Utopianism or to return to the western European system of private Capitalism. It can at once retain the fruits of the revolution and resolutely modernize itself. All these advantages are certainly only to be achieved if two preliminary conditions are fulfilled: First, the establishment of dogmatic absolutism in Russia, which will forbid all independent critical thought on the subject of Marxism and Socialism. For from the moment the Russian people no longer believe that Stalin's Socialism is the true Socialism all the old difficulties will revive. Hence Stalin and his Party refuse to tolerate any theoretical deviation from the official beliefs that are declared to be the sole true doctrines of Lenin. Second, the theory of national Russian Socialism meant the final separation of Soviet Russia from the world revolution, notwithstanding the fact that Stalin has preserved the façade of the Third International.

At first, Stalin's new theory effected no practical change in industrial conditions in Soviet Russia. During 1925–7 the work of reconstruction went on with whatever materials were at hand, and accompanied by a rigorous regard for economy and the stability of the Soviet currency. Of greater importance were the changes that occurred in the agricultural districts of Russia. Stalin, like all other Bolsheviks, knew that the Kulaks—the village money-lenders—were enemies of the Soviet State, and that the very poor peasants for the most part sympathized with the town proletariat. The decisive influence among the Russian peasantry was, nevertheless, neither the Kulak nor the very poor peasant, but the class of so-called 'middle' peasants who could live comfortably on the produce of their farms without, however, having any surplus. In 1925 Stalin urged upon the Communist Party the extreme importance of making firm friends of the 'middle' peasants. These 'middle' peasants, or small farmers, were not merely to be obedient to the Government officials but also to become convinced and enthusiastic supporters of the Soviet State. Once that had taken place it would be easy to induce them voluntarily to form co-operative societies. Stalin demanded that the last vestiges of war-time Communism should be made to disappear from the villages. Party and Government officials were not to make these farmers conscious of their authority. Free elections should be held for country Soviets. In those districts where elections had already been held under pressure from the Government officials the results were to be declared null and void and new elections held.

Stalin's object was to strengthen Soviet democracy at any rate within the realm of local government. The Bolshevik Party in any case continued to enjoy the monopoly of being the only political Party in Russia, and the foundation or promotion of any new Party continued to be forbidden. The peasants were now to be free to elect non-Party men from their own ranks to serve on the village councils, and these village Soviets were to have freedom of action within the limits of Soviet law. This unquestionably denoted a relaxation of the Party dictatorship. All harshness was to be avoided in the collection of land taxes, and the greater part of the receipts from these taxes were allocated to the local administration in order that the peasants in the village Soviet might decide for themselves what use was to be made of their own money. Stalin's object in making these concessions was to isolate the anti-Soviet Kulaks from the main body of the peasants and to oppose to them a front of small farmers and poor peasants who were loyal Government supporters. The success of this policy pursued by the Soviet Government between 1925 and 1927 is highly questionable. It became evident again and again in the free elections for the village Soviets that the Kulak was the ruler of the village, was followed by the other peasants, and was master of the local Soviet. In districts where the Kulak controlled the local administration the poor peasant was treated more harshly than the rich in the assessment of taxes, and the State subsidies for the promotion of agriculture went to swell the pockets of the Kulak. Even as early as 1925 the Kulaks in a great part of Russia were not afraid to buy up the produce of the poor peasants and small farmers. The corn thus purchased was then stored away in their barns and retained until a shortage of bread caused the price of wheat to rise to fantastic heights.

Nevertheless, in the years 1925-7 Stalin hesitated to take forcible measures against the Kulaks. He was afraid that the small farmers would fail to understand the purpose of police action against the Kulaks, and that they would think that

war-time Communism with its use of force had once more
returned to their midst. Once this belief took root and spread,
the masses of the peasants would be seized with panic and
would adopt an inimical attitude towards the Soviet Government that would render impossible the peaceful winning
over of the small farmers for Socialism. Whilst the Kulaks
were organizing first economic and then political counter-
revolution in the villages, Stalin continued his methods of
educating the peasants by gentle means. In districts where
speculation in corn on the part of the Kulaks was specially
notorious the Government threw on the market, at low prices,
large quantities of grain from its own grain stores. Prices
were thus forced down and the Kulaks were at least in part
compelled to disgorge their stocks. This warfare between
the omnipotent Soviet Government and the Kulaks had a
tragi-comic aspect. If it continued for some years, what
would be left of the dictatorship of the proletariat?

Winning the goodwill of the peasants was in Stalin's eyes
not an end in itself. His desire was to make the peasants
anxious to accept Socialist improvements. At the same time
his policy was capable of another interpretation. A group
specially friendly to the peasants grew up within the Russian
Communist Party and was referred to in its discussions
as the Right. At the head of this Right Wing was Rykov,
the Chairman of the Council of People's Commissars, and
Bukharin, the most highly respected Marxist thinker in the
Party, and the author of important scientific books. These
men were of the opinion that Russia was and would remain
an agricultural country, notwithstanding all the progress
that had been made towards its industrialization. The prosperity of Russia therefore depended wholly upon agriculture,
and everything possible must be done to improve the productivity and standard of life of the peasants. The development
of a rich peasantry would from this standpoint be anything
but a misfortune for the Soviet Government, since if the
Soviet State held in its hand the control of heavy industry,
foreign trade, and the entire banking system, a wealthy
peasantry could not injure it. Where was the peasant to take
his savings? All he could do was to purchase Government
stocks bearing a good rate of interest or put his money into

the nearest State Savings Bank. No matter what happened, the accumulated profits of the Kulak or the successful trader must eventually return to benefit the Soviet State.

Bukharin, Rykov, and their intimate friends accepted without reservations Lenin's and Stalin's theory of the possibility of realizing Socialism in a single land. This justified them in designating the economy of Soviet Russia, despite its many inner contradictions, as 'Socialist'. In 1925, in the course of a speech addressed to the wealthy peasants Bukharin gave them as a motto 'Enrich yourselves!' This phrase coming as it did from the lips of the Government theorist made an enormous impression. For the first time the purpose of the new policy became clear. Many Russian workmen and old-time Bolsheviks said to themselves that the Kulak's lust for profits should now be proclaimed to be true Socialism. A cynical use was being made of the word 'Socialism' and the way was being prepared for Russia's return to Capitalism. In order to calm the excitement in the Party and among the working class Stalin declared officially that he disapproved of the phrase 'Enrich yourselves'. And in truth Stalin was wholly opposed to the group led by Bukharin and Rykov which wished to perpetuate the conditions created by the NEP of 1921 and the concessions made to the wealthy peasants. This group looked upon the perpetuation of the existent state of affairs in Russia as the sole means to the pursuit of a Socialist policy. Stalin, on the contrary, wished the existent conditions merely to serve as a basis upon which it should and would be possible to erect something new in the future. Moreover, Stalin and the aged Lenin were not free from responsibility for this misunderstanding, since if Marxian Socialism is replaced by the arbitrary theory of 'Socialism in a single land' there is small cause for wonder when people of all sorts and conditions read into this 'Socialism' whatever they wish it to mean.

A singular chance willed that the most prominent leader of Russian Trade Unionism, Tomski, was also to be found among the followers of Bukharin and Rykov. Tomski was a sceptic and a realist politician who reconciled himself to the agricultural character of Russian economy as an unalterable fact. The Russian worker, in Tomski's opinion, should not run after wild visions and should devote himself to obtaining as good a livelihood as possible in the existent circumstances. If the country were ruined by Utopian Socialist experiments, the workman would suffer more than anybody in that he would again experience the pangs of hunger. Tomski represented the views of a minority of skilled and better-paid Russian workmen who had grown weary of revolution and refused to listen any longer to Socialist fables. Their desire was to defend and to improve their living conditions with the assistance of the Trade Unions. If the Soviet State were to take on a semi-middle-class character that would not cause them any anxiety, since the skilled workmen as a professional class would not be likely to suffer from the change. Tomski regarded the Soviet State after the fashion in which a western European Socialist Trade Union leader looks upon his middle-class capitalist State. For this reason it is easy to understand why in the years 1925–7 Tomski was the most enthusiastic worker for an alliance between the Russian workers and the Socialist Trade Unions in Europe.

It is obvious that the Right group in the Bolshevik Party —the group led by Bukharin, Rykov, and Tomski—made use of the theory of 'Socialism in a single land' in order to free themselves from the Socialist-Communist myth. On the other hand, Stalin wanted to use this theory to lend an appearance of reality to the myth itself. Moreover, the seemingly insuperable inability of the Soviet Government to deal with the Kulaks and traders aroused new hopes in the middle-class Russian intellectuals. These men were in part to be found in the service of the Soviet State and in part in exile. It seemed to them that Russia was now increasing the pace of her return journey to a middle-class order of society that had begun in 1921 and that Stalin and Bukharin, notwithstanding their Socialist formulas, would either themselves restore the middle-class nationalist State in Russia or that the evolution would proceed irresistibly by way of the Right Wing Communists until the old conditions had been restored. There thus came into existence within and without Russia a group of Russian intellectuals who supported Stalin and the Soviet Government. These men openly wrote their articles in support of Stalin from the standpoint of Russian middle-class patriots, and did not deem it necessary to make any profession of faith in Socialism and Communism. A minor Soviet official named Ustryalov became famous in these years as the mouthpiece of Stalin's middle-class followers. The support of these men gravely compromised the Soviet Government in the eyes of the Party and the workmen. A single article in praise of the Government from Ustryalov's pen did more harm to Stalin than a hundred spiteful attacks in the newspapers published by the exiled White Guards. For it seemed as if the middle-class counter-revolution could claim the leading men in Soviet Russia as its supporters. Hence Stalin was forced in his great speeches before the Party Congresses—the most ceremonial occasions in the life of the Soviet State—to point out time and again at great length the divergences of opinion separating him from the minor official Ustryalov.

After Trotsky had been defeated in the Party debates and excluded from power towards the close of 1924 Stalin propounded his theory in the form of a violent attack upon Trotsky's conception of the permanent international revolution. At first Trotsky kept silence and waited to see how the Party would react to Stalin's ideas. He had not long to wait. In 1925 the crisis came in a disruption of the Committee of Three. The Bolshevik Old Guard, led by Zinoviev and Kamenev, rejected Stalin's theory of Socialism in a single State and his agrarian policy as an Opportunist deviation from Marxism and Leninism. Thanks to the support of the Right Wing, led by Bukharin and Rykov, Stalin obtained a majority in the Central Committee, and thus became sole head of the Party and the Government. Dissension, nevertheless, increased within the Party. Hundreds of old-time Bolsheviks, among them Lenin's widow, Madame Krupskaya, joined the opposition to Stalin and Bukharin in the belief that the Revolution had not been undertaken merely to enable the Kulaks to grow rich. The Leningrad Bolshevik Party revolted against the Central Committee. Violent debates took place at the celebrated Fourteenth Congress of the Russian Communist Party in December 1925. Since he had the Party machine firmly under his control, Stalin was successful in securing the election of the majority of his supporters as delegates to the Party Congress, although their election was no true indication of the state of feeling among the members of the Party and the working class. Trotsky continued to maintain silence. It was not until 1926 that Russia was suddenly electrified by the news that Trotsky had allied himself with Zinoviev in waging war on the Soviet Government and the Party leaders.

The fact that it was the Bolshevik Old Guard who now turned to him for help afforded Trotsky great personal satisfaction. These men had for twenty years been his greatest opponents in doctrinal matters. In the discussions in 1923 and 1924 Zinoviev and Kamenev had directed a fierce bombardment upon Trotsky and his doctrines that had been answered no less fiercely. Stalin had in those days refrained from appearing in the forefront of the attack upon Trotsky and had prevented his expulsion from the Russian Communist Party on the motion of Zinoviev and Kamenev. Now two years later Trotsky and his former opponents were walking arm-in-arm. It was, moreover, obvious that Trotsky alone was the intellectual inspiration of the Opposition, since he alone had a theory fundamentally opposed to that of Stalin. The old-time Bolsheviks could not reproach Stalin in matters of principle, but only accuse him of mistakes and backslidings in matters of detail. In spite of internal differences of opinion this Left Wing solidly opposed Stalin in 1926-7 with an ever-increasing sharpness. Stalin was accused of preparing the Thermidor of the Russian Revolution. On November 9, 1794, Robespierre had been overthrown by the French capitalists, and it now seemed that a similar occurrence was imminent in the history of the Russian Revolution.

Stalin still retained control of the Party machine and the State administration and was supported by the Secretaries of the Party, by Ustryalov, the Kulaks and NEP men (successful traders and profiteers), and the young 'Red' professors who had been taught by Bukharin to reconcile Leninist doctrines with the slogan 'Enrich yourselves'. Stalin was opposed by Trotsky and Krupskaya, Zinoviev and Kamenev, the senior members of the Party, and all who had been prisoners in Siberia or fought in the battles of the Civil War.

In 1927 Stalin saw himself in danger of being compelled to fight on an untenable front, i.e. in alliance with all the partly and wholly middle-class elements in the country against the proletariat and the ideals of the Russian Revolution. From such a struggle Stalin could only emerge defeated, or in the event of victory would be compelled to open the gates to the counter-revolution. The sharpest criticism of the Opposition was directed less against Stalin's domestic than against his foreign policy. The history of the Third International has been narrated above up to the winter of 1923–4, in which the KPD found itself in danger of dissolution as a result of its decisive defeat in the March Action. The dissatisfaction felt by the members of the Party with Brandler's policy had resulted in giving the Left Opposition the majority in the Party. If this Left Opposition had publicly and resolutely proclaimed that the International was to blame for the disaster in Germany, the Party would have been split in twain, a cleavage that would have been accompanied by serious consequences for the Executive and the Bolshevik leaders. The Left Opposition was, nevertheless, not as powerful as it seemed. Although its leaders were under no illusions regarding the Russian myth, they had not imparted their knowledge to their followers. The members of the KPD still believed in Soviet Russia. They blamed the Central Committee of the KPD for the mistakes of 1921–3, and believed that the Executive and the Bolshevik leaders had been kept in ignorance of the facts. Since the Left Opposition leaders had up to 1923 not ventured to denounce this Russian legend, they now found themselves its prisoners.

The logical members of the Left—called in reproach Ultra-Left by their opponents—were unable to gain acceptance for their views. The friends of a compromise with Russia were in a majority and the Left came to an understanding in 1924 with the Executive. The Executive and the Left then joined in placing the entire responsibility for the mistakes made in Germany upon Brandler's shoulders. The revolutionary glory of the Executive and the Bolshevik leaders was unimpaired in the eyes of German Communists and the Executive in return permitted the Left to take over the leadership of the KPD. The Pyrrhic victory of the

German Left at the Party Congress in Frankfurt in 1924 bore in it the seeds of the coming disaster in that the Left was deprived of all independent beliefs and contributed to strengthen in Germany the authority of the Third International.

The Fifth World Congress of the Communist International met in 1924 in Moscow, and was the scene of an orgy of rhetorical Radicalism that was wholly unmeaning. Zinoviev now retrospectively damned the 'Opportunist' policy of Brandler and designated the Saxon policy of 1923 'a banal parliamentary comedy'. As a reply to this denunciation the Left Wing Central Committee of the KPD declared itself in opposition to Trotsky and passed a vote of confidence in the Russian Committee of Three. In truth the policy of the united front that had been pursued in 1922-3 could no longer be maintained in the same fashion. Zinoviev laid emphasis upon the fact that a Labour Government could only be looked upon as another expression for a dictatorship of the proletariat. From a practical standpoint the notion of a Labour Government ceased to have any importance, and the policy of the united front between Communists and Social Democrats broke down as a result of the internal dissensions in the Third International. When Stalin developed his theory of Socialism in a single land, it was obvious that this must have a decisive influence upon the future of the International. Stalin's theory was that Russia could achieve Socialism alone if the working class abroad could prevent an armed capitalist foreign intervention in Soviet Russia. Since, however, the Communists as a minority in the world proletariat are not able themselves to guard Russia against such a danger, it is necessary to achieve direct connexion between Soviet Russia and the Social Democrat majority of the international proletariat. Scarcely had the policy of a united front been buried in its old dress than it was resurrected and clad in a new garb. This new garb was the international solidarity of Trade Unions. If necessary the International of the Red Trade Unions would be sacrificed for this purpose. This International comprised the Russian Trade Unions together with larger and smaller individual Trade Unions in France, Czechoslovakia, Germany, Asia, &c. The great

majority of the Trade Unionist workmen in Europe belonged
to the so-called Social Democrat Amsterdam Trade Union
International. The Red International now proposed to the
Amsterdam International the holding of a World Congress
of Trade Unions for the purpose of achieving their unification.

If the Congress had ever assembled it would have marked
a decisive stage in the breakdown of international Communism. It is true that the Bolshevik leaders hotly denied,
in 1925–7, that they had in view the dissolution of the Third
International. Suppose, nevertheless, that this World Congress of Trade Unions had held a meeting and decided upon
achieving the international unification of the Trade Unions.
The Central Committee of the new World International
would comprise English and German Social Democrats as
well as Russian Communists. The new World International
would be responsible for all international working-class
action and, in the several countries comprised in the International, Socialists and Communists would jointly conduct
the daily economic struggle. The separate existence of the
Communist International and the individual Communist
Parties would be rendered so unnecessary that the workers
themselves would put forward an irresistible demand for
political unification.

Stalin and his supporters cannot have been ignorant of
the inevitable results of their proposal for bringing about
the international unification of the Trade Union movement.
Their aim was to make the bonds uniting Soviet Russia to the
international proletariat as tight as possible. If the organized
workmen in all European countries sympathized with Soviet
Russia, there would no longer be any cause to fear a foreign
invasion. The payment made by Soviet Russia for this
incomparable service was very slight and consisted in fact in
the renunciation of an outworn revolutionary Romanticism
that was no longer regarded seriously by leading circles in
Russia. It is also comprehensible that it should have been
especially the Right Wing in the Russian Communist Party,
led by Bukharin and Tomski, that worked in the interests
of international proletarian solidarity. The Right hoped in
this manner to free themselves of the remains of the proletarian revolutionary myth that hindered them in their

domestic policy. Obviously the Communist International must continue to reflect faithfully the hesitations and tactical manœuvres of Moscow for as long as it remained in existence. Disturbances were, however, to be expected from the side of the KPD under its Left Wing leadership. Hence the Left Wing was deprived of its leadership by the Executive as a result of a manœuvre carried out by Bukharin in 1925 with brilliant diplomatic skill. A part of the Left Wing—the Thälmann Group—unconditionally submitted to orders from Moscow and established a new Central Committee prepared loyally to carry out the wishes of the Bolshevik leaders. The other leaders of the former German Left were driven out into the political wilderness and expelled from the Party in succeeding years. The majority of the members of the KPD had lost all revolutionary spirit after the defeat of 1923, and consequently believed all the more firmly in the Russian fable. The Left Wing leaders were followed into political exile by only a few small sections in the Party and these Left Communist groups that formed outside the official Parties in Germany and other countries endeavoured to establish relations with Trotsky and his followers. Thus the Russian line of battle grew longer. Pamphlets in which Trotsky and Zinoviev criticized Stalin's policy were zealously distributed by Left Communists in 1926 and 1927 in Germany and France.

The Social Democrat leaders in Europe looked with grave mistrust upon Russian endeavours to promote international unity among the Trade Unions. A greater degree of success attended their efforts in England. English Trade Union officials made a tour of Russia, published glowing reports of their Russian impressions, and pronounced themselves in favour of an alliance with the Russian workmen. A separate agreement was concluded between Russian and English Trade Unions by which both parties pledged themselves to work in common in the interests of the international proletariat and in the campaign for international unification of Trade Unions. Tomski was the moving spirit in this Anglo-Russian united front. Trade Union leaders from both countries met on several occasions during the years 1925–7 to exchange views on the international situation. The

English Trade Unions are for all practical purposes identical with the English Labour Party. Hence the tiny English Communist Party was, in truth, excluded from this united front of Russian Bolsheviks and English Socialists. The friendship of the English workmen was at this time of great value to the Soviet Government because events in Asia had strained Anglo-Russian relations to breaking-point and the English Conservatives threatened to make war on Russia.

A general strike occurred in England in 1926 which ended in defeat for the English Trade Unions. The consequences of this defeat were overcome with extraordinary rapidity by the English workmen. The Russian Government and Tomski refrained from criticizing the policy of the English Trade Union officials for fear lest they should offend them and lose the friendship which they needed so badly. In truth the Labour movement in England from the World War to the present day has made amazing progress and has no need of Russian teachers. Nevertheless, in the customary phrases employed by the Communist International, the English Trade Union leaders who called off the general strike were styled 'Strike-breakers, agents of the middle class, and betrayers of the workmen'. The leaders of the Opposition in Russia, Trotsky and Zinoviev, now made use of these polite epithets when speaking of the leaders of the English Labour movement. The Opposition accused Stalin of concealing the 'betrayal of the workers' on the part of the English 'Reformists' out of consideration for less important interests of State. The criticism of English Social Democracy by the English Communists was rendered valueless, and the entire work of the Communist Party in England rendered hopeless, because the Social Democrat leaders of the English Labour movement could always secure the approval of Soviet Russia and the Bolsheviks for their actions. The double-dealing of official Bolshevik policy was indeed mercilessly revealed by the events in England in 1926–7. Either the Bolsheviks must admit the English Social Democrats to be in the right and therefore dissolve the Communist International, or they must continue to prove themselves Communists by pursuing an independent Communist policy and by breaking with the

English Social Democrats. Stalin thus found himself at a cross-roads in 1927, both in foreign and domestic policy.

All the paradoxes characterizing the English policy of the Bolsheviks appeared still more sharply and with tragic results in the Chinese Revolution. In the years following upon the World War the rise of Soviet Russia had been greeted with enthusiasm in all Asiatic lands. The patriots in the various districts in Asia where a struggle was being waged with foreign rulers and European-American Imperialism, saw their natural allies in the Bolsheviks. Soviet Russia had renounced all the unfair treaties which had been forced upon Asiatic countries in Tsarist days. Soviet Russia had retained her rights only in the North Manchurian Railway—and by doing so created a fruitful source of trouble. In no other Asiatic country was there such a feeling of sympathy with the Russian Revolution as in China. The nationalist movement for liberation in China found its embodiment in the Kuomintang Party founded by Dr. Sun Yat Sen. The Party was animated by the ideas of the young intellectuals and especially of students who had been educated in Europe. In their struggle against foreign Imperialism the Kuomintang had the support of the masses of Chinese workmen and peasants as well as of patriotic business men and estate-owners. The attitude of the Kuomintang in social questions was as ambiguous as that of European democracy before 1848. Sun Yat Sen had himself declared that China was still in a pre-Capitalist stage of development. A clever policy on the part of the Kuomintang could prevent the development of private Capitalism of the European type in China. The development of China's productive forces could proceed under State Capitalism and thus the Chinese nation would be spared the danger of being poisoned by the struggle between Capital and Labour. Unhappily in the years following on the World War an industrial proletariat numbering millions came into existence whose cares and demands could not be overlooked. Sun Yat Sen's ideas were of as little avail in talking away the existence of Capitalism in China as those of the *Naródniki* in destroying its existence in Russia.

The principal enemies of the Kuomintang in China were the foreign Powers with their settlements and men-of-war.

There were in addition the native Chinese millionaires, who were involved in the ramifications of international capital, and, finally, adventurers, styling themselves Generals and Marshals, with their armies. The Kuomintang had indeed overthrown the monarchy in China before the World War. But authority in the majority of the provinces had fallen into the hands of the generals who joined with the foreigners in brutally repressing the national movement for liberation. At the time of Sun Yat Sen's death his Party only ruled over Canton and the surrounding provinces in southern China. In the rest of China the generals and their armies were the rulers. During the years 1924–5 the Bolsheviks were the stronger party in the relations between Soviet Russia and the Kuomintang. The Bolsheviks were the rulers of a great and powerful Empire with all its possibilities of help for China. The Kuomintang barely maintained itself in a single Chinese province. Nevertheless, the Soviet Government recognized that the future belonged to the Kuomintang. Although belief in the possibility of spreading the world revolution from land to land by the sword had been abandoned, it was obvious that once a Russophil National Government came into power in China that vast country with its 400 million inhabitants would become the political and economic ally of Soviet Russia. That would mean an enormous support for the international position of Soviet Russia and this would be an object that would repay much sacrifice. For this reason the Soviet Government supported the Kuomintang generously with advice and assistance.

The Kuomintang was willing in 1924 to enter the Third International. Soviet Russia politely refused its request. Although Lenin had laid upon the Bolsheviks the duty of stirring up nationalist revolutions among the oppressed Asiatic peoples, it was impossible for the Bolsheviks to bring themselves to admitting a middle-class party like the Kuomintang into the proletarian International. Their refusal led to the foundation of an independent Communist Party in China. Its membership remained small up to 1927, although it exercised a profound ideological influence upon millions of workmen and peasants, for in the years prior to 1927 Soviet Russia and Bolshevism meant to the masses of the people in China approximately what it had meant to European workmen in the years 1919–20. The Bolsheviks were given an opportunity throughout the years 1924–7 to pursue one of two policies in regard to the Chinese Revolution. The first policy was based firmly on the belief that only a middle-class nationalist revolution was possible in China—and nothing else. In that case the leaders of the Kuomintang must be unconditionally and unreservedly supported even if the middle-class element should completely dominate the Kuomintang. A distinguished soldier, General Chang Kai Shek, had become Chairman of the Kuomintang in succession to Dr. Sun Yat Sen, and he felt himself to be politically a representative of the middle-class Right Wing of the Party. If the Soviet Government believed this policy to be right, it should have unquestioningly supported Chang Kai Shek and instructed the Communist Party in China to follow its example. The second policy was based on the belief that the Chinese Revolution could be carried on beyond the limits of the middle-class stage within a reasonable time. In that case the Kuomintang should only be supported in so far as it really fought against military despotism and foreign Imperialism. At the same time the Communist Party in China must ruthlessly pursue its own policy. It must place itself at the head of the workmen and peasants, organize Soviets of armed workers of all classes throughout China, overthrow the Kuomintang in the course of the revolution, and establish a democratic dictatorship of the peasants and workers.

Fate decreed that Stalin and the Chinese Communists should not make any serious attempt to adopt either of these alternative policies, but that they should endeavour to effect a weak compromise that involved them in complete disaster. It is unquestionable that the Soviet Government was from 1924 to 1927 inspired with the sincere desire to make common cause with Chang Kai Shek and the leaders of the Kuomintang. The Communists in China were organized in two ways: they became members of the Kuomintang and undertook to support it loyally in addition to being members of the Communist Party. A vast wave of discontent swept over the masses in China during the years 1924–7. The workmen refused any longer to accept the miserable existence of coolies that was forced upon them by their employers. The peasants rebelled against the intolerable burden of rents and taxes. Nevertheless, the Communist Party in China never contemplated placing itself at the head of these discontented masses. Instead it hindered, in so far as it lay in its power, insurrections on the part of peasants and workmen, prevented the proletariat from arming, opposed strikes and allowed officials of the Kuomintang to deal cruelly with peasant extremists. All this was done in the name of the political truce between the Communists and the Kuomintang. The united front of all patriotic classes in China in the struggle against Imperialism must not be broken up. The Chinese Communist Party anxiously avoided suggesting the establishment of Soviets to the masses of the population.

At the same time the Chinese Communist Party had certain duties as a Communist Party and belonged to the proletarian International. The Kuomintang was itself not a united Party. There was a Left Wing composed of sympathizers with the workmen and peasants which was in opposition to Chang Kai Shek's Right Wing. The Communist Party began to intrigue against Chang Kai Shek in alliance with the Kuomintang Left Wing. In 1926 the Kuomintang won a number of astonishing military successes. Chang Kai Shek set out on his famous march northwards that led him from one province to another as far as the Yangtse-Kiang valley and Shanghai. The Chinese Communist Party endeavoured to impede his progress by all sorts of intrigues. Chang Kai Shek was, nevertheless, successful in reaching Shanghai. He now became convinced that Soviet Russia and the Communists were his enemies and in the spring of 1927 he took action against them. The Chinese Communist Party and its subsidiary and associated organizations were dissolved and the opposition of the workmen broken by force. For a brief moment it appeared as if the Left Wing in the Kuomintang would fight against Chang Kai Shek in alliance with the Communists. In the result all groups in the Kuomintang united against Russia. The ban on the Chinese Communist Party remained in force, all Russian helpers and advisers were expelled from China, and the Kuomintang Government broke off relations with Soviet Russia.

Thus Stalin's Chinese policy ended in disaster. Everything that had been gained in Asia in the way of authority and prestige had been lost. The sympathies of the Chinese National Party for Soviet Russia had been changed into bitter enmity. The Communist International had not wished to wage class warfare in China. Instead it had manœuvred and intrigued. The result was that the masses were defeated and the middle-class element in the Kuomintang won the day. The Opposition in Russia bitterly attacked Stalin's foreign policy. In May 1927 Trotsky and Zinoviev drew up an indictment of Stalin and the Central Committee of the Russian Communist Party that criticized with unparalleled sharpness the foreign and domestic policy of the rulers of Russia. The indictment was signed within a short space of time by five hundred of the oldest members of the Bolshevik Party. In this indictment the writers say *inter alia*:

'The question at issue is not whether we have sustained a terrible defeat in China but why, how, and for what reason we have sustained it. . . . No Marxist will deny that the false policy in China and in the matter of the Anglo-Russian Committee [the joint Committee of Russian and English Trade Unions] was not a matter of chance. It is a continuation and enlargement of the mistaken domestic policy. . . . The economy of the Soviet Republic has in the main come to the end of its period of reconstruction. Real results have been achieved in the course of this period of economic reconstruction.

'Grave difficulties arose simultaneously with these achievements as a result of this period of economic reconstruction. These difficulties, which arose out of an insufficient development of productive forces and out of our economic backwardness, were increased by being concealed from the broad masses of the Party. Instead of being given a Marxian analysis of the true situation of the proletarian dictatorship in Soviet Russia the Party was put off with the petty middle-class "theory of Socialism in a single land" which has nothing in common with Marxism and Leninism. This gross desertion of Marxism resulted in rendering it harder for the Party to discern the nature of the economic process in progress from a class standpoint. It is, nevertheless, in the rearrangement of classes to the disadvantage of the proletariat, and in the misery in which broad masses of the people are living, that there exist the negative phenomena of the period of revolution that we have experienced.'

The Declaration of the Five Hundred continues:

'This mistaken policy accelerates the growth of elements inimical to the proletarian dictatorship—the Kulaks, NEP men, the bureaucrats. Our entire Party policy suffers from taking a swing to the Right. . . . The self-satisfied officials who toady to their superiors; the petty middle-class men who have wormed their way up to posts of authority and look down arrogantly on the masses—these find the ground growing steadily firmer beneath their feet and raise their heads higher and higher. . . . Under the NEP the new *bourgeoisie* has become a powerful element in the towns and in the country.'

The Declaration warned the Central Committee of the Party against attempting to discredit or destroy the Left, proletarian, 'Leninist' Wing. Their destruction would inevitably result in a speedy increase of strength to the Right Wing and in opening up the prospect of a no less inevitable 'subjection of the interests of the proletariat to those of other classes'.

In these words Trotsky and the old Bolsheviks uttered their warning against the approaching Thermidor of the Russian Revolution. Towards the close of 1927 Stalin recognized that his entire policy had led Russia up a blind alley. He sought and found the way out in December 1927 at the Fifteenth Congress of the Russian Communist Party.

'SOCIALISM IN A SINGLE LAND', 1927-32

AMONG the Russian proletariat in the years 1926 and 1927 confidence in the Soviet Government was severely shaken. This want of confidence was caused by the belief that the Soviet Government was the friend of the Kulaks and lacked the desire to promote Socialism. In order to regain the confidence of the Russian workmen Stalin was compelled to prove to them that he was in earnest in seeking to realize Socialism in the form laid down by his theory of 'Socialism in a single country'.

At the Fifteenth Congress of the Party Stalin adopted a resolute and confident manner of speech. He demonstrated to his listeners that Russia was an industrial country, and set before the Party the task of furthering its industrialization by all possible means. He then proceeded to draw the conclusion: 'Our country advances unerringly and swiftly towards Socialism inasmuch as it forces the capitalist elements into the background and gradually excludes them from the national economy.' Stalin continued:

'This fact confronts us with the fundamental problem: Who shall be attacked and by whom? This question was asked by Lenin in 1921 after the introduction of the New Economic Policy. Should we be capable of allying our Socialist economy to peasant economy, of driving out the private trader and private capitalist, and of learning to trade ourselves, or would private Capital be too strong for us and create a chasm between the proletariat and the peasants? Such was the question in those days. Now we are able to say that we have already achieved a decisive victory in this direction. The truth of that statement can only be denied by madmen and the blind. Now, however, the problem of "Who" and "By whom" takes on quite a different character. Now the problem is transferred from the sphere of trading to that of production, manual production and agricultural production, in which private Capital has a certain definite importance and from which it must be systematically uprooted.'

Stalin admitted in this speech that the situation in the country districts was unsatisfactory, and that hitherto too little effort had been made to destroy the influence of the Kulaks. He went on to describe severe measures that were about to be put into operation against the village money-lenders. Police measures—he added—would not alone suffice; it would be necessary to find a satisfactory solution to the problem presented by Russian agriculture. Stalin continued:

'This solution is to be found in the transformation of the tiny scattered peasant farms into a vast and centralized industry on the basis of co-operative farming and in the adoption of collective farming based on a new and higher technical knowledge. The solution consists in the incorporation through example and as the result of conviction, but not of force, of the smaller and smallest farms in a great industrial organization for communal, collective, and co-operative farming, employing agricultural machinery and tractors, and making use of scientific methods to intensify agricultural production. There is no other solution. Our agriculture will in no other way be able to catch up with and surpass the agricultural methods of the most highly-developed capitalist countries (Canada, &c.).'

The Soviet Government, in conformity with the resolutions passed by the Fifteenth Party Congress, greatly increased the pace of industrial construction. A Five-Year Plan to cover the period October 1, 1928 to October 1, 1933, was put into operation. Industrial and agricultural production was to attain a certain level within this period. The progress achieved in the first year caused the Government to announce its intention of completing the Five-Year Plan in four years. This meant that this stage in the industrialization of Russia was to terminate at the close of 1932. It has already been stated above that Soviet Russian industry had in 1927 already achieved the level of pre-War production. By the end of 1930 industrial production had been doubled, and in 1931 production had been increased by 20 per cent. in comparison with the previous year. A further increase was to be expected in 1932, and by the close of that year the output of Soviet Russian industry should have trebled that of Russian industry in pre-War years. Although this is doubtless an immense achievement, Russian industry has, nevertheless, not attained to the level of the leading industrial countries in Europe or to that of the United States. A few significant statistics may not be out of place here. In 1913 the coke production of Russia totalled 27 million tons, in 1926, 20 million tons, and in 1931, 58 million tons. For the purposes of comparison with the coke production of western Europe it is necessary to select a year previous to the present great economic crisis. In 1927 Germany produced 154 million tons of coke and 151 million tons of brown coal. The petroleum output of Russia in 1913 was 9 million tons, in 1925, 7 million tons, and in 1931, 22 million tons. The United States in 1926 produced 106 million tons. The Russian production in pig-iron in 1913 was 4,600,000 tons, in 1926, 2,400,000 tons, and in 1931, 4,900,000 tons. In 1927 Germany produced 13 million tons. In 1913 Russia produced 4,200,000 tons of raw steel, in 1926, 3 million, and in 1931, 5,300,000 tons. Germany in 1927 produced 16 million tons of steel. Great praise must be given to Russia for the steady increase that has taken place in her industrial production in recent years. Soviet Russia will, nevertheless, have to carry out many Five-Year Plans before it attains even to the industrial level of Germany.

Interesting comparisons can be made between the number of factory workers, and indeed of all paid workers and employees, in Russia, and in the modern industrial States of western Europe. The percentage of paid workers and employees to the total population, or to all engaged in work of any kind, affords an approximate index figure for the rate of proletarization or for the disappearance of the self-supporting small industries and occupations. In 1927 there were 2,300,000 factory workers actually employed in the great industries. The total number of persons in receipt of wages or salaries amounted to 10,300,000. Among these were no less than 3,300,000 brain workers—employees, officials, civil servants of all descriptions. The balance was made up of railwaymen, transport workers, agricultural labourers, and those employed in small industries or businesses. In consequence of the growth of Russian industry the total number of industrial workers in Russia had risen, in 1931, to 5,400,000 and the total of wage-earners in the widest sense to 18,500,000. The increase in the latter class is to be accounted for by the increase in the number of employees and officials as a result of the concomitant growth of industry and also of the over-organization that was a consequence of the attempt to complete the Five-Year Plan in four years. Out of a wage-earning population of 32 millions in Germany in 1925 there were no less than 21 million workmen. If the population of Germany of 65 millions be compared with that of Russia of 160 millions, the following result is obtained. In Germany every third person is in receipt of wages, or a salary, and in Russia every eighth person. The total number of wage-earners, inclusive of working members of families, can to-day be reckoned in general at half the total population. According to this rule two-thirds of the industrial population of Germany are wage-earners, or employees, and in Russia only a fourth. These figures prove that even to-day the self-supporting lower middle class are in the majority in Russia even though they are concealed behind the veil of so-called peasant 'collectives'. Here, again, many and successful Five-Year Plans will be necessary in order to transfer the centre of gravity of Russian economic life from the country to the town, and from the peasantry to the proletariat.

The vast growth of Russian industry since 1927 has necessitated the expenditure of immense sums of money. The circulation of money has in consequence steadily increased. This form of inflation can, nevertheless, be justified from an economic standpoint, since the goods produced in Russia increased in proportion to the increase in the amount of currency in circulation. The sound principles on which Russian foreign trade has been conducted have not been departed from in recent years. It is true that Russian imports have notably increased in consequence of the necessity to import from abroad the machinery necessary for the expansion of industry. Foreign currency was also necessary to pay the foreign experts employed in Russian factories. This increased demand for foreign currency was in great part balanced with the help of the proceeds of Russia's export trade.

Soviet Russia has made use of all possible means to increase its export trade in recent years. Russia not only sold her natural products like naphtha, timber, furs, and corn, but also products of which her own population had an insufficient supply, such as butter, fish, poultry, &c. These heavy sacrifices were required of the Russian population, especially of the proletarian population of the towns, in order to acquire foreign currency. The economic crisis throughout the world and the diminishing purchasing power of the international market at present places difficulties in the way of Russian export, and therefore of the acquisition of the foreign currency necessary for the further industrialization of Russia. Nevertheless, the Soviet Government obstinately continues to carry on its work of industrialization and the entire State and Party machinery works unceasingly to increase industrial production. The working capacity of the factory workers is strained to the uttermost—the Trade Unions co-operate in this endeavour—for, according to the official Party belief, the industrialization of Russia means the realization of Socialism. The demands made of the factories by the Party and the Government are so great that they cannot possibly be fulfilled. It is in this connexion significant that the production of the year 1931 has failed to reach the projected figures. 83,500,000 tons of coal were to have been produced and only 58 million tons were actually obtained. 8,800,000 tons of steel were stipulated for, and only 5,300,000 were produced. Even the naphtha industry, which had undergone an especially rapid and successful increase in productivity, only produced 22,300,000 tons instead of the projected 25,500,000 tons. For 1932, extraordinarily high demands have been made of the individual industries and in general the figures exceeded those stipulated for in 1931. It is unnecessary to add that the quality of the manufactured article suffers from hasty production.

The plan for the industrialization of Russia lays the greatest stress upon heavy industry and upon increased production of raw materials and machinery. Judged from the standpoint of national economy this is right, since it is only by this path that Russia can arrive at having a modern self-supporting industry, but it involves at least temporarily neglect of production of the necessaries of life and of ready-made goods. For this reason the vast growth in the industrial production in Russia in recent years has not diminished the lack of commodities from which the population is suffering.

Unemployment has indeed been overcome by the great increase in employment necessitated by the rapid growth of Russian industry, transport, &c.; and this achievement of the Soviet Government is all the more noteworthy in view of the unemployment prevalent throughout the world. The Soviet Government may justifiably pride itself upon the fact that unemployment no longer exists in Russia. This is an important achievement for the Russian workman from a psychological standpoint, since as long as there were a million unemployed in Russia the contrast between the official Socialist legend and the reality was glaring in the extreme.

Ever since 1928 Stalin's policy has been directed towards a steady repression of the Kulaks and the development of peasant co-operative societies. Stalin was anxious to avoid anything in the nature of a startling interference on the part of the Soviet Government in the peasant life of Russia, because he feared that it would have catastrophic effects upon Russia's food-supplies. His object was to increase the number of peasant co-operative societies and he hoped that within the five years 1928-33 approximately a fourth of the Russian peasantry would be organized in societies for co-operative production. The object of the State was to favour these societies in such matters as the payment of taxes and the granting of credits. The co-operative societies were to be given tractors and all other necessary modern farming implements and machinery. The peasants who still remained in their archaic isolation would thus be induced to abandon it gradually by the sight of the work accomplished by the co-operative societies for production (the 'collective' farms).

Class distinctions in the Russian village proved too strong in the years 1928-9 for even a slow rate of development to be maintained. The Kulaks observed that the Government wished to take still sharper measures against them in taxation, local administrative questions, &c., and they intensified their obstructive tactics. They systematically held back grain supplies with the result that in 1928 Russia was forced to purchase foreign wheat in order to relieve the worst sufferings of the population. In many districts in Russia the Kulaks organized a regular terror. Village correspondents for Communist newspapers who reported the true state of affairs were in danger of their lives. Many of them were murdered. Stalin found himself compelled to make use of the entire resources of the Soviet State in his struggle with the Kulaks and the order went forth that they were to be exterminated as a separate class in society. Their properties were confiscated in many cases and presented to the peasant co-operative societies. Kulaks who had been specially active in a counter-revolutionary sense were exiled from their native districts. It is unquestionable that many injustices were done to them and that there was much suffering. Although it is possible to argue that the Kulaks were only punished because they wanted to make money, and that the Soviet Government itself had for years stimulated their cupidity, the truth is that the struggle with the Kulaks in the years 1929-30 was a struggle for the preservation of the Russian Revolution.

All concessions on the part of the Soviet Government had proved unavailing in satisfying the wealthy peasants and the village usurers. In the first place they asked that in return for their grain they should be given manufactured goods at prices that were not higher than those obtained for the same goods in foreign countries. A domestic policy that would have satisfied the Kulaks would have finally resulted in the destruction of the Government's monopoly of foreign trade. The abolition of this monopoly would have had for its consequences the flooding of the Russian market with cheap foreign manufactured goods and the ruin of Russian industry. All progress in civilization that had resulted from the Russian Revolution would have been destroyed as a result of the decay of the great industrial towns. If the Kulak had in reality been stronger than the Soviet Government, he would have become the autocrat of the village, have allied himself with the reactionary elements in the State administration and the Red Army, and thus have brought about a real Russian Thermidor and a White Guard military dictatorship. The struggle with the Kulaks of necessity involved the country in unpleasant economic consequences. Since the small farmer and peasant as a general rule only produced sufficient supplies for his own needs, the country as a whole was forced to rely upon the bigger farmers—the Kulaks—for its supplies.

The expropriation and dividing up of the Kulak farms at first resulted in producing a state of confusion in the villages and a complete disorganization of the food market. In a large number of instances the Kulaks slaughtered their cattle wholesale before their lands were confiscated and the panic thus created seized upon large numbers of the small farmers.

In the course of the single year 1929 Russia's stock of cattle sank by a quarter and her stock of pigs by more than a third. The consequences of this catastrophic shock to Russian agriculture in 1929 have not yet been overcome. The Soviet Government was once more forced to introduce food rationing, and in conjunction with it came State control and high prices, to the exclusion of free trade. The results were similar to those experienced by Germany during the World War—shortage of food-supplies, profiteering, lowering of agricultural production. The Soviet Government was forced to restore liberty to trade by the May Decrees of 1932.

The action taken by the GPU against the Kulaks aroused the fear in many small farmers that a persecution of the Russian peasantry was about to begin. Stalin and the Soviet Government never entertained the slightest intention of taking action against the Russian peasants as a whole. Local mishandlings on the part of over-hasty officials occurred that were hardly to be avoided in a process of this kind. The small farmers sought and found protection in the 'collective' system of farming. Any one quick to join a Collective Society was not only assured of his personal safety but was changed from being an object of suspicion to the Soviet Government into a co-worker with it in the cause of Socialism. As a member of a Collective Society the peasant no longer had cause to fear the police and could even approach the State with all manner of requests. Thus the years 1929 and 1930 beheld the Russian peasants flocking in crowds to join the Collective Societies. As early as 1930, 37 per cent. of the agricultural land of Russia was in the possession of the Collectives, 3 per cent. in that of the great State farms, and 60 per cent. remained in the hands of individual and uncollectivized peasants. At the close of 1931 the Collectives were in possession of 62 per cent. of all peasant farms and 79 per cent. of the arable land, and the process of collectivization was proceeding uninterruptedly.

Although the Soviet Government proudly pointed in its official publications to this triumph of the co-operative ideal among the Russian peasants, the rulers of Russia must in truth have watched the mass movement of the peasants into the co-operative societies with mixed feelings; for the Soviet Government did not possess sufficient tractors and other agricultural implements to supply the colossal needs of the Collectives. In 1930 only 17 per cent. of the arable land in the possession of the Collective farms was cultivated by means of tractors. In 1931 it was hoped to raise this figure to 19 per cent. and in 1932 to 44 per cent. At present the majority of Soviet Collective farms are still using the old primitive methods of agriculture of the peasants. In other words, these Collective farms exist only on paper. In the normal type of Russian Collective farm the arable land and the means of production are the property of the Co-operative Society. The farm-house, domestic animals, and garden remain the property of the peasant. The produce belongs to the Society and is annually divided up among the members. The taxes paid by a Collective farm are very small. The Collective farms have to hand over a settled proportion of their produce to the State authorities at State-controlled prices. It was decided in 1930 that the Collective farms in the good grain districts after an average harvest must surrender to the State a quarter to a third of their gross production. In districts where the land is poorer the proportion is less. In practice this does not place a too heavy burden upon the Collectives. The May Decrees of 1932 lowered the amount of produce to be surrendered to the State and the taxes to be paid by both the Collectives and the non-collectivized peasants. At the same time smuggling was in a sense legalized in that the peasants after they had given the required quota to the State were free to sell their surplus stocks of grain, cattle, &c., in the open market at whatever prices they could obtain. It is indeed not intended to permit private trading to develop, and instead the Collectives are to open their own shops for the sale of their surplus produce.

The vast extent of the Russian State and the enormous

number of its peasant inhabitants renders impossible any effective State control of agriculture. The Collectives can easily prove themselves an excellent cloak for the development of a new class of Kulaks. If the members of the Soviet Russian Collectives were not inspired by agrarian selfishness but by a Socialist communal feeling, Russia would not to-day be experiencing any shortage of food-supplies. Once successful Collectives have turned into shopkeepers the business instinct will soon seize upon them. Moreover, there is also the serious problem of what is to happen to those poor peasant families that have failed to gain a footing either in a prosperous Collective or in industry. Signs are not wanting to show that a new poverty-stricken class is coming into existence in the Russian country-side.

The change in Soviet policy brought about by Stalin in December 1927 altered his relations with the various groups inside the Russian Communist Party. Stalin's so-called 'Left course' split the Opposition. The old-time Bolsheviks led by Zinoviev and Kamenev made their peace with the Soviet Government. At the same time they were no longer given responsible posts. Trotsky and his intimate friends were once more alone in their opposition. Nevertheless, Trotsky did not allow himself to be discouraged by Zinoviev's defection and instead only attacked Stalin and his policy with greater bitterness. In 1929 Trotsky was forcibly expelled from Russia by the police and handed over to the Russophil Turkish Government, who gave him asylum on an island near Constantinople. Here Trotsky has devoted himself untiringly to literary activities and waged war to the death on the theory of Socialism in a single country. He has criticized the mistakes of the ruling bureaucracy in Soviet Russia and demanded that it should accord the Russian workman the right to decide his own fate. He has also demanded the pursuit of a resolute, internationalist, proletarian policy.

Since 1928 the great majority of Russian workmen and members of the Communist Party have remained faithful supporters of Stalin and the Central Committee. But the Radical agrarian policy of the Soviet Government led to a breach with the 'Right' group of peasant sympathizers in the Communist Party. Stalin overcame their opposition with little difficulty. Rykov, Bukharin, and Tomski were removed from their responsible posts. Indeed it is remarkable that the Right Opposition put up so poor a fight against Stalin. For this nationalist Conservative group could not only have mobilized the masses of the peasantry but also a large number of civil servants and a part of the army; and Tomski himself represented important sections of the working class. It must, however, not be forgotten that Rykov's group was in reality only a buffer between Stalin and the group whose opinions can best be symbolized by the name of Ustryalov. In their first assault upon Stalin's position the Right would have found themselves the prisoners of the middle-class-peasant-military counter-revolution. The leaders of the Right recognized this danger and preferred to submit to the majority in the Party. Police measures such as were employed against Trotsky and his followers have never been used against the Right.

In order to make clear to the Russian proletariat his conversion to unqualified Socialism, Stalin at the close of 1927 abandoned the foreign policy that had caused him to become the object of so much criticism. Soviet Russia broke off relations with the English Trade Unions and also relinquished its propaganda for international Trade Union solidarity. It declared war to the death upon the Kuomintang in China and made no further attempt to restrain the masses of the population from revolutionary action. Ever since Chang Kai Shek's victory in the spring of 1927 the fighting strength of the revolutionary masses in China had been broken and armed insurrections could now only be in the nature of wild adventures. Nevertheless, in December 1927, Communist workmen revolted in Canton and proclaimed a Soviet Republic. The insurrection was put down after bloody fighting. This insurrection in Canton was the tragic conclusion to the Communist International's Chinese policy. Events in China between 1924 and 1927 display a remarkable similarity with those in Germany between 1921 and 1923. In both cases Soviet Russia judged conditions in a foreign country from the standpoint of her own State interests. In Germany her policy was based on the Treaty of Rapallo and friendship with a middle-class Republican Government; her policy in China was founded on the agreement with the Kuomintang Government and with Chang Kai Shek. The Soviet Government refused in both instances to believe in the possibility of an independent proletarian revolution in the near future, and by so doing paralysed the KPD in Germany and the Communist Party in China. The Bolsheviks could, nevertheless, not bring themselves to give up their pseudo-Radical manner of speech and their intrigues. Hence they failed in Germany to work in sincere collaboration with the Social Democrats and their friendship with the Kuomintang in China was not of a permanent nature. It was only when it was already too late that it was discovered that in both countries the situation was favourable for revolution. Hamburg and Canton were the achievements of this policy.

Ever since the foundation of the Third International the Bolsheviks attempted to exercise an influence over the course of the world revolution. They did this in the years 1919-21 by directly stirring up an international Communist revolution, and from 1921 to 1927 by their pursuit of a policy of a united front with the Social Democrat workmen in the West and the movement for national independence in the East. Both policies successively proved mistaken and their failure caused the Soviet Government to draw the natural conclusions. After 1928 it abandoned all attempts to influence the international Labour movement and to assist colonial and oppressed countries in their struggles for national freedom. And it sought at the same time to maintain its hold over the minority of the international proletariat that still believed in Soviet Russia and to fill their minds with a meaningless pseudo-Radicalism.

The new policy of the Communist International was laid down at the Sixth World Congress in the summer of 1928, and at the Fifth Congress of the Red Trade Union International in 1930. The Sixth World Congress made the discovery that a 'third period' had begun in the international Labour movement. The first period, from 1917 to 1923, was that of direct revolutionary struggle; the second covered the years 1923-8. In the summer of 1928 the United States was still enjoying great prosperity, and even Germany was experiencing economically an Indian summer, brought about by the foreign credits she had received since 1924. The resolutions of the Sixth World Congress made no attempt to deny the relatively prosperous economic condition of the capitalist world. Although it was always possible from a Communist standpoint to entertain doubts of the permanence of capitalist prosperity, and to prophesy new crises and upheavals on a vast scale, it is very difficult to understand why the 'third period' should have been said to have begun in the summer of 1928. It was stated that the typical characteristic of this 'third period' was the appearance of Social Democracy as an ally of world Capitalism and its assumption in certain respects of Fascist ideas. Any form of united front with Social Democrat Parties and leaders was therefore out of the question during this 'third period'. This judgement upon international Social Democracy will be accepted or otherwise by the individual critic according to his own personal political beliefs. The Social Democrats can be praised or condemned according to the political standpoint from which they are judged. It is, nevertheless, impossible to prove that in matters of principle Social Democracy had undergone any change between the summer of 1927 and that of 1928.

Hence it is only possible to explain the resolutions passed by the Sixth World Congress by the same methods that were employed above to explain those of the Third World Congress in 1921. Soviet Russia and not the world at large had changed. A new attitude towards the international situation is always the consequence of a change in Russian domestic policy. The policy of compromise pursued in Russia itself at the time of the NEP and the concessions to the Kulaks, found its international expression in the policy of a united front. Since, however, Stalin had embarked on his so-called 'Left Course' in domestic policy, it became necessary to reveal this new radicalization of Bolshevism in the International's policy by abandoning the policy of a united front with the Social Democrats and by burdening the Sixth World Congress with the notorious 'third period' theory in order to advance a pseudo-practical reason, based upon conditions within the International, for the disruption of the united front. The task of the Communist International since 1928 has been to attract to itself a minority of the workmen by means of radical formulas unaccompanied by purposeful actions. The Utopian Radicals among the international proletariat are the most receptive of this propaganda. Hence the policy of the Communist International was framed in such a way as to appeal to them. The theory of a working-class aristocracy put forward, before 1917, by Lenin in his isolation in the midst of the World War, was revived—a theory that had been abandoned in favour of an attempt to win the support of the Trade Union workmen at the time in 1920 when the Communist International was making a serious effort to obtain the leadership of the proletariat.

The Communists are for the present content to remain a minority of the proletariat. They have no longer any real hopes of achieving power and have therefore abandoned their struggle for the control of the Trade Unions. The resolutions of the World Congresses in 1928 and 1930 did indeed declare that Communists were to continue their activities in the Trade Unions. At the same time, however, the task was given to them of organizing the non-Unionist workmen for the purpose of leading them in economic conflicts without regard for the wishes of the Unions. In practice this implied the creation of new organizations in competition with the old Social Democrat Trade Unions and the promotion of a split within the Trade Union movement. Important successes have, nevertheless, been denied to the Communists since 1928 in their work of organizing a Red Trade Union Opposition in Germany and other countries. Although it is true that they have secured the support of at least a part of the unemployed by means of their Utopian Radical propaganda, it is also true that the Utopian Radical workmen are the most unreliable element in the whole proletariat. This section of the proletariat, composed chiefly of unemployed, and actuated mainly by purely emotional considerations, is capable of changing its convictions with great rapidity, and could within twenty-four hours abandon the Communists and join the Fascists, National Socialists, &c. Recent elections in Germany have testified to the truth of this statement. The Communist International could not indeed achieve any real success with such a policy. The result of a parliamentary election is in this connexion relatively unimportant. But what is of decisive importance is that in all those places where the world revolution is in progress the Communists are without any influence. The Spanish Revolution was carried out without the help of the Spanish Communist Party. The English Communists exercise no influence upon the great struggles of the English working class. The Communist Parties in India and China are completely insignificant, notwithstanding the fact that on occasions the European press describes the insurrectionary Chinese peasants as 'Communists'.

At the time of the Third World Congress the Communist International was still supported by the majority of the workmen in France, Czechoslovakia, and Norway. The Communists have long ago lost the support of the majority of the workmen in all three countries. They have sunk to the level of an unimportant minority in France. There are to-day 6 million unemployed in Germany, and if their families be added to the calculation, the total is at least 9 million voters. The largest Communist vote in the elections in 1932 totalled 5 millions. The KPD probably comprises at present barely 50 per cent. of the German unemployed, and only a very small percentage of the employed workmen. That is a catastrophic condition for a Party that seriously aims at the leadership of the majority of the proletariat. At the same time the KPD is relatively the strongest Party in the Communist International.

During 1925-7 the Communist bureaucrats in control of the Party forced the so-called Left to leave its ranks. After 1928 the Right met with the same fate. Thus the Communist Parties are for the present freed from all unwelcome independent criticism and are in the undisputed control of the bureaucracy. These bureaucratic officials endeavour to conceal the failure of the policy of the Communist International by narrating to their supporters the victories won by Socialism in Russia.

This is not the place in which to discuss whether Socialism is better than Capitalism. It can, nevertheless, be discovered whether a country is organized in an economic sense in accordance with the doctrines of Marx. In order that Soviet

Russia should be truly Socialist there are at least three preliminary conditions that must be fulfilled: Industry must be organized into great industrial associations under the free control of the producers; agriculture must be organized in a similar fashion; and production must be regulated solely by demand and not in accordance with market and trade interests. Soviet Russia to-day does not fulfil any one of these three preliminary conditions. Although industry is organized into the modern big industry system, the producers have no part in the management and no voice in the determination of industrial policy. Socialism is inconceivable unless accompanied by the exercise of self-determination on the part of the people. For Socialism is the rule of freedom under which the State disappears. An over-bureaucratized administration based on the employment of force, and which the masses must obey, is irreconcilable with the Socialist organization of society and can only be regarded as a middle-class institution.

In the agricultural organization of Soviet Russia only a small part of the production is organized on a large scale. The predominant agrarian type is the Collective farm. At present the State cannot supply the majority of these farms with agricultural machinery. The peasant therefore continues to make use of his old-fashioned plough and aged horse to till the piece of ground that has been in the possession of his family for generations. The communal division of produce in the Collectives serves only to veil the traditional petty middle-class system. On the Collective farms where State tractors are working the peasant has less work and a far better result from his labours. The Collective farm system as a whole serves no other purpose than to work well in the interests of its members, to sell as little produce as possible at State-controlled prices, and to dispose of as much as possible in private trading at far higher prices. That is a typical petty middle-class method of production.

There is as little trace in the State industries as in the Collectives of a system of working solely for the production of necessaries. Here trade interests are also predominant; and this without taking into account the influence daily exercised upon Soviet Russia by the movements of the capitalist world market. The same conditions prevail in the domestic economy of Soviet Russia. The individual State Trusts and heavy industries are legally independent. A Russian machine factory must find a market for its goods and pay for its raw materials exactly as is done by a similar factory in Europe. It has its overdraft at the State Bank; the management must fulfil all obligations; and, in the event of its becoming bankrupt, its credit ceases with the State Bank and its supplies of steel are discontinued. The latest decrees of the Soviet Government, published in the second half of 1931 and the beginning of 1932, lay upon the State industries an obligation to organize themselves on a purely business model, acquire capital, and to make profits. At present it is theoretically impossible, however, for a badly managed Soviet undertaking to go bankrupt. All this is trading on a modern financial and capitalist basis.

There is a great difference from an economic standpoint in whether Russia produces 20 or 60 millions of coal annually, or whether her vast and fertile cornlands are ploughed up with a wooden plough or a tractor. Nevertheless, increased production, and the abandonment of outworn methods of production, have not helped to bring Russia an inch farther along the path leading to true Socialism. Soviet Russia still belongs to the same social and State category to which she belonged in 1921. Russia is a peasants' and workers' State, organized in accordance with a system of State Capitalism by means of which the governing bureaucracy contrives to maintain its hold over both the basic classes in society. The proletarian influence shows itself in the fact that private trading for profits is inadmissible. The governing bureaucracy, which owes its existence to the support of the peasants, issues its commands, nevertheless, to the workmen, and organizes industry on a trading and financial and capitalist basis. The proletarian influence prevents the emergence in the country districts of a class of private landowners. The power of the peasants, however, is shown in all the concessions which the State has made to the Collectives; and their existence indirectly justifies the dictatorship exercised by the Party and State machinery over Soviet Russia.

It is only possible to avoid delivering false judgements on

the subject of Soviet Russia by according full recognition to the mixed character of its social order. It is as mistaken to ignore the part of the proletariat in present-day Russia as it is to under-estimate the importance of the middle-class and peasant element. Official Soviet statistics published in 1930 show that deposits amounting to 722 million roubles were credited in the books of the Russian Savings Bank. Of this total only 91 millions belonged to workmen, 205 millions to employees and Government officials, 134 millions to 'special' workers, i.e. members of professions, manual workers, &c., and only 46 millions to peasants as individuals. To these figures must be added, however, 246 millions belonging to 'legal persons', behind which designation were concealed chiefly Collectives and other co-operative societies. This statistical panorama serves admirably to reveal the multiplicity of classes in modern Russia no less than the fact that, in standard of living and opportunity for saving, the working class are by no means favoured above the rest.

State Capitalism is for Russia an excessively modern form of social and economic organization. Such an organization of society demands a modernist civilization. Soviet Russia can therefore dispense with religion in public life, use the latest pedagogic methods, and make an inestimable contribution towards knowledge of maternity and child welfare. The complete intellectual freedom that is characteristic of a true Socialist society is certainly not to be found in Soviet Russia, where the ruling Party dictatorship could not continue to exist without a rigidly dogmatic doctrinal system known as Leninism, which all citizens are compelled to believe in.

The wages of the Russian workman have risen in recent years. At the same time his real standard of living has been lowered in comparison with the years before 1927, since the supply of manufactured goods available for the town population has not improved and the supplies of food have diminished. Nevertheless, there is no actual famine, unemployment is virtually unknown, and the Soviet Government should find it possible in the near future by the employment of all the means at its disposal, and after its latest concessions to the peasants, to bring the national food-supplies once more into order. Moreover, the Soviet Government in taking action against the Kulaks has for the time being suppressed all open enmity among the country population. The situation of the small farmers and peasants organized in the Collectives has improved wherever modern machinery could be placed at their disposal. There has never been any question of a persecution of the peasantry by the Soviet Government.

The Socialist theory put forward by Stalin has given the Soviet Government freedom of action in the immediate future. A new Five-Year Plan is now being drawn up. The collectivization of Russian agriculture and the simultaneous raising of the level of industrial production to a respectable height is possible within the next few years. The Soviet Government will then be able to declare that the 'realization of Socialism' has been achieved and the 'class-free society' brought into existence. It would then be possible to lessen the present too intense pace of industrialization. The Party dictatorship might even be relaxed and more freedom accorded to self-government; for in a 'class-free society' the dictatorship of the proletariat is clearly superfluous. Substantial concessions to the peasants could also be justified by the argument that 'peasants' in a private capitalist sense no longer existed but only agricultural producers within the framework of the perfected Socialist order of society.

Class distinctions in Russia cannot be concealed permanently. If the present and the succeeding Five-Year Plan prove an economic success, improved living conditions will strengthen the class-consciousness both of the workers and the peasants. In a distant future Russia will not be spared decisive class-warfare, and *Naródnik* 'Socialism' will not avail to postpone the conflict indefinitely.

In their endeavours to overcome Russia's backwardness the Bolsheviks feel themselves the executors of the testament of Peter the Great. On November 19, 1928, in a speech before the Central Committee of the Russian Communist Party, Stalin said:

'We are not responsible for the technical and economic backwardness of our country. It has existed for centuries and has come down to us as an inheritance from our entire history. This backwardness was also felt to be an evil in pre-Revolutionary days and it continued to be so after the Revolution. Peter the Great's

attempt, after his experience of developed Western States, fever-
ishly to build factories and other works to supply the army and
to increase the defensive strength of the country, was a unique
attempt to burst the bonds of this backwardness. It is only
natural that neither of the old classes—feudal aristocracy or
middle class—was able to solve the problem provided by the
backwardness of our country. Indeed these classes were not only
incapable of solving this problem but even of visualizing it
properly. The centuries-old backwardness of our country can
only be overcome by successful Socialization and only the proletariat, which had established its dictatorship and directs the
destinies of the country, is able to accomplish it.'

The historic mission thus placed before Bolshevism has
in the main been fulfilled by it. Bolshevism in Russia
overthrew the Tsar with the help of the proletariat and
completed the middle-class revolution. It overcame the
shameful backwardness of the country and brought it up to
the level of a modern middle-class European State. Indeed,
thanks to the power of the working class, Bolshevism could in
Russia replace private Capitalism and its accompaniments
in social and economic life by a modern system of State
Capitalism.

The successes achieved by the Bolsheviks from a Russian
nationalist standpoint were precisely the cause of their
international failures. It is not an accident that Soviet
Russia has advanced steadily and uninterruptedly since 1921,
whilst the Communist International has in the same years
gone steadily down hill. Bolshevik doctrines and methods
were modern and progressive in comparison with the ideas
and methods of Tsarist Russia. But they were reactionary
when applied to the industrial lands of the West, where the
middle-class revolution has virtually reached its completion,
where the peasants are no longer the most influential element
in the population, and where the proletariat has already
learnt to create and control its own organizations. The
heroic deeds of the Russian workmen from 1917 to 1920
temporarily threw a veil over Bolshevik backwardness and
awoke the feeling that Bolshevism was the predestined form
of the universal proletarian revolution. Important sections
of the European proletariat were at that time anxious to ally

themselves with the Bolsheviks in an attempt to seize the reins of government. In the course of time, however, the impossibility of entrusting the leadership of the world proletariat to the Government of the agrarian Russian State became more and more evident. The Russian State and the international working class once more parted company, and Stalin's theory of 'Socialism in a single land' is only the verbal expression of an accomplished fact. An isolated, nationalist, Russian Bolshevism was not even capable of leading the Asiatic peoples in their struggle for freedom.

The historic deeds of the great Russian Revolution still fascinate some small sections of the international working class. But the Communist International has no longer any influence upon the course of the world proletarian movement. The achievements of Bolshevism in the Russian Revolution will live for ever in history. If to-day the international middle class still fears Bolshevism, it does so because it misunderstands the present nature of Bolshevism. It may have cause to fear the international Marxian proletariat and the world revolution: but these are not 'Bolshevism'.

BIBLIOGRAPHY

Translator's Note

In his bibliography Professor Rosenberg refers to German translations of Russian works and to works by German writers upon his subject. The Translator has therefore deemed it better to preserve the German titles. A list of Russian works used by Professor Rosenberg that are available in English has been appended for the reader's convenience.

CHAPTER ONE

For the correspondence between Marx and Ruge, cf. Marx-Engels, Gesamtausgabe, herausgegeben vom Marx-Engels-Lenin Institut in Moscow, Erste Abteilung, Band I, Erster Halbband (Frankfurt a. M. 1927), pp. 557 f.

Marx, *Zur Kritik der Hegelschen Rechtsphilosophie*; cf. ibid., pp. 607 f.

Engels's letter of 13. xi. 1851; cf. Gesamtausgabe, Dritte Abteilung, Band I (Berlin, 1929), pp. 148 f.

Marx and the Commune; cf. Karl Korsch, *Revolutionäre Kommune*, in the review *Die Aktion*, 1929, Nos. 5–8, and 1931, Nos. 3–4.

Marxism in general; cf. Karl Korsch, *Marxismus und Philosophie* (2. Auflage, Leipzig, 1930), and his *Die materialistische Geschichtsauffassung* (Leipzig, 1929).

CHAPTER TWO

All references made here and throughout this work to Lenin's writings and speeches are taken from the publication in which they are most readily accessible to German readers, i.e. the great collection of his writings and speeches entitled *Ausgewählte Werke* (Vienna, Verlag für Literatur und Politik, 1925). Reference is also made to various writings published individually in German translations. The standard collection of Lenin's writings in the original Russian has now appeared in a second edition. A part has already been translated into German under the title W. J. Lenin, *Sämtliche Werke* (Vienna and Berlin, Verlag für Literatur und Politik). The Russian and German versions are arranged in chronological order. Hence it is easy for the reader to discover in either edition the passages to which reference is made here.

For Lenin's early life cf. N. K. Krupskaya, *Erinnerungen an Lenin* (Vienna and Berlin, Verlag für Literatur und Politik, 1929), p. 5, where Lenin's widow writes: 'Vladimir Ilyitsh came to Petersburg in the autumn of 1893. Although I did not make his acquaintance in those days, I was told by friends that a very well-informed Marxist had arrived from the Volga,' &c.

Lenin was born in 1870.

The quotations from Lenin's writings in 1902 are taken from the pamphlet entitled *Was tun?* cf. *Sammelband*, pp. 45, 49, 52, 78.

For Lenin's speech at the Party Congress in 1903 cf. *Sammelband*, pp. 80 f.

For Lenin's *Rede über die Revolution von 1905* (delivered in January, 1917) cf. the publication bearing that title published by Verlag für Literatur und Politik in Vienna in 1925.

L. Trotsky, *Die russische Revolution 1905* (2. Auflage, Berlin, 1923. The first edition was published in Dresden in 1909), pp. 87 f. and 168 f.

For Lenin's article on the Soviets cf. *Sammelband*, pp. 170 f.

Lenin *versus* Martynov in 1905, cf. *Sammelband*, pp. 132 f., 135, 147 f., 150 f.

Zinoviev, *Vom Werdegang unserer Partei* (Berlin, 1920), p. 26: 'Historians cannot suppress the fact that the Councils of Workers' Delegates in Petersburg were the creation of a group of Mensheviks who sought the support of the non-party masses of the population against the "narrow circle" of professional revolutionaries.'

CHAPTER THREE

Lenin and Zinoviev, *Gegen den Strom* (containing articles written in the years 1914–16, and published by the Verlag der Kommunistischen Internationale, 1921), pp. 30 f., 272 f., 291 f.

Trotsky's articles for the years 1909 and 1915 are to be found in an appendix to his book *Die russische Revolution 1905*, pp. 228 f., 230 f., 232 f.

CHAPTER FOUR

Lenin and Zinoviev, *Gegen den Strom*, pp. 6, 277 f., 281 f., 341 f., 521 f.

P. Frölich, *10 Jahre Krieg und Bürgerkrieg* (Berlin, 1924), p. 150 f.

Spartakusbriefe I, (Berlin, 1921, Vereinigte Kommunistische Partei Deutschlands) pp. 57 f., 132 f.

CHAPTER FIVE

Lenin, *Sammelband*, pp. 345 f., 369 f., 423.

Lenin, *Staat und Revolution* (3. Auflage, Berlin, 1919).

Lenin, *Die drohende Katastrophe und wie soll man sie bekämpfen?* (Vienna, 1920), pp. 9, 10, 12, 17, 25, 40.

Trotsky, *Von der Oktober-Revolution bis zum Brester Friedensvertrag* (written in 1918 and published in 1919 in Berlin).

Bukharin, *Der Klassenkampf und die Revolution in Russland* (Berlin, Kleine Bibliothek der russischen Korrespondenz, Nr. 19–21. 1920. It was written in 1917).

CHAPTER SIX

Trotsky, ibid.; cf. especially pp. 43, 52 f., 61 f., 89 f.

Trotsky, *Die Geburt der Roten Armee* (Vienna, Verlag für Literatur und Politik, 1924. It was written in 1922), pp. 10 f., 133 f.

Trotsky, *1917. Die Lehren der Revolution* (Berlin, 1925. It was written in 1924), pp. 45 f., 54 f. Trotsky reveals in these pages the part played by Zinoviev and Kamenev in 1917.

Lenin, *Sammelband*, pp. 425 f.

Lenin, *Die Kinderkrankheit des Radikalismus in Kommunismus* (Berlin, 1925. It was written in 1920). For the elections to the National Assembly cf. pp. 64 f., 104 f.; and for the situation in regard to the peasants cf. p. 55.

Larin and Kritzmann, *Wirtschaftsleben und wirtschaftlicher Aufbau in Sowjet-Russland 1917 bis 1920* (Berlin, 1921), pp. 132, 136.

Milyutin, *Zwei Jahre ökonomischer Diktatur des Proletariats in Russland* (Verlag der Kommunistischen Internationale, 1920), p. 4.

Die Verfassung der Russischen Sozialistischen Föderativen Sowjetrepublik, Beschluss des 5. Allrussischen Sowjetkongresses vom 10. Juli 1918 (Berlin, 1920. Kleine Bibliothek der russischen Korrespondenz, Nr. 22). This also contains the 'Deklaration der Rechte des werktätigen und ausgebeuteten Volkes' dated January, 1918.

CHAPTER SEVEN

Rosa Luxemburg, *Die russische Revolution. Eine kritische Würdigung. Aus dem Nachlass herausgegeben von Paul Levi* (Berlin, 1922. It was written in 1918), p. 113.

Lenin, *Sammelband*, pp. 512, 542, 570 f. (on Italy).

Lenin, *Die Kinderkrankheit des Radikalismus in Kommunismus*, pp. 61 f., 69 f., 91 f., 97.

Lenin, *Die Weltlage und die Aufgaben der Kommunistischen Internationale* (speech delivered in the first session of the Second World Congress. Verlag der Kommunistischen Internationale, 1920).

Leitsätze und Statuten der Kommunistischen Internationale (passed by the Second World Congress. Verlag der Kommunistischen Internationale, 1920). For the twenty-one conditions, cf. *ibid.*, pp. 26 f.

Zinoviev, *Die Weltrevolution und die III. Kommunistische Internationale.* A speech delivered at the USPD Congress in Halle on October 14, 1920. (Verlag der Kommunistischen Internationale, 1920.)

CHAPTER EIGHT

Lenin, *Sammelband*, pp. 588 f. (Trade Union Debate), 638 f. (NEP), 712 f. (co-operative societies).

Steinberg (a former Social Revolutionary People's Commissar) *Gewalt und Terror in der Revolution* (Berlin, Verlag Rowohlt, 1931), pp. 189 f. (Cronstadt revolt).

244   BIBLIOGRAPHY

Trotsky, *Die neue Etappe. Die Weltlage und unsere Aufgaben.*
(Verlag der Kommunistischen Internationale, 1921), p. 59.

*Taktik und Organisation der revolutionären Offensive. Die Lehren
der März-Aktion.* Herausgegeben von der Zentrale der Vereinigten
Kommunistischen Partei Deutschlands (Leipzig and Berlin, 1921).

*Thesen und Resolutionen des III. Weltkongresses der Kommunis-
tischen Internationale* (Verlag der Kommunistischen Internationale,
1921), cf. especially pp. 8 f., 45, 48, 52 f.

Gorter, *Die Moskauer Internationale* (Berlin, Verlag der KAPD,
1921).

CHAPTER NINE

Karl Korsch, *Zur Geschichte der marxistischen Ideologie in Russland,*
in the review entitled *Der Gegner* for February 5, 1932.

The preface to the Russian edition of the Communist Manifesto,
cf. *Kommunistisches Manifest* herausgegeben von Kautsky (Berlin,
1918), pp. 20 f.

Ryazanov, *Briefwechsel zwischen Vera Sassulitsch und Marx* in
Marx-Engels, *Archiv,* I, pp. 309 f.

Rykov, *Die Wirtschaftslage der Sowjet-Union* (Berlin, 1924).

Rykov, *Bericht über die Wirtschaftslage der Sowjet-Union und die
Ergebnisse der Parteidiskussion in der KPR* (Referat auf dem 5. Welt-
kongress. Moskau, 1924. Herausgegeben vom Pressbüro des Kon-
gresses).

For the views of the Third World Congress on the situation in
Russia cf. *Thesen und Resolutionen des III. Weltkongresses,* p. 104.

Radek, *Genua, die Einheitsfront des Proletariats und die Kommunistische Internationale* (Verlag der Kommunistischen Internationale, 1922). Radek's account of the development in Germany
and of the KPD from 1921 to 1924 is based in the main upon his own
experiences. It is useful to compare with this Paul Levi's *Unser
Weg. Wider den Putschismus* (Berlin, 1921).

*Die Lehren der deutschen Ereignisse. Das Präsidium des Exekutiv-
komitees der Kommunistischen Internationale zur deutschen Frage,
Januar 1924* (Verlag der Kommunistischen Internationale, 1924).

Zinoviev, *Bericht über die Tätigkeit des Exekutiv-Komitees der
Kommunistischen Internationale* (presented to the Fifth World Congress in Moscow in 1924).

*Bericht über die Verhandlungen des 9. Parteitages der Kom-
munistischen Partei Deutschlands, abgehalten in Frankfurt a. M. vom
7. bis 10. April, 1924* (Berlin, 1924).

CHAPTER TEN

Lenin on Stalin; cf. *Briefe an Maxim Gorki* (Vienna, 1924), p. 75.

Stalin, *Probleme des Leninismus* in *Sammlung von Stalins Reden
und Aufsätzen aus den Jahren 1924 bis 1925* (Vienna, Verlag für
Literatur und Politik, 1926).

Plattform der russischen Opposition, published by the Verlag 'Fahne des Kommunismus' in Berlin in 1927.

Der Kampf um die Kommunistische Internationale, Dokumente der russischen Opposition, veröffentlicht vom Verlag der 'Fahne des Kommunismus' (Berlin, 1927). The declaration of the Five Hundred is to be found here; cf. pp. 149 f.

Lozowsky, *Der Kampf für die Einheit der Welt-Gewerkschafts-bewegung* (Berlin, 1925).

Sun Yat Sen, *The International Development of China* (New York and London, 1922).

Wofür kämpft China? herausgegeben von der chinesischen Nachrichten-Agentur in Europa (Berlin, 1927).

Wie die chinesische Revolution zugrunde gerichtet wurde (Brief aus Schanghai. Verlag der 'Fahne des Kommunismus'. Berlin, 1928). On this subject my remarks are based on my personal experiences in the years 1924–7.

CHAPTER ELEVEN

Stalin, *Probleme des Leninismus*, Zweite Folge (Vienna, Verlag für Literatur und Politik, 1929). This volume contains Stalin's articles and speeches in 1927–8.

Stalin and Peter the Great; cf. *ibid.*, p. 248.

Trotsky, *Die politische Lage in China und die Aufgaben der Bolschewiki-Leninisten* in the review *Die Aktion*, 1929, Heft 5–8.

Trotsky, *Entwurf einer Plattform der internationalen linken Kommunisten zur russischen Frage* in the review *Die Aktion*, 1931, Heft 3–4.

Protokoll des VI. Weltkongresses der Roten Gewerkschaftsinternationale. Moskau, 1930.

The best source of information on the present economic situation in Russia is *Die Ostwirtschaft. Organ des Russland-Ausschusses der deutschen Wirtschaft.* Herausgeber: R. Glanz. (Cf. especially the issues from January to May, 1932.) Another source is the review *Die Volkswirtschaft der Union der Sozialistischen Sowjet-Republiken*, herausgegeben von der Handelsvertretung der UdSSR in Deutschland (Berlin).

On the subject of the Savings Banks in Russia cf. Nagler, *Die Finanzen und die Währung der Sowjet-Union* (Berlin, Rowohlt, 1932), p. 40; also the *Zeitschrift der Handelsvertretung*, 1930, Nr. 16, pp. 53 f.

The following works among others mentioned in the above bibliography are now available in English translations from the original Russian texts. All the translations mentioned below are published by Messrs. Martin Lawrence, Ltd., 33 Great James Street, London, W.C. 1.

Lenin's Collected Works. An edition of thirty volumes based on the revised edition published by the Marx-Engels-Lenin Institute in Moscow.

Lenin, *Was tun?* translated under the title 'What is to be done?'
— *Die drohende Katastrophe, etc.*, translated under the title 'The Threatening Catastrophe and how to avert it'.
— *Staat und Revolution*, translated under the title 'The State and Revolution'.
— *Rede über die Revolution von 1905*, translated under the title 'The Revolution of 1905'.
Krupskaya, N., *Erinnerungen an Lenin*, translated under the title 'Memories of Lenin'.

INDEX